The

Milano Papers

Essays in Societal Alternatives

The Milano Papers

Essays in Societal Alternatives

Volume 7
Critical Perspectives on Historic Issues

Edited by Michele Cangiani

BLACK ROSE BOOKS

Montréal/New York
London

Black Rose Books No. 242
Hardcover ISBN: 1-55164-022-8
Paperback ISBN: 1-55164-023-6
ISSN: 1195-1869
Library of Congress Catalog Card Number: 96-86088

Canadian Cataloguing in Publication Data

The Milano papers: essays in societal alternatives

ISBN 1-55164-022-8 (pbk.)
ISBN 1-55164-023-6 (bound)
(Critical Perspectives on Historic Issues, ISSN 1195-1869; v. 7)

1. Economics—Sociological aspects. 2. Economic development.
I. Cangiani, Michele. II. Series

HC59.15   330.9   C96-900897-X

Mailing Address		
	BLACK ROSE BOOKS	
C.P. 1258	250 Sonwil Drive	99 Wallis Road
Succ. Place du Parc	Buffalo, New York	London, E9 5LN
Montréal, Québec	14225 USA	England
H2W 2R3		
Canada		

To order books in North America: (phone) 1-800-565-9523
(fax) 1-800-221-9985
In Europe: (phone) 081-986-485 (fax) 081-533-5821
Our Web site address: http://web.net/blackrosebooks

A publication of the Institute of Policy Alternatives of Montréal (IPAM)
Printed in Canada

TABLE OF CONTENTS

I: THE SEDUCTION OF THE MARKET AND THE SOCIALIST ALTERNATIVE

II: ECONOMY AND POLITICS IN THE POSTWAR TRANSFORMATION

III: CRITICAL PERSPECTIVES AND ALTERNATIVE PATHS

Notes on Contributors

Juan Martinez-Alier is a professor of economics and economic history at the Universitad Autonoma de Barcelona in Spain and visiting professor at the FLACSO, Quito. He is the author of *Ecological Economics* (Blackwell, 1990).

Samir Amin is the director of the African Office of the Third World Forum in Dakar, Senegal. He is the author of numerous books including, *Accumulation on a World Scale, Unequal Development, Neo-Colonialism in West Africa, The Future of Maoism*, and *Eurocentrism*, all published by Monthly Review Press.

Zygmunt Bauman is Emeritus Professor of sociology, University of Leeds, England. Recent Publications: *Postmodern Economics* (1993); *Life in Fragments* (1995).

Gérald Berthoud is a professor at the Institut d'anthropologie et sociologie, Faculté des sciences sociales, Université de Lausanne, Switzerland. His most recent book is *Vers une anthropologie générale: Modernité et altérité* (1992). He is a frequent contributor to *La Revue de MAUSS* (Paris).

Ayse Bugra is a professor of economics, Bogazici University, Istanbul, Turkey. Her publications include *On Economists and Human Behaviour* (in Turkish, Istanbul, 1989; 2nd ed., 1995) and *State and Business in Modern Turkey: A Comparative Study* (State University of New York Press, 1994). She has translated *The Great Transformation* by Polanyi into Turkish.

Michele Cangiani teaches economic sociology at the Università di Venezia, Italy. He translated and edited a selection of Karl Polanyi's articles (Cronache della grande tranzformazione, Torino, Einaudi, 1993).

Gian Primo Cella is a professor of economic sociology at the Università di Brescia, Italy. His books include *La solidarietà possible* (1989) and *Non di solo mercato* (1994), both published by Edizioni Lavoro, Roma. He is the editor of *Stato e mercato*, a political and economic journal.

Alfredo L. de Romaña is a research fellow at the Karl Polanyi Institute of Political Economy, Concordia University, Montréal, Canada. He has been working on a long term synthesis entitled *The World Beyond Development*, of which he has published two progress reports: "Post-crisis equilibrium" (Institut Interculterel de Montréal, 1989) and "Third World debt and the informal sector, New responses to the modern crisis."

Pat Devine teaches in the School of Economic Studies at the University of Manchester, England. He is a joint author of *An Introduc-tion to Industrial Economics* and author of *Democracy and Economic Planning*. He is currently working on the prospects for a green-socialist future and is a joint author of *What on Earth is to Be Done?*

Alain Lipietz est Directeur de Recherche au CNRS, Paris, France. Il est l'auteur de nombreaux ouvrages, soit d'analyse de l'économie mondiale. (*The Enchanted World, Inflation, Credit and the World Economy*, Verso, 1985; *Mirages and Miracles: The Crisis in Global Fordism*, Verso, 1987), soit de propositions pour une économie alternatif (*Towards a New Economic Order: Postfordism, Ecology, Democracy*, Polity Press, 1992; *Green Hopes: The Future of Political Ecology*, Polity Press, 1995). Il anime la Commission Économique des Verts français.

Abraham Rotstein is professor of economics and political science at Massey College, University of Toronto, Toronto, Canada. He is a former student and collaborator of Karl Polanyi.

Jean-Michel Servet, est professeur de Sciences Économiques à l'Université Lumière-Lyon 2 et Directeur de Recherche au CNRS (Centre Walras), France. Il a publié plusieurs articles sur la finance informelle et en histoire comparée des théories et des systèmes économiques. Il est co-éditeur des Oeuvres complètes d'Auguste et Léon Walras (Paris, Economica).

Claus Thomasberger, is professor of economics at the Fachhochschule für Technik und Wirtschaft (FHTW), Berlin, Germany. He is the author of *Europäische Währungsintegration und globale Währungskonkurrenz* (Tübingen: Mohr, 1993) and the editor of *Europäische Geldpolitik zwischen Marktzwängen und neuen institutionellen Regelungen* (Marburg: Metropolis, 1995).

PREFACE

The Third International Karl Polanyi conference, held in Milan, November 1990, proved to be an ambitiously wide-ranging review of world problems and prospects.

Alfredo Salsano, who organized the conference on behalf of the Karl Polanyi Institute of Political Economy, played a decisive role in this achievement, one which was paralleled at the following conferences promoted by the Institute (Montréal 1992 and Vienna 1994).

This book is comprised of papers presented at the Milan Conference, organized around selected themes. It does not include many excellent papers on a variety of other important themes.

Funds for the translation of the Introduction and Jean-Michel Servet's chapters were provided by the Italian Ministry of the University and Scientific Research.

I would like to thank Margie Mendell, Kenneth McRobbie and Ana Gomez for their precious assistance in the preparation of this book.

Michele Cangiani

INTRODUCTION

Michele Cangiani

The institutional order or mode of regulation which asserted itself in the postwar period was characterized by mass production; neocorporatist *concertation*; "Keynesian intervention" by the State; international equilibrium guaranteed by the dollar standard; and, also by the economic, political and military hegemony of the United States. The working class accepted Taylorist forms of control in return for a share of the gains in productivity (Lipietz). Welfare policies and State-supported effective demand favoured growth and employment, while facilitating collective bargaining. The market system, no longer self-regulating, experienced unprecedented development in which, furthermore, the whole world was involved. World War Two alone had made it possible to overcome the recession. The ensuing cold war was to convince even conservative American circles to accept State intervention, all the more so as growing expenditures on arms were becoming a fundamental factor in economic growth.

Karl Polanyi's remarks on other ways in which "transformation" was realized (for example, fascism and the New Deal) also apply to this present form of a capitalism that has been preserved through the introduction of new economic and political institutions which have replaced those of liberal capitalism. Even considering the greatest achievements of postliberal capitalism, such as the maintenance of pluralistic interest representation and the Welfare State, there was never any reason to believe that these in themselves would open the way toward a fuller measure of democratic control over the economic system. Although the market system was over in its "self-regulated" nineteenth-century form, it survived in new forms. The interlocking of two analytical levels—at the more general level, modern capitalist society as such; at the less general one, the historic phases of its development—is typical of Polanyi's *The Great Transformation*.

For many years now, it has been the turn of the postliberal institutional order to be in crisis. Following Polanyi's method, we must ask ourselves two questions. First, what are the reasons for the crisis, and what are the characteristics of the new phase, the new transformation? Second, how may we understand the significance of the historical process we are witnessing in relation to the more general context of market capitalism? It may further be asked: what new questions does the present transformation oblige us to pose about development, economic rationality, the destiny of democracy, and even the modern condition of man in the world?

Keynesianism "protected" the market system; it attempted to ensure its stability, by means of State institutions regulating the monetary system and the labour market (Thomasberger). With the onset of the 1970s, however, this institutional structure entered a critical phase. The labour market proved to be too rigid. It became difficult, given the contractual and political power obtained by the workers, to keep the increase in real wages at a level below that of the increase in productivity, as well as to control increases in monetary wages and prices. The decline in profits lead to a corresponding decline in investment and increased unemployment, which inflationary policies are no longer able to counteract. As competition becomes stiffer, firms try to augment productivity and to reduce the labour force. While the social costs of such cutbacks are laid on the State, the taxation necessary for the State to be able to finance transfer payments for social services and unemployment benefits begins to be perceived by the productive system as an intolerable burden. This is the "fiscal crisis of the State" which many governments try vainly to overcome by large-budget deficits. The international system Bretton Woods, which was an integral part of the Keynesian model, revealed its weakness in August 1971, when the convertability of the dollar, which had served as the international reserve currency, was suspended.

In the 1970s the anti-Keynesian reaction began. Monetary theories advocated the reintegration of both the labour market and the rates of exchange of national currencies according to the logic of supply and demand. Of the two alternatives—bringing the economy under the control of society *beyond the limits of the Keynesian model*, or returning to a form of self-regulation of the market—it is the latter that prevails.

However, this is not purely and simply a return to the self-regulating market, to nineteenth-century separation of the political and economic spheres. With deregulation, self-regulation did not return. The concentration and centralization of capital have continued. Now that the epoch of more-or-less competitive capitalism is no more, the economic system can no longer function as a system of self-regulating markets. The alternative involves only the *form* of organization: more-or-less political or economic, more-or-less democratic or managerial, more-or-less managed directly by and in the interests of the big corporations. Economic liberalism continues to be theorized about and imposed, but concrete reality contradicts its principles: not only do the strategies of several key enterprises regulate the markets, both economic and political systems are by now irreversibly interlocked. The only issue now is the extent of the marginal independence of political institutions from the direct influence of economic forces, and the degree (if any) to which *democratic political life* is still possible. It is a problem concerning not only the State but also international institutions, like the International Monetary Fund (IMF) and the World Bank, which play a decisive role in coordinating the monetary and economic policies of many countries. The "institutional vacuum" left by the collapse of the Bretton Woods system has not been filled by supranational autonomous institutions (Thomasberger). In the meantime, the investments and financial interests of the multinational firms become more and more extensive and important.

The globalization of the economy has also contributed to rendering untenable the "Keynesian compromise," both economically and politically. From the economic point of view, the competition of the "newly industrializing countries," and the movement of investments toward the periphery not only directly contribute to unemployment in the central countries; they also negatively influence world effective demand, to the extent that well-paid workers are replaced with poorly-paid workers (Lipietz). A negative influence is also exerted by the increasing mass of financial capital, which is destined not for investment but for speculation. Finally, the quest for equilibrium in the trade balance leads each country to apply deflationary policies; attempts are made to lower wages and global demand in order to improve the trading balance; rates of interest are kept high to support the rates of exchange of national currencies. These policies are also an effect of the above-mentioned deregulation of the international monetary system, and of the increase in the volume of speculative capital. Such effects reinforce the causes.

From the political point of view, these developments in the world economy lead to the decay of the State as primary subject and main sphere of politics. Both labour and monetary markets escape the possibility of control by individual States. The volume of capital roaming about the world has become ungovernable. It seems that at this point the central banks can no longer control the rate of exchange, and that the latter have even become insensitive to variations in the bank rate. The function of States, naturally, remains important, but their autonomy is radically reduced compared with the powers, on a world scale, of market forces, financial capital, and big corporations. The scope of democratic political life is consequently reduced.

After the debt crisis and the world recession of 1981-82, programmes of structural readjustment, as recommended by the IMF, affected some eighty countries. International financial institutions assumed a kind of economic tutelage of parallel government. Governments have been asked to reduce budget deficits, to control prices and trade, and to limit welfare expenditures; they also have had to give up many public enterprises. The policy of stimulating exports requires low wages. This world strategy reinforces the structure of the world economy—grounded on unfair terms of trade and unequal wages—which is at the root of indebtedness. On the peripheries and semi-peripheries of the world, while only a small minority of people become richer, the number of the poor increases as a consequence of low wages, confronted with "dollarization" of prices, and the decay of premodern and nonmarket modes of life and work. The "cultural catastrophe," as Polanyi argued, is continuing.

Putting neoliberal prescriptions into practice and becoming territory favourable for penetration by international finance did not save Mexico from near bankruptcy in December 1994. The need to protect foreign creditors (mainly North American) caused the United States and the IMF to immediately prepare a rescue plan: but at the cost of limiting the sovereignty of Mexico, which had to accept budgetary controls and a mortgage on petroleum exports. It therefore cannot be said that no form of organization, no form of world government is responsible for the economy. There is the General Agreement on

Trades and Tariffs (GATT) and its accompanying institutions, such as the World Bank and the new World Trade Organization, in addition to the G7 group, and regional organizations such as the European Community and the North American Free Trade Agreement (NAFTA). We know, furthermore, how concerned certain diplomatic services and secret services are to oppose reforms and (to use an expression of Polanyi's) any "popular governments" which might be adversely inclined to international financial interests. And yet, perhaps precisely for this reason, the need is increasingly felt for an alternative organization, one that is more autonomous and truly international; one that allows for at least a minimum of control of speculative capital flows. But how realistic is such an alternative? Anyway, it ought to come about as a result of intervention and collaboration on the part of various nations; therefore, it would presuppose the development of democracy inside those nations. But the existing economic system and the current economic situation make such a development increasingly difficult

As Polanyi emphasized in 1934—with reference to the crisis of liberal democracy and the spread of fascism in Europe—democracy and the developing capitalist market system tend, at a certain point, to become incompatible. It seems that the crisis of the "Keynesian" transformation has also rendered untenable the system of democratic equilibrium between different social forces, needs, and institutions. It is symptomatic that the latest trend in the field of industrial organization studies is to ignore the existence of power conflicts in favour of a premodern interiorization of the hierarchical principle, and an organic identification of workers with the organization and the goals fixed by the management.

In the "central" nations of the world capitalist system, the impact of creeping crisis, deregulation (that is, neoliberal rules), and insecurity of the monetary and international financial system militate against the possibility that States and international institutions may continue to guarantee, as in the "Keynesian" phase, social protection, and the appearance (at least) of that individual liberty, and democratic politics originally viewed as an integral part of the "liberal creed." While the autonomy of the economy is reinforced, the scope and instruments of a democratic political life become ever more limited. And the separation of economy and politics is no longer possible at this point. The new liberalism implies State intervention and a corporatist context: collaboration on the part of all for would-be common goals decided by an elite. Politics, under such conditions, tends to be less the coordination of independently expressed interests and increasingly a "political design" process moulding the very nature of such interests.

As far as peripheral or semi-peripheral nations are concerned, the development of the market, or of industrial production does not imply the assertion of individual freedom and political democracy, such as occurred in the early days of bourgeois society. In the newly industrializing countries, the political system often plays an important role in shaping the organization of production, and the direction of development, considered as *the* national goal. The determinative importance of the State and corporative involvement in the name of developmentalist ideology combine with the quasi-governmental role of big firms, resulting in "privatization of the planning process" (Bugra). Businessmen depend on State intervention and coordination, but have direct and exclusive access to government. Informal and particularistic ties, according to Bugra, characterize the relationship between the State and big business. Institutional checks and balances are lacking, and the behaviour of public bureaucracy is discretionary rather than rule-based and legally-bound as in the "rational" Weberian model. A tendency in this direction also exists in the older industrialized countries, representing a significant aspect of the decadence of democracy.

There is no doubt that the predominance of the neoliberal alternative—compared with that of managed capitalism, neocorporatist *concertation*, "Keynesian" and welfare policies—has increased polarization, in terms of wealth and power, both within and between nations. Unemployment, poverty and social marginalization have increased. The grave consequences of ecological destruction, waste of resources and deterioration of social life are more and more noticeable.

This outcome compels us to question not only neoliberalism, but also the preceding phase. At the end of the war, when the United States fully embarked upon its hegemonic role, "universal capitalism" (Polanyi's phrase, 1945) imposed itself and policies aimed at "third world" development systematically began. Considering the last half-century as a whole, there was a first phase characterized by Fordist-Keynesian compromise, the neocorporatist State, the dollar standard, and the resulting State regulation of labour and currency markets which now appears as a mode of capitalist development subsequently left behind by development itself. Therefore, this institutional order can no longer be an alternative. Currently, the very existence of a neoliberal economy, in the context of global competition, hinders a return to institutions of the previous phase. Gains in productivity can no longer be redistributed; wages must be kept as low as possible. Moreover, postwar development, characterized by mass production and the Fordist-Keynesian "mode of regulation," has overexploited natural and social resources on such a massive scale, and without bothering to replace them, so as to make expanded reproduction of capital more and more difficult. Social costs, exhaustion of resources and pollution are setting ecological limits to growth. Thus, in a global-ized economic system, "Fordism is not a realistic prospect for the 'periphery' of the world, where most people live" (Martinez-Alier).

These considerations lead us to think also that there is no going back to the institutions of the previous phase, in the more general sense, in that it seems by now necessary to dispute capitalist devel-opment itself, of which both the Fordist-Keynesian and the neolib-eral phases are modes of operation.

We have come to realize (de Romaña) that growth can be jobless, that with it the cost but not the standard of living increases, and that gross national product (GNP) figures do not take into account autonomous economic powers and goals that are incompatible with any exercise of choice (beginning with the definition of needs) adher-ent to the experience and interaction of individuals. The success of neoliberalism signals something which goes beyond a contrast with the institutions and policies of the preceding phase: for it repre-sents abandonment of the hope that, after the crisis of liberal capi-talism, society would steadily follow the path of a *democratic* politi-cization of the economy. For Polanyi, too, this was in fact only *one* of the alternatives.

The ideology of both development and economic liberalism today is society's answer to its problems, as was the reformulation of the Poor Law at the end of the eighteenth century. The social system tends to react in a manner consistent with its organization, even though, since the organization itself is the source of the problem, the result is a positive feedback of increased imbalance and aggravation. While the global domination of financial capital is reinforced, the possibility of contrasting entropy, of stopping or reversing the increasing disorder, is diminished. Society must relinquish political-democratic consideration of any *alternative choices*.

Although a radically alternative system seems for the moment unlikely and even difficult to imagine, there exist currently in society ideas, attitudes, and even accomplishments which, although only partially and sometimes illusorily, appear nevertheless as alternatives to the system in force. At the same time, there exist tentative plans to resolve both the problem of unemployment and the lack of those services which would be of use, but which do not allow for profit as such; services which the State has either never offered, or no longer offers. There is the question, for example, of building a new, alternative sector of activity, dedicated to socially useful tasks and only partially supported by the State (Lipietz). Such a sector could be a testing ground for new social relations, nonmarket forms of organization, and democratic forms of control by customers, local communities and State agencies.

Servet's paper examines lending organizations widespread in Africa which demonstrate the capacity of individuals to manage collectively their own resources in opposition to the State and the market. Individual interest expresses itself in a collective dimension which counteracts the "cultural catastrophe." Elements of the traditional culture are revitalized within more modern forms of voluntary reciprocity and social protection.

The link between individual economic choice and social institutions within complex "Western" societies, is the subject of Cella's paper. Polanyi's "forms of integration" are employed as sociological models for the analysis of different kinds of social determinants of economic action. In a market society there exist also forms of "reciprocity and redistribution," which, although useful for its reproduction, refer to different patterns of social interaction and economic reality. Cella also discusses such important problems of sociological method as relations between micro and macro levels, and utilization of the concept of "embeddedness" by neoinstitutionalist economics.

It is true that the structures of vested interested remain fundamental; also important however are the signs, albeit slight, of autonomous cultural reconstruction as an alternative to utilitarianism; the economistic conception of development, the pervasiveness of the dominion of capital and the market. The signs extend all the way from the introduction of indicators of welfare in national accounting (de Romaña), to proposals for alternative forms of an "informal" economy, and even a cultural fabric of convivial relations and a new kind of moral economy. All this is, so to speak, "small but beautiful."

It is as important as the efforts of the ecologists. The decadence of politics, the lack of faith in the possibility of democratic control of the economic system, seem for the moment, to leave room only for small and indirect escape routes, or for sometimes overly generic criticism of "instrumental rationality."

Half a century after the publication of Polanyi's *The Great Transformation* the economy is no less "disembedded" and prevalent, although the liberal nineteenth-century system has been irreversibly supplanted. Subordination of the economy to democratically defined social objectives remains but a utopia. The world is more than ever unified by the market. Even defences against the market mechanism, especially those previously won by the working classes, have been attacked and partially dismantled. Therefore, while Polanyi's analysis of the characteristics and history of the market system continues to be valid and contributes toward understanding the current situation, it may be asked whether the political prospects, delineated for example in the closing pages of *The Great Transformation*, constitute little more than wishful thinking.

In fact, Polanyi not only raises the problem of the different phases of modern capitalist society, but also the problem of this kind of society in general, and thorough-going alternative can be conceived. Placing themselves in this more general perspective, Berthoud and Rotstein ask why we are witnessing the "resurgence of market institutions," and what "the secret of the market's seductive power" is. They seek to answer these questions by considering market society as a particular form of externalization, or as an expression of man's realization in social institutions. Current society rests on the illusion of freedom from the constraints of society, on the illusion of "a purely individualizing and rationalizing externalization." In fact, the opposite is true, such a society being characterized by "technical and market heteronomy."

Moreover, the illusion of freedom reinforces the heteronomy: the "fetishism of commodities" concept thus acquiring a deeper meaning, allowing us to better understand the success of liberal ideologies. All the more so since the end of really existing communism "disqualifies, in advance, any doubts about the unchallengeable superiority of the really existing regime of freedom and the consumer market" (Bauman). Is, then, the market system "without alternatives?"

The end of communism has meant that the modern grandiose dream "of a transparent, monitored, supervised, and deliberately

shaped order" (Bauman) is definitely out of the question. The sociological characteristics of postmodern society furthermore lead to "privatization of dissent." Discontent stops short of merging with social
movements. All that remains for individuals is illusory participation
in the enchanted society of commodities and mass media. Communism was unable to meet the challenge of a world where seduction of
the consumer has become the most important way of securing social
integration.

The absence of the communist alternative, however, can damage
the market system since it no longer recognizes the necessity to
carry out institutional transformations (like the welfare and neocorporatist State) to prevent the the accumulation of "lethal dysfunctions" (Bauman). The problem will more and more become one, in
Polanyi's well-known phrase, of "how to organize human life in a
machine society": one that capitalism will prove increasingly incom-
petent to solve.

The continuation of the critique, then, is more imperative than
ever. We do not know whether socialism has a future; what is certain is that, if we at least wish to have a future, we cannot accept
the "end of history" thesis (Devine); we must pursue a critical analysis of "really existing capitalism." The reality of capitalism as a
world system does not confirm, indeed contradicts, liberal ideology,
according to which only the market can guarantee economic rationality; only capitalism can guarantee democracy; and only free trade
can guarantee development (Amin). The basis of socialism is analysis of the historical limits of capitalist "rationality," its characteristic economism, the constraints it exerts on democracy, and the
polarization it produces between classes and nations. This is the scientific foundation of socialism, not a blueprint for a new society. The
choice between alternative institutions must be left to the creativity
of future generations.

The experience of previous socialist regimes has taught us that
neither bureaucratic planning nor the "antidemocratic political
monopoly of a ruling party-State" (Amin) can be an alternative. In
addition, the "regional planning," which in 1945 Polanyi posited in
contrast to "universal capitalism," should not result in regional
autarky; polycentralism and democratic regional governments
should go hand in hand with international cooperation and some
kind of democratic world government.

The emancipatory ideals of socialism, brought into disrepute by the Soviet-Statist model, permit us both to carry out a critical analysis of that model (Devine), and to polarize our judgement and choices. These ideals are to be found, in a utopian sense, beyond the horizon of economic ideology which is as pervasive as it is unilateral and incapable of facing the real problems of our world. Even the ecological point of view, which sees the "entropic character" of the capitalist market economy as contrasting with the "anti-entropic properties of life" (Martinez-Alier), ends by consistently proposing some kind of democratic socialism. The problem of organizing the "livelihood of man" at the global level, while taking account of the needs of future generations, cannot be resolved either by the market or by ecomanagerialism, by central planning or by little "ecotopian" communes. It could, however, be resolved by "ecological socialism," "defined by equality, internationalism, and social and communal control over the means of production." It is in this direction, according to Martinez-Alier, that we should seek an effective solution to the need for embedding economic decisions in the political sphere.

The fundamental thesis of *The Great Transformation* is that the liberal utopia had been rendered obsolete by the very development of capitalist society. Thereupon, conscious and democratic control of the economy could now present itself as a topical need. This had been the object of Polanyi's analyses in the early 1920s, when he used to make explicit reference to Otto Bauer's "functional" socialism and to guild socialism. The processes and current consequences of the domination and globalization of the market-capitalist system again suggest the same need, but also disenchanted consciousness of the difficulty in satisfying it. "Social control of the polity and the economy through self-government" (Devine)—or, as Polanyi wrote, the development of democracy toward "planned intervention of the producers and consumers themselves"— seem to be more than ever the only means of facing economic, ecological, and social entropy. But this objective, to be pursued through the conscious participation of the people, seems as necessary as the actual possibility of realizing it seems remote.

I.

THE SEDUCTION OF THE MARKET AND THE SOCIALIST ALTERNATIVE

1.

THE SEDUCTIVE MARKET

Gérald Berthoud and Abraham Rotstein

"In retrospect our age will be credited with having seen the end of the self-regulating market."[1] So wrote Karl Polanyi in 1944 when he looked hopefully toward the promise of the postwar period. In that work he portrayed the self-regulating market system as an ephemeral network that ran blindly in its own autonomous grooves. The system was seen as inimical to the flourishing of a genuinely human society. After the Great Depression had signalled a devastating conclusion to the nineteenth-century market system, Polanyi foresaw the coming of creative new adaptations for the economy in the period of social reconstruction that was to follow the peace.

In its pristine form, the system of self-regulating markets, Polanyi argued, was inoperable. As the spreading market system threw its net over the factors of production such as labour and land, man reacted spontaneously to protect his social relationships and his habitat. A countermovement arose to safeguard these, the fabric of human society, against inadvertent destruction or erosion by the market. But such safeguards created serious disruptions of the system and ultimately led to its breakdown during the Great Depression. This marked the end of the utopian dream of a self-regulating market economy that was intended to guide the course of the human economy smoothly, harmoniously and justly.

For the postwar period, Polanyi foresaw the re-embedding of this runaway economy within the transcendent social purposes of society. The market would have a place within that social framework but it would be subordinated to society's overall objectives. This was in fact the challenge to which the term the "great transformation" also pointed. Were these prophesies of the 1940's wishful thinking? Today, almost a half-century later, we see instead a global panorama of a resurgent market system in both East and West. In the liberal democracies, anything and everything are being turned into commodities, accompanied by the widespread process of privatization and deregulation. In the East European countries, traditional planning is being abandoned in the expectation that "laws" of supply and demand will instantly fill the vacuum. Third world countries are being swept into the process by an expanded planetary liberalism under the aegis of such agencies as the International Monetary Fund (IMF) and the World Bank.

How are we to understand the great chasm that has opened up under socialism in Eastern Europe, the Soviet Union, and even China? The great rush to exit from the system of centrally planned regimes in the direction of the market system has been spurred by its own ideological upheaval. For the moment, the renewed liberal perspective in Eastern Europe goes far beyond the actual institutional changes that have so far taken place. With all the impetus of a Hegelian dialectic in reverse gear, the new rhetoric has seemingly swung back about a century and a half to reinvent the fervent crusade of Manchester liberalism.

What is the secret of the market's seductive power? Are Polanyi's arguments undermined or negated by present circumstances?

The key to his analysis was the fate of the three factors of production: land, labour and capital. Each has now been subjected to new global forces that should be explored. Moreover, the power of the Nation State, that traditional bulwark against the market, is being subverted by independent trends toward globalization spearheaded by the new circuits of communications technology.

How can we account for this unexpected turn of events? Was Polanyi spectacularly wrong? The resurgence of the market on the wings of the new global electronic technology seems to belie and negate much of the humanist thrust of *The Great Transformation*. The original countermovements toward the market to which Polanyi had pointed, now seem to be countered in their turn. It is as if a "counterreformation" has been set in train.

Can Polanyi's analysis be reconciled in some way with comtemporary developments? Some revision and amplification of his views is, we believe, now necessary given that almost five decades have elapsed since his book appeared. In particular, a more extended analytical and theoretical perspective on the genesis of the market as an institution is warranted. Whence does it derive its siren-like qualities that seem to entrance a whole generation of disenchanted socialists?

What we propose here is a new mode of analysis of the "archeology" of the market: that is, its emergence as an institutional artifact embodying a simulated version of a hybrid archaic gift. While this mode of analysis is speculative, it is nevertheless linked to what Hegel, Marx, and Polanyi himself referred to as the process of "externalization" or "exteriorization" as a driving force of social development, and fundamentally a way of being human.

In attempting to trace the genesis of the market as institution we may pose the following question. In what way do the forms of integration (reciprocity, redistribution and market) derive, however indirectly, from certain ontological aspects of man? We shall address this question in the following section drawing on the domains of paleontology and psychoanalysis, treating it under the broad rubric of the process of externalization. Such a review of Polanyi's "forms of integration" will help our understanding of the durable and seductive market as it reemerges once more. If we are indeed at the present time reliving the 1920s with renewed faith in the market utopia, should we anticipate a new set of countermovements in the realm of land, labour and capital, or even another global collapse as end result?

In the *Economic and Philosophic Manuscripts* of 1844 Marx first put forward the notion of *äusserung,* translated literally as "externalization," the process whereby man came to realize himself through his creative talents and activities. In this Marx was following Hegel, the original proponent of the notion that institutional evolution was the external expression of the phenomenology of mind. For Hegel, human history and human society proceeded as an unfolding of the "inner" within and into the "outer."

Originally, the term externalization had a fully positive connotation; but Marx introduced significant qualifications to the original Hegelian perspective. Marx highlighted the antinomies and contradictions of social evolution. He proceeded to contrast this *äusserung* with its opposite, *entäusserung* (usually translated as estrangement or alienation, particularly as it related to modern society). This was the initial disease that he diagnosed in the capitalist (or market) system, one that subverted all that was human and worthwhile in man's natural mode of self-expression, and turned it into the source of his oppression.

Of the two, much of Marx's attention was taken up with the latter, *entäusserung*, and little thought was given to the initial proposition, the process of externalization itself. How in fact does man embody himself not only in his artifacts but in the social institutions that express his person, his goals and his aspirations? The (capitalist) market system was only treated as a form of subversion of man's human capacities and authentic forms of his self-expression, even though it was regarded as a necessary stage of historical development through which he had to pass. Inner contradictions of the social process would produce the forces of its own eventual destruction and bring forward the next phase of development that was to follow capitalism.

The pendulum of the dialectic "overshot" with virtually every swing. The immediacy of the social process as an authentic form of man's self-expression was lost. It was partly shrouded in the mists of some aboriginal stage in time when a natural or idyllic state existed. But in history, mobilization for the struggle required denigration of the tainted forms of social existence which for Marx constituted virtually all of history. Man could hardly recognize the pristine elements of his being and personality any more in the externalization of the social processes now surrounding him.

In attempting to distinguish the effective features of the process of externalization and to analyze its role in social evolution, we may examine how the issue was treated in the works of Leroi-Gourhan and Castoriadis.

We shall start with the features that were essential for the development of the human being. In Leroi-Gourhan's *Le Geste et la Parole*, the fundamental basis of this human condition is vertical posture with its two corollaries of a low-situated face and free hands, thereby following the two poles that are constitutive of the human condition, language and technique. The first comprises both thought and symbol, while technique includes gesture and tool. Tool and symbol stem from the same mental phenomenon. "Man makes concrete tools and symbols, both emerging out of the same process or rather resorting from the same basic source of the brain."[2]

These two constitutive poles, "hand-tool" and "face-language," define the essential conditions of a world made human. Put differently, through language and technique man is from the very beginning liberated from his immediate experience and its physiological limitations. At bottom, what is properly human is "the faculty of symbolization or more generally that property of the human brain that interposes some distance between actual experience and his organism."[3] Consequently, "all of human evolution combines to locate outside of man the specific adaptation to which the rest of the animal world responds."[4] Thus man may be conceived as an animal whose mode of being, thinking and acting beyond some rudimentary activities, externalizes, through symbols and tools, what lies within himself. Further, "the technical function is externalized into the movable tool" and "the perceived object shifts externally into a verbal symbol."[5] But this would become a reductionist argument, if this movement were regarded merely as one-way, that is from inside to the outside. It is here that our second source applies, because for Castoriadis the question turns on what it is that is intrinsic to the human being.

While acknowledging the importance of Leroi-Gourhan's approach, Castoriadis insists that externalization "remains unintelligible if it is severed from its own interior source, even though the latter may not be accessible."[6] Such an interior source is nothing less than mind in the fullest sense, including both cognitive and affective components. For Castoriadis, such a human psyche is inherently "asocial" or "arational" and "sees everything in relation to itself."[7] Of course, such a human being would be unable to survive, were he or she under the constraints of reality. But there is always an antinomy between the psychic universe and the social world. The result is a compromise between the two which constitutes the individual's social being.

The conjunction of these pale ontological and psychoanalytical views renders the human condition as a constantly unstable balance between liberty and social attachment; alternatively, between self-interest and moral obligation. Man's self-realization occurs within such a basic contradiction.

It is within this context that the market can be perceived as one of the definitive forms of institutional externalization *en route* from primordial community to modern society. In other words, what is essential for understanding the seductive power of the market is the realization that men do not set up direct relations among themselves except within small groups and for limited time periods. The human being projects a part of his interior existence outward as a social being. For some this liberation of the individual from the natural and social environment is evidence of continuing progress. Ever more effective mediation between man and nature, accompanied by a more articulated mediation between man and man, results in an increasingly artificial universe.

For further consideration of this process, we turn to Mauss as our point of departure. In his famous *Essay on the Gift*, he underlines the anthropological wisdom of the primordial community and highlights the archaic gift. With the latter, Mauss insists, "we touch upon fundamentals."[8] The primordial community is the matrix from which other social systems emerge, and thus it plays a constitutive role.

The gift, viewed in such a manner, embodies a social logic, an integrative social form, or better still is a "sort of hybrid."[9] But the gift as object and symbol is a mediation between persons and groups. As such it is of course a proxy for the giver. Thus such a formula expressed by Mauss as "by giving one is giving oneself,"[10] is a way to reduce gift-exchange to confusing persons with things, ignoring any distinction between them. To insist only on the unifying component of the gift is to forget that human communication occurs through a symbolic mediation. Consequently, exchange allows one at the same time to express one's subjective identity and to show one's social membership. In other words, a gift, just like a commodity, must be considered within a generalized movement of externalization characteristic of the human condition. Both gift and commodity are particular forms of objectification, essential conditions for man to build his social universe. He can thus insure also his personal survival against the violence of his own nature, that of the "arational" or "asocial" psyche, as Castoriadis would express it.

But the main difficulty is how to outline, even in a speculative way, the logical transformation of gift into commodity. There is no doubt that the gift, viewed as the original form of exchange and pristine expression of the social link, is a combination of elements which are institutionally separated and modified today.

The archaic gift may be viewed as consisting of three parts combined in various ways. Gift can be simultaneously a constraining act to manifest one's membership within a total community, an affirmation of one's individuality, particularly in the competitive practices seeking prestige, and also an expression of generosity.

The separation of the gift into its economic and social components results in the well-known distinction between contract and moral obligation, as has been clearly defined by Mauss. On the one hand, the so-called independent individual, centered on his or her own utility or interest, engages in free exchange. On the other, a person involves himself in the practice of pure gifts to maintain the foundations of the common life of a group.

Within the market context, however, the economic order tends to take the place of the society as a whole, subordinating the political order to its own objectives and reducing the social order to a residual status. The distinction between commodity and "pure" gift exemplifies quite adequately the opposition between the economic and the social. This tendency to confound economy and society is a permanent feature of economic liberalism. Such, by our purposes here, is the view of Adam Smith: "society may subsist among different men, as among different merchants, from a sense of its utility, without any mutual love or affection; and though no man in it should owe any obligation, or be bound in gratitude to any other, it may still be upheld by a mercenary exchange of good offices according to an agreed valuation."[11]

For the "new economists," such a view is so widespread that everything is transformed into commodities, and every social link is regarded as a market exchange. The independence of the private sphere seems the most desirable state for the individual. This withdrawal into oneself is understandable as we consider the process of externalization. In the movement from gift to commodity, there is a change from a personified to a reified objectification. The social totality is no longer expressed in spiritual terms but in things available for so-called independent individuals.

Today, man hopes to be released from any obligation towards nature, persons and particular groups, except such as may result from contractual relationships. It is becoming not only acceptable but more and more desirable that everything be rendered into artifact and thus sold as a commodity. Even symbols of social identification are produced by the mass media. In this case, we reach the ultimate step of externalization by transforming our social membership into a commercial product to be consumed in the private sphere.

Technique is seductive, as Polanyi had already noted in his

unpublished essay "Freedom and Technology,"[12] because it is possible with it "to promise the solution of all problems, the implementation of all ideals." The market is of course also viewed as a liberating force. With technology the human being may hope to escape from the constraints of the natural environment; with the market this same human being may believe he can free himself from the constraints of society. Such is the prospect of a modernity which was assuming the aspect of ineluctable process. Such a movement of externalization, pushed to the extreme, could lead to a generalized separation of individuals, in order to allow anyone to manipulate things and persons according to his commercial dictates, whims and desires.

Here we confront a deeply rooted illusion. The mutual direct dependence of individuals in traditional systems is not replaced by independence, but fundamentally by indirect dependence within the market system.

At first sight, a commodity seems to be an object free from any symbolic tie, thus depersonalized and consequently easily alienable. The individual himself is also free of any nonvoluntary obligation, and his relationships remain ephemeral. Even rules of good conduct are cut back to a minimum, when market codification is internalized. The market universe is a homogenized world of strangers often moved by generalized indifference. Within market relationships intentions do not matter, only results are taken into account. The market is thus an emancipatory device for avoiding any affective or emotional constraints and misunderstandings so common in human communication. The market is still assumed to consist of pure exchanges strictly determined by the calculus of private interests. the artifice of price imposes reason and measure on its protagonists. Moreover, impersonal market exchange is designed to keep the other at arm's length.

The individual, thus constituted by his economic role, is neither too near nor too far from the other. He or she is consequently in a position to preserve his or her independence, this heteronomous form of freedom. As a substitute for interpersonal links, implied for example by reciprocity, the market tends to replace internalized norms of behavior by objective and quantifiable criteria. Up to a certain point, there is a progressive shift from comprehensive internalization to the primacy of codification. Such is of course the meaning of the saying the "truth of prices."

The individual is then strongly inclined to believe that he is free to choose from among things external to everybody and thus available to anyone. But subsequently this liberating force of the market is seen to be at variance with the mystification it creates. And here, although Marx seems to be no longer fashionable, we would have to start with the fetishism of commodities, and more widely with the whole question of social reification or social artifact.

The present extension of technical and market dominance produces, strictly speaking, individuals whose main characteristic is their impersonality and thus their total lack of self-creativity. In a startling summary, Leroi-Gourhan insists on the correspondence between technical externalization as exemplified in "the liberation of culinary art by tinned food," and symbolic externalization from direct social participation to passive reception "through the window of the television set and the lips of the transistor radio."[13] Again, the market can supply an affective and emotional artifact, replacing in a simulated way familial intimacy, provided of course that such a private sphere is not itself ruled by market norms.

Within such a situation, how do we preserve within each of us what is properly human, when the technical and market mediation tends to become our mode of being and acting? How do we avoid being transformed individually and collectively into instruments and victims of a system which is however of our own construction?

Are we subjected only to the requirements of the market and technology only so that may be regulated by our behaviour? We are compelled to answer in the affirmative. With increasing conformism, which endangers any expression of inner freedom, people are mesmerized by the very words "technology" and "market," and adhere almost exclusively to their injunctions. However difficult it may be to question the irreversibility of this condition, it is particularly urgent within the present global context, to argue against its "absolutization."

Finally, we must ask what is more likely: a global collapse or the rise of new countermovements? In the previous section we tried to indicate to some of the ontological or internal sources of the origin of the market. We now turn to the events of recent years centering on the resurgence of market institutions. The most dramatic case is that of the former communist countries; but important developments are occurring also in the global economy, particularly in the financial field. Accordingly, it may be asked whether markets are an expression of the process of externalization in the social or institutional field.

Do the events in Eastern Europe mean that the clock has been turned back, restoring the nineteenth-century world of markets?

That would not be an appropriate interpretation of events. *The Great Transformation* portrayed the dramatic confrontation of two giant protagonists. Under Polanyi's broad rubric of "economy and society," the self-regulating market economy confronted the resilience of human community. But in the postwar period, new protagonists have intruded of a sort not easily accommodated in this schema. They included secular forces such as the pace and calibre of technological change, the nuclear threat at the heart of the cold war, the decades of political repression that resulted from the nuclear threat, and breakthroughs in industrial production and electronic communication. All of these new factors intruded into the traditional realm of "economy" and "society" and spawned in turn new stresses and disruptions as well as new ways of restructuring the world economic system.

Beyond the specific shocks and the political stringencies, as well as the immediate reactions to them, the underlying secular trends should be examined. Over the long term we may discern a widespread, underlying process of externalization that has helped shape modern society. In that sense many other systems outside of the economy, social as well as sociotechnical, are woven into the fabric of what we term the "complex society."

A striking parallel to the economy, for example, lies in the evolution of the legal system. This system evolves from an internalized code linked to the magic and religion of tribal society, into an objectified external code of law. This is proudly proclaimed as "the rule of law and not of men." Is there a parallel here (albeit a positive one) to the emergence of the autonomous self-regulating market system? In short, as the externalization process envelops modern society, we may see parallels in other social spheres, such as law, to the process of separation and emergence of the economy as an autonomous sphere.

This self-regulating market system is better understood (particularly by economists) in terms of its process rather than its origin. How and why did its main features come about? Polanyi's "catallactic triad," the convergence of trade, money and market within the modern market system, is itself a substantive institutional development of enormous importance. But how are its origins to be understood, except as a major illustration of systemic convergence and externalization of our social structures. This is indeed the essence of "self-regulation."

The modern currency system provides another striking example. Briefly put, the blending of the three money uses into the modern all-purpose money that Polanyi set out so well, offers a further illustration of a process of systemic convergence and externalization with a new power of its own to spin out of human control.

If we examine a few of the recent developments in the area of *haute* finance, we find that there has been an extraordinary expansion of market-type devices on a global level. These rely on the new communications techniques of electronic banking used in the currency and bond markets, and on computer-based "program trading" on the stock market.

One trillion dollars in global currencies move in tides through the world's currency and capital markets each week. Such markets operate around the clock and induce massive and instantaneous responses as hundreds of thousands of players monitor their computer screens and send huge sums cascading around the globe. Financial markets have become a global casino for its own sake, leaving far behind their traditional purpose of serving the needs of trade and investment.

There are still further strains on the global economic system to be taken into account: the accumulated budgetary deficits of Western countries; the outstanding debt of third world countries; the renewed volatility of oil prices; the crisis of local banks in the United States (Savings and Loan bailouts may approach $500 billion), and ensuing global economic recession. Under the circumstances, the volatility of currency, capital and stock markets grows, and along with it the risk of major disruption in the global financial system.

We may skirt catastrophe in most of these areas most of the time. But the risk remains that the strained and overextended financial system is in increasingly precarious equilibrium. It may not be able to sustain a particularly heavy shock and this may create a series of disruptions throughout the global economy. There are few institutional controls to modify or counter these disruptive effects, or to compensate for severe losses.

Another new area of major concern is the environment. The commitment to exponential economic growth puts a fragile world ecology under increasing strain. Capitalism is in its very essence oriented toward traditional (exponential) rates of economic growth. If these cannot be sustained, capitalism will be in dire straits. Doing something serious about the environment will involve a major deceleration or possibly elimination of what we normally mean by growth. We have hardly begun to face up to this impasse.

The social drama recalled in *The Great Transformation* should alert us to the possibility of new countermovements to maintain the integrity of society amid these new threats. But at the beginning of the last decade of this century, these countermovements are barely under way.

The erosion of the economic powers of the Nation State seems also to have weakened the potential for a response in the field of the new communications technology on which global financial markets depend. A firm international countermovement would be the most effective level of response, but the requisite international networks are still absent and the channels of intervention such as the International Monetary Fund and the World Bank are still weak; resources they have available are inadequate to the task.

Only in the area of the environment can we detect a new global consciousness of the threat to man's habitat posed by the new industrialism. The remarkable development of the Green movement signals a new spontaneous countermovement around "land." The growing momentum of this movement, carried along by organizations such as Greenpeace, may before long begin to contain indiscriminate industrial depredations, and renew the old battle of "habitat versus improvement."

The countries of Eastern Europe appear poised to live through a speeded-up version of nineteenth-century Europe's travail as recounted in *The Great Transformation*. But many of those who rush to embrace the liberal society may come up against their own exaggerated expectations, particularly of those implicit features that add a special lustre to Western economies. The whole apparatus of the Welfare State is today assumed to be present as an implicit support system. Many of these welfare provisions had emerged out of the travails of the nineteenth century and its double movement. They are now taken for granted in Western countries as an intrinsic part of the market economy.

But can the populations of Eastern Europe rely on such welfare provisions when in their turn they shift, under very difficult economic circumstances, to a market economy? When dramatic price increases are imposed on the population (e.g., in Hungary or Poland),

and effective support systems are absent or fall short, disillusionment may set in. This may be followed by open rebellion when it is realized that the new market economy fails to provide the expected bonanza, even perhaps falling short in performance of that of the old socialist regime.

CONCLUSION

The Great Transformation heralded a more benign society in the postwar period within which market institutions would be subsumed. In subsequent work, Polanyi anticipated the extent to which this challenge of institutional reform would be overtaken by technological stringencies.

The complexities have multiplied in many directions since the antinomies of "economy and society" were set out in *The Great Transformation*. If we widen our view of the spectrum of social and political forces at work, we may discern the underlying secular trends and the proliferation of the more sophisticated systems that permeate our lives. Events in the 1980s and the beginning of the 1990s have outrun what Polanyi foresaw in the 1940s. Yet his themes from that period are interwoven with our present concerns.

In the last decade, the anticipated social equilibrium was upset by the new technologies of *haute* finance and communications. The dark underside of globalization became apparent in the threats to the planet's ecological systems.

What was not anticipated was the resurgence of market systems to displace the failed methods of central planning in Eastern Europe and the Soviet Union. Does this passionate embrace of market institutions have more than a fleeting chance of success in creating a stable and more productive form of livelihood?

The countermovements that begin to make their appearance are as rudimentary in this new phase of the expansion of the market economy, as were the countermovements against labour and land markets in the 1840s and 1850s at the onset of the first round of *laissez-faire*. Their ability to contain the new forms of unbridled technological innovation and environmental depredation is only just being tested. The drama of *The Great Transformation* may be replayed on a larger screen with human protagonists now contending with robotic forces rather than with each other.

How can we account for the recurrence of this old drama writ larger than ever? We have pointed in a forgotten direction—that of the process of externalization. Here we see the contrast between the inner imperative, a process of self-objectification through market institutions, and the disruptive results for a complex society as sketched out above. The social consequences take on an unexpected and contradictory shape from what was initially intended. Perhaps this is a further illustration of the perils to which Polanyi pointed when he singled out the problems of power and economic value as the abiding moral concerns of modern society.

NOTES

1. K. Polanyi, *The Great Transformation. The Political and Economic Origins of Our Time* (Boston: Beacon Press, 1957 [1944]), p. 142.
2. A. Leroi-Gourhan, *Le geste et la parole. La mémoire et les rythmes* (Paris: Albin Michel, 1965), p. 162.
3. *Ibid.*, p. 33.
4. *Ibid.*, p. 34.
5. *Ibid.*, p. 87.
6. C. Castoriadis, *Les carrefours du labyrinthe* (Paris: Seuil, 1978), p. 221.
7. C. Castoriadis, "Institution de la société et religion," *Esprit* (May 1982), p. 116.
8. M. Mauss, M. *The Gift. The Form and Reason for Exchange in Archaic Societies* (London: Routledge, 1990), p. 70.
9. *Ibid.*, p. 73.
10. *Ibid.*, p. 46.
11. A. Smith, *The Theory of Moral Sentiments* (Oxford: Clarendon Press, 1976), p. 86.
12. Karl Polanyi, "Freedom and Technology," unpublished essay (Karl Polanyi Archive, Karl Polanyi Institute of Political Economy, Concordia University, Montréal, Québec).
13. *Le geste et la parole*, pp. 202-3.

REFERENCES

Castoriadis, C. *Les carrefours du labyrinthe* (Paris: Seuil, 1978).
———. "Institution de la société et Religion," *Esprit* (May 1982), pp. 116-131.
Leroi-Gourhan, A. *Le geste et la parole. Technique et langage* (Paris: Albin Michel, 1964).

————. *Le geste et la parole. La mémoire et les rythmes* (Paris: Albin Michel, 1965).

Mauss, M. *The Gift. The Form and Reason for Exchange in Archaic Societies* (London: Routledge, 1990 [1924]).

Polanyi, K. *The Great Transformation. The Political and Economic Origins of Our Time* (Boston: Beacon Press, 1957 [1944]).

Smith, A. *The Theory of Moral Sentiments*. Edited by D. D. Raphael and A. L. Macfie. (Oxford: Clarendon Press, 1976 [1759]).

2.

LIVING WITHOUT ALTERNATIVE

ZYGMUNT BAUMAN

Communism has died. Some say, of senility. Some say, of shameful afflictions. All agree that it will stay dead for a long, long time.

Official opinion (whatever that means) in the affluent West greeted the news, arguably the least expected news of the century, with self-congratulating glee. The theme of the celebration is well known: "our way of life" has once and for all proved both its viability and its superiority over any other real or imaginable form. Our mixture of individual freedom and market consumerism has emerged as the necessary and sufficient, truly universal principle of social organization; there will be no more traumatic turns of history, indeed no history at all to speak of. For "our way of life" the world has become safe. The century hitherto remarkable for choosing between alternatives on the battlefield has come to an end ten years before its appointed time. From now on, there will be nothing but more of the good things that already are.

Amid the din of celebration, the few voices of doubt are barely audible. Some doubts they do not dare to voice. Some inarticulate worries have not yet congealed into doubts fit to be put into words. One can only guess what they are.

Those who made use of communism as a bogeyman with which to

frighten disobedient children ("look what will become of you if you do not do what I tell you to") and bring them to their senses, feel slightly uneasy. Where are they to find a substitute for the service that communism—now no more—had rendered? How are people to be kept feeling thankful for however little they have if one can no longer take credit for defending them from having less still?

Some categories of people have more basic and more immediate reasons to be worried: the huge warfare bureaucracy, for instance. It had lived off the threat of the communist evil empire; the more terrifyingly real it could make the threat look, the better it lived. That bureaucracy presided over and derived its livelihood from the biggest peace time arms industry that even existed in history. This was an industry that did not need actual warfare to thrive: the initial stimulus of the communist threat sufficed to assure continuous, exponential development. Thereafter, it acquired its own momentum of self-perpetuation and growth. Producers of defensive weapons competed with merchants of offensive ones, navies with air forces, tanks with rocket units. New weapons had to be developed today because yesterday's weapons made inadequate or downright obsolete the weapons deployed the day before. Or, new weapons had to be developed because the laboratories, staffed with high-class brain power, kept constantly at the highest pitch by tempting commissions, ambition, and professional rivalry, could not stop spawning ever new ideas; and also because there were spare or idle technological resources eager to absorb them. And yet this cozy arrangement needed the communist threat to secure the steady inflow of funds. The weapons industry is less able than any other to survive without an enemy; its products have no use value when no one is afraid and no one seeks to frighten the others.

And there is yet another powerful industry that may bewail the passing of the communist enemy: those thousands of university departments and research institutes, worldwide networks of congresses, conferences, publishing houses and journals all dedicated to "Soviet and East-European Studies" are now, like the warfare bureaucracy, facing the prospect of redundancy. As with all well-established and viable organizations (including the warfare bureaucracy), *sovietology* will certainly attempt to find a new topic to justify its continued existence, which it can only do by construing new targets to match its impressive human and material resources. And yet one doubts whether new targets, however defined, will attract as in the past the funding and benevolence of the powers that be in amounts sufficient to maintain the industry at its recent level of material wealth, academic prestige, and self-congratulatory mood.

These and similar worries may be serious enough for the special interests directly affected, yet the global nature of any disaster to which they point is, to say the least, debatable. There are, however, other consequences of the demise of communism which may have truly global deleterious effects for the survival of that "form of life" whose ultimate triumph they ostensibly augur.

It is widely assumed, particularly on the extreme right of the political spectrum, that the bankruptcy of the communist system must have delivered a mortal blow not just to the preachers and outspoken devotees of the faith, but to any cause however loosely related to the leftist tradition of disaffection, critique and dissent, to any value-questioning, to any alternative vision. It is assumed that the practical discrediting of communism—construed as "the other" in respect of *our form of life*, the *negative* totality which injects meaning into *our positivity*—preempts by proxy and disqualifies in advance any doubts about the unchallengeable superiority of the really-existing regime of freedom and consumer market; that it discredits, moreover, any suggestion that this regime, even if technically more viable, may be still neither entirely flawless, nor the most just of conceivable orders (indeed that it may be instead in urgent need of overhaul and improvement). I will argue, however, that the assertion that the collapse of communism threatens the survival of the "Left alternative," and the Left critique *alone* is invalid, a *non sequitur*; that such dangers arise in the world which has abandoned the socialist alternative in its universally decried communist variant, apply to "our way of life" (that is, to the *really-existing regime* of free consumers and free markets) in the same (perhaps even greater) measure as they do to its Left critique—and hence may only render the continuation of a critique even more imperative than it otherwise would have been.

THE HISTORICAL MEANING OF THE COLLAPSE OF COMMUNISM

What lies buried beneath the debris of the communist system? A number of totalitarian states, of course; specimens of a regime which left rule-unprotected individuals at the mercy of rule-free power, and which insulated the self-reproduction of the political power-holders from all, and any intervention by the powerless. The demise of the totalitarian State cannot, however, be said to be final or complete, for communism was just one of many political formulae of totalitarianism. Noncommunist totalitarianism is neither logically incongruent as a notion, nor technically inoperative as a practice. Even a cursory survey of the panoply of extant political regimes would show that to issue a death certificate to totalitarianism just because its communist version has disintegrated would be, to say the least, premature and unwise. Even if every former communist State were to adopt parliamentary-democratic procedures and to guarantee individual rights (not by any means a foregone conclusion), this would not mean that "the world has become safe for democracy" and that the struggle between liberal and totalitarian principles previously existing within the contemporary body politic has been settled. To suggest that the communist utopia was the only virus responsible for totalitarian affliction would be to propagate a dangerous illusion, one that is both theoretically incapacitating and politically disarming; one that would be, for the future prospects of democracy, a costly and perhaps even lethal error.

There are, however, other graves hidden beneath the rubble still waiting to be uncovered. The fall of communism was a resounding defeat for the project of *total order*, an artificially designed, all-embracing construct of human actions and their setting, one following the rules of reason rather than emerging from the diffuse and uncoordinated activities of human agents. It was also the downfall of a grandiose dream of *remaking nature*, forcing it to yield ever more of whatever human satisfaction might require, while disregarding or neutralizing those unplanned aspects of it which could not yield any sensible human benefit. It demonstrated also the ultimate frustration of the ambitions of global management; of replacing spontaneity with planning; of a transparent, monitored, supervised and deliberately shaped order in which nothing is left to chance and everything derives its meaning and *raison d'être* from the vision of a harmonious totality. In short, the fall of communism signaled the final retreat from the dreams and ambitions of *modernity*.

One of the most conspicuous traits of modernity was an overwhelming urge to replace spontaneity, seen as meaningless and identified with chaos, by an order devised by reason and constructed through legislative and controlling effort. That urge gestated (or was it gestated by?) what has become a specifically *modern State*, one that modeled its intentions and the prerogatives it claimed after the pattern of a gardener, a medical man, or an architect: a *gardening* State, a *therapeutic / surgical* State, a *space-managing* State. It was a gardening State, in so far as it usurped the right to select a final model of harmony which made some plants "useful" and others "useless," and to propagate some while exterminating others. It was a therapeutic/surgical State in so far as it set standards of health and disease, casting its subjects in the role of patients embodying ailments, incapable of defeating the malady without the intervention of a knowledgeable and resourceful tutor. It was a space-managing State in so far as it was busy landscaping territory which it regarded as wasteland, subjecting all local features to one unifying (homogenizing) principle of harmony.

As it happened, it was communism that took the precepts of modernity most seriously and set out to implement them in earnest. Indeed, its logic as system had been geared to gardening/therapeutic/architectural functions to the detriment of all and any prerequisites or demands not justified by the enterprise's rationale. From the start, communism was a system one-sidedly adapted to the task of mobilizing social and natural resources in the name of modernization: a nineteenth-century steam and iron ideal of modern plenty. It could—at least to its own satisfaction—compete with capitalism, but only with a capitalism engaged in the same pursuits. The trouble and its ultimate undoing, as transpired later, was that what it could not do, and did not ready itself for doing was to match the performance of a capitalist market-centred society once that society abandoned its steel mills and coal mines, and moved into the postmodern age—once it passed, in Jean Baudrillard's apt aphorism, from *metallurgy* to *semiurgy*. Stuck at its metallurgical stage, Soviet communism—as if to cast out devils—went on spending much of its surplus energy on fighting wide trousers, long hair, rock music and any other manifestation of semiurgical initiative.

Throughout its history, communism remained modernity's most devout (pious to the point of simplicity), vigorous and gallant champion. It also claimed to be its only true champion. Indeed, it was under communist, not capitalist, auspices that the audacious dream of modernity, freed from obstacles by the unsparing and seemingly omnipotent State, was pushed to its radical limits: grand designs, unlimited social engineering, huge and bulky technology, total transformation of nature. Deserts were irrigated (but they turned into salinated bogs); marshlands were dried out (but they turned into deserts); massive gas pipelines criss-crossed the land to remedy nature's whims in distributing its resources (but they kept exploding with a force unequaled by previous natural disasters); millions were lifted from the "idiocy of rural life" (but they were poisoned by the effluvia of rationally designed industry, if they did not perish first on the way). Raped and crippled, nature failed to deliver the riches once hoped for; the totality of the design scale made the devastation total. Worse, life did not seem to become more comfortable, more happy: needs (even those acknowledged by State tutors) did not seem to be satisfied better than before; the kingdom of reason and harmony seemed to be more distant than ever.

Even if communism could claim (erroneously, as it turned out) to be capable of *out-modernizing the modernizers*, it has become apparent that it cannot seriously contemplate facing the challenge of the postmodern world. For that may be seen as a world in which consumer choice is simultaneously the essential systemic requisite, the main factor of social integration, and the channel through which individual life-concerns are vented and problems resolved—while the State, grounding its expectations of discipline on the seduction of the consumer rather than on the indoctrination and oppression of the subject, could (and had to) wash its hands of all matters ideological and thus make conscience a private affair.

Communism could perhaps coexist with other forms of modern life as their "less developed," inferior sibling, and even offer a beacon of hope to those many who entertained the dream of joining, belatedly, the feast of modern plenty. But it could not survive the advent of the postmodern condition and its attendant values. It was the advent of this abandonment of modern ambitions and *de-étatization* (often wrongly described as "privatization") of social problems, this enthronement of seduction as the principal means of social control, this replacement of State-structuring with the self-constructing of individual and tribal identities that delivered to communism its *coup de grace*. Not so much by exposing yet again the inefficiency of its services, as by devaluing in no uncertain terms the purpose those services were meant to serve.

What, in fact, the affluent West is celebrating today is the official passing of its own past, with a last farewell to modernity's dream and arrogance. If the joyous immersion in postmodern fluidity and the sensuous bliss of aimless drift were poisoned by the residues of modern conscience—the urge to do something about those who suffer and clamour for something to be done—they seem unpolluted now. With communism, the ghost of modernity has been exorcized. Social engineering, the principle of communal responsibility for individual fate, the duty to commonly provide for individual survival, the tendency to view personal tragedies as social problems, the commandment to strive collectively for shared justice—all such moral precepts, once used to legitimize (some say motivate) modern practices—have been compromised beyond repair by the spectacular collapse of the communist system. No more guilty conscience. No scruples. No supraindividual commitment contaminating individual enjoyment. The past has descended into its grave in disgrace.

POLITICAL SIGNIFICANCE OF THE COLLAPSE OF COMMUNISM

The demise of the communist system was also a defeat for the overambitious and overprotective State, being in effect the final, dramatic act of a protracted and tortuous process of demise that makes credible the description of such states as *overambitious* and *overprotective*. Such a State seemed to give its last breath at the Vaclavske Namesti and in the city square of Timisoara, though it survived, albeit temporarily, Tiananmen Square. What discredited that State more than anything else *(de facto* if not in theory) was that it revealed unbelievable inner weakness; it surrendered to an unarmed crowd which ostensibly threatened nothing more than its resolute refusal to go home. Such weakness seems to be the sole property of a communist State; it can be easily, gladly, ascribed to everything it stood for. Can one imagine any similar effects of a public gathering in Trafalgar Square? Or in the Champs Elysées? Can one even imagine such gatherings?

The subjects of the communist State, because of the factors spelled out above, could have more reason to express disaffection than the populations of most Western countries. The point not stressed strongly enough, if at all, is that they also had greater possibility to make their disaffection effective and reforge it into systemic change. There was a price the overbearing State had to pay for the formidable volume of its concerns and entitlements, that price being *vulnerability*. To assert the State's right to command and control the means to assume responsibility for effects. The doorstep at which to lay blame is publicly known and clearly marked, and for each and every grievance it is *the same* doorstep. The State cannot help but cumulate and condense social dissent; it cannot help turning the edge of dissent against itself. The State is the major (and sufficient) factor in forging in often incompatible complaints and bids into a unified opposition, at least long enough for a dramatic showdown. The State that assumes the right to structure society also induces a tendency to political polarization: the conflicts that otherwise would remain diffuse, and fragment the population in different directions tend to be subsumed within unified opposition to the State.

It has not been proven that the illusionary nature of State power, its incapacity to survive the mere refusal of obedience, is the sole property of the communist State alone. Rather, what has been proved is that the communist regime created conditions most propitious for calling the bluff of State omnipotence. Most directly related to the nature of the regime was the possibility that refusal of obedience would be synchronized, involving if not all then than at least a sizable part of the population.

From the point of view of political sociology, by far the most important consequence of the present Western tendency to *de-étatization* of the growing number of previously State-managed areas is the *privatization of dissent*. With the balance of social activities and the logic of the life-process split into finely sliced and mutually autonomous functions, disaffections arising along separate task-oriented activities have no ground on which to meet and merge. Disaffection tends to generate one-issue campaigns; dissent, functionally dispersed, is either depoliticized or politically diluted. Seldom, if ever, is grievance directed against the State, the frantic efforts of political parties notwithstanding. More often than not it stops short even of blending into a social movement; instead, it rebounds as even greater disillusionment with collective solutions to individual troubles, and back again upon the sufferer in the form of feeling guilty on account of unfulfilled potential. The difference between the two systems consists not so much in the size of the sum total of disaffection, as in the propensity of dissent to accumulate to the point of the delegitimation of the system and its condensation into a system-subverting force.

It is for this reason that the sham of State omnipotence (sometimes represented in political theory as "legitimacy"), even if it really were nothing more than that, would tend to remain invisible.

Whether communist and liberal-parliamentary States (one presiding over the command economy, the other letting loose the market) do or do not share the inner weakness that only the communist States recently demonstrated, is bound to remain a moot question; it is unlikely to be put to a practical test. Hence the repeated assertions of the "end of history," of the "end of conflict," of "from now on, more of the same" may boast immunity to empirical criticism. However much such assertions *feel* wrong, detractors can find little in the political life of the apparently victorious system to give credibility to doubts.

Indeed, what is often called *Western civilization* seems to have found the philosophers' stone which all other civilizations sought in vain, and with it the warranty of its own immortality. It has succeeded in reforging its *discontents* into factors of its own *reproduction*. Whatever could be described in other systems as aspects of "dysfunctionality," manifestations of crisis and imminent breakdown seem to add to its strength and vigour. Deprivation breeds and further enhances the alluring power of the market, instead of gestating politically effective discontent. Public risks and dangers spawned by "single task" technologies and narrowly focused expertise supply further legitimation for problem-oriented action and functional subdivision, while generating demand for more technology and specialized expertise instead of questioning the wisdom of "problem-limited" thinking and practice. Impoverishment of the public sphere boosts the search for, and the seductive power of private escape from public squalor, and thus further decimates the ranks of potential defenders of the common weal. Above all, system-generated discontents are as subdivided as the agencies and actions generating them. At most, such discontents lead to "single-issue" campaigns commanding intense commitment to the issue focused upon, while the surrounding area becomes a vast no man's land of indifference and apathy. Party-political platforms do not reflect integrated group interests, real or postulated; instead, they are carefully patched together following scrupulous calculation of the relative popularity (that is, vote-generating capacity) of each issue that has caught the public's attention. Party-political mobilization of votes does not detract from the volume of voter apathy; indeed, one may say that the success of mobilization-through-single-issues is conditional on the voters' paying no attention to the topics left out of focus.

As a result of all this, the current Western form of life with its market-sponsored production of needs, privatization of grievance, and single task action seems to be strikingly different from that of previous regionally localized civilizations. Lacking either effective enemies inside or barbarians knocking at the gates from outside, it has only adulators and imitators. It has practically, and apparently irrevocably, delegitimized all alternatives to itself. Having done so, it has made it uncannily difficult, even impossible, to conceive of a different way of life in a form that would resist assimilation and hamper rather than boost the logic of its reproduction. Its courtly bards may therefore credibly pronounce it universal and *sub specie aeternitatis*.

THE COSTS OF VICTORY

One aspect of the situation in which the Western way of life has found itself after the collapse of the communist alternative is the unprecedented freedom it will from now on enjoy in construing "the other" in respect of itself, and, by the same token, in defining its own identity. We do not really know what effects such freedom may bring: little can we learn from history, as it did not contain any similar situation. For most historically formed civilizations, "the other" had self-constituting power. Alternatives appeared as real contenders and resourceful enemies, as threats to be reckoned with, adapted to and actively staved off. In such forms alternatives were sources of at least temporary dynamism, even if capacity for change proved in the end too limited to avoid ultimate defeat. For the larger part of the twentieth century, communism seemed to perform successfully the role of such an alternative. Even before that, virtually from the beginning of capitalist modernity, such a role was played by socialist movements. Such vital demonstration of social organization focused on the ends which capitalist modernity neglected, called for the broadening of the systemic agenda, and enforced corrections to prevent the accumulation of potentially lethal dysfunctions (the Welfare State being the most conspicuous though by no means the only example). This relative luxury of an autonomous, self-constituted critique is now no more. The question is where its functional substitute may be found, if at all.

The most immediate answer is that it is to be found now, at least in part, in the drastically enhanced role of the intellectuals' rational analysis and critique; the latter would now need to shoulder a task shared in the past with contenders in the political battle of systemic alternatives. What is at stake here is not merely an extension and intensification of the former role of the intellectuals.

Throughout the modern era, with states relying for their operative capacity mostly on ideological legitimation, intellectuals together with their institutions (universities most prominent among them), whether in conformist or rebellious mode, were first and foremost suppliers of current or potential legitimating formulae. These goods are not much in demand today, as the State by and large cedes the integrative task to the seductive attractions of the market—this absence of demand is behind the process dubbed the "crisis of the universities," namely the relentless erosion of the cultural role from which they derived their high status in the past. This loss of State-assisted status, however alarming at the moment, may yet prove a blessing in disguise. Prized away from automatically assumed or ascribed legitimizing (or, which amounts to much the same, delegitimizing) function, intellectual work may share in general freedom of cultural creation derived from the present irrelevance of culture for systemic reproduction.[1] This opens up in front of intellectual work a chance for considerable autonomy: indeed, a radical shift of balance inside the modern power/knowledge syndrome becoming a distinct possibility.

On the other hand, the waning of the communist alternative exposes the inner shortcomings of the market-centred version of freedom, previously either deproblematized or played down when confronting less alluring aspects of the system of comparative reference. Now, however, less can be forgiven it; less is likely to be placidly endured. An immanent critique of the maladies of a freedom reduced to consumer choice will be less easy to dismiss through the old expedient of imputing approval of a discredited alternative, and inanities which the critique discloses will be more difficult to exonerate as "the lesser of two evils." Market freedom would need to explain and defend itself on its own terms; these are, admittedly, not particularly strong or cogent, especially when it comes to justifying its social and psychological costs.

The costs are, indeed, enormous. And they cannot now be minimized by appeal to the fact that attempts to rectify them, such as were undertaken elsewhere, only increased instead of diminishing the total volume of human suffering. Such attempts are no more on the agenda. Yet the costs show no sign of abating, and call for action no less loudly than before; only the call is now more poignant than ever, as failure to act cannot be apologized for by proxy. The continuing polarization of well-being and life at risk cannot be made any less repulsive by pointing to the general impoverishment resulting elsewhere from efforts to remedy it. The traumas of privatized identity-constructs cannot be easily dispelled by pointing to the stultifying effects of the totalitarian alternative. Indifference only thinly disguised ostensibly as tolerance cannot be made more acceptable by the salient impotence of power-enforced coexistence. Reduction of citizenship to consumerism cannot be justified by reference to the even more gruesome effects of obligatory political mobilization. Ironical dismissal of dreaming of a better future loses much of its cogency now that the discredited promotions of "total order" and gardening utopias cease to be its most conspicuous and tangible incarnations.

All this points to an opportunity, though one that does not necessarily guarantee success. (I have discussed elsewhere the astonishing ability of the postmodern habitat to absorb dissent and avant-garde-style critique, and deploy them as the sources of its own renewed strength.) We residents of the postmodern habitat live on a territory that admits no clear options and no strategies which can even be *imagined* as being incontrovertibly correct. We know better than before just how slippery were the roads once pursued with single-minded determination. We know how easily critiques of "market-only" freedom may lead to the destruction of freedom as such. But we know as well (or we will soon, if we do not know it already) that freedom confined only to consumer choice is blatantly inadequate for the performance of the life-task confronting privatized individuality (for instance, for the self-construction of identity); that it tends to be supplemented by the renascence of the selfsame irrationality which grandiose projects of modernity wished to eradicate while succeeding, at best, in its purely temporary suppression. Dangers lurk on either side. A world without alternative needs self-critique as a condition of its survival and decency. But that does not make living the critique any easier.

NOTES

1. I have discussed this process more extensively in the third chapter of *Freedom* (London: Open University Press, 1989).

3.

THE FUTURE OF SOCIALISM[1]

Samir Amin

It is surely time to raise the issue of the future of socialism once again. Since the beginning of the 1980s, the ideological offensive of the ultraliberal Right has forced the predominantly social-democratic elements of the Western Left to fall broadly into line. In the third world, autonomous development has been systematically undermined in favor of the demands of world capitalism. Last but not least, the sudden collapse of East European regimes may pave the way for integration of these countries into the same capitalist world system. Triumphant liberal ideology proclaims the definitive failure of socialism.

For those who believe, as we do, that socialism offers a system of values never fully achieved, and in no way a constructed model on display in any particular place, the issue is infinitely more complex. Quite frankly, today's real danger is that the illusions of the peoples of the West, East, and South can only mean that the inevitable failure of today's triumphant liberalism may be disastrous for the popular classes, once they are ideologically and politically disarmed. More than ever, I would urge that the choice lies between "socialism or barbarism."

PART ONE

It might be helpful to begin this analysis with a critique of the three fundamental bases of the fashionable liberal thesis.

1. First liberal axiom: the "market" represents economic rationality *per se*, outside any specific social context. (In its extreme version: without the market, only chaos.)

This erroneous postulate expresses the "economistic" alienation essential for capitalist "legitimacy." Nothing more. The "market" does not in fact rationalize social relations. On the contrary, the framework of social relations determines how the market will operate. From an alienated, "economistic" standpoint, economic laws are analogous to laws of nature and exert external forces on every human action, and the economy is the product of determinate social behavior.[2] There is no economic rationality *per se*, but merely the expression of the demands of a social system at the level of economic management.

But no such social system is rational from a humanist point of view if it fails to meet the needs of the human beings subject to it. Unemployment, polarization in world development, and ecological waste and manifestations of the irrationality of this system—*really existing capitalism*. These negative phenomena are, purely and simply, necessary products of the market. The rationality of the market reproduces the irrationalities of the social system.

2. Second liberal axiom: Democracy equals capitalism. (Put more emphatically: without capitalism, no democracy.)

This is mere trickery. Contemporary trends of opinion, broadly typified by Anglo-American evolutionism, impoverish the debate by treating democracy as a set of narrowly-defined rights and practices, independent of the desired social result. This democracy can then stabilize the society by leaving the "evolution" to "objective forces." The latter are in the last resort governed by science and technology,[3] operating independently of the human will. Hence the functional role of the revolutionary process in history can be played down.

Socialist thought lies poles apart from this line of argument. The analysis of "economistic" alienation provided by Marx, central to any scientific and realistic understanding of capitalist reproduction, rehabilitates the crucial function of revolutions, moments of qualitative transformation, and the crystallization of potentialities inconceivable without them. In each of the three great revolutions of the modern world (the French, the Russian, and the Chinese), the play of ideas and social forces at moments of radicalization succeeded in moving far beyond the requirements of historical, objectively necessary social transformation. Hence Jacobin democracy did more than merely establish bourgeois power. Although the democracy operated in a framework of private ownership, its anxiety to establish power genuinely at the service of the people clashed with the merely bourgeois needs. At this stage of social development the bourgeoisie looked for little more than a qualified democracy such as occurred elsewhere in the nineteenth century. They were furthermore willing to compromise with the monarchy and the aristocracy. The aspirations of the "people"—the crowd of peasants and artisans—went further. The people wanted something more than "free trade," to such an extent that, during the convention, they launched the astonishingly modern slogan, "liberalism is the enemy of democracy!" This was a foretaste of a socialist consciousness yet to come. In the same way, the USSR in the 1920s and China in the Maoist period expressed a communist vision well beyond the requirements of the national and popular reform on the agenda. Certainly these moments of radicalization are fragile. In the end, narrower concepts more consonant with "objective" needs win the day. But would it be quite wrong to underestimate their significance as an indication of the way the movement is bound to continue.

Bourgeois democracy is the product of the revolution that dethroned "tributary metaphysics."[4] It establishes "equal rights" and personal liberties, but not equality, except under the law. As late as the latter half of the nineteenth century, the labour movement could impose unqualified political democracy and seize social rights, but only in the framework of a compromise based on acceptance of capitalist management of the economy, itself made possible by world polarization to the benefit of the industrial centers. Western democracy is thereby restricted to the political domain, while economic management continues to be based on nondemocratic principles of private ownership and competition. The capitalist mode of production does not in and of itself *require* democracy, but its characteristic oppression is *in fact hidden*, in economic alienation. By contrast, the socialist project of a classless society, free of economic alienation, *implies* a democratic structure. Once capitalist reliance on competition is broken, social relations based on cooperation among workers and not on their subjection, are inconceivable without a full-flowering of democracy.

If what are known as the third world countries have almost never seen their political systems in a genuinely democratic form, this is not a hangover from their "traditional culture."[5] What I call "really existing capitalism"—that is, *capitalism as a world system and not as a mode of production*—taken at its highest level of abstraction has until now always generated polarization on a world scale. Unfortunately, this dimension has always been underestimated in socialist thought, including Marxism. International polarization inherent in this expansion brings in turn a manifold internal polarization: growing inequality in income, widespread unemployment, marginalization, etc. Seeing the world system as the only ultimately meaningful unit of analysis is crucial to understanding what is at stake in the struggles, namely that the essential reserve army of capitalism is to be found at the peripheries of the system.

Hence instability is the rule in the political life of the peripheries. The political norm of the vicious dictatorship (whether military or not), broadly amenable to the expansion of world capital, is occasionally shaken by explosions, which rarely lead to real political democracy. The communist response is the "populist" model. Such regimes genuinely address at least some aspects of the social problem and try to develop strategies to reduce the tragic consequences of peripheralization, but they do not break with capitalism.

Between the right wing dictatorships and the popular movements, there is a middle ground onto which "petty democracy" can sometimes sneak. Such regimes recognize the principle of multi-party elections, and grant a measure of free speech, but fall short of addressing fundamental social problems and/or challenging relations of dependence and subjection to the world system. These "democracies" are little more than expressions of the crisis of the despotic system of capitalism. Latin America, Korea and the Philippines provide examples of contradictions unresolved by such regimes. Democracy imposed in such circumstances faces a striking dilemma. Either the democratic political system surrenders to the demands of world "adjustment"—it cannot then consider any substantial social reforms, and the democracy soon reaches crisis (as in Argentina) or the popular forces take charge of the democracy and impose the reforms. But the political system then comes quickly into conflict with world capitalism and must shift from its national bourgeois project to a national and popular project.

The areas of the periphery most affected by capitalist expansion are in a more desperate plight. The historical record of capitalist expansion must own up to much more than the "development" it has engendered. Actually existing capitalism has a destructive side that is invariably omitted from its flattering self-portraits. Here the usual pattern of power is the Tontons Macoutes in Haiti, the Somozas in Nicaragua, and a disturbing number of dictatorships of the same stamp in contemporary Africa.

3. Third liberal axiom: a wide-open door to the world system is an unavoidable constraint, the *sine qua non* of any development. (Put more emphatically: free trade, or no development.)

The underlying hypothesis is that "development" depends essentially on *internal* circumstances peculiar to each society, with integration into the world economy *a positive factor if only one knows how to use the opportunities it provides*. This thesis is not only contradicted by the history of five centuries of capitalist expansion—incessant polarization reproduced and intensified up until the present and for the foreseeable future—but is also scientifically unsound. The "world market" in question is truncated, and restricted to goods and capital. Despite international migrations there has never been any suggestion of a "world labour market," and no prospect of one. Liberal economic theory demonstrates that mobility of a single factor of production (capital)—while two other factors (labour and natural resources) are imprisoned by natural and political geography—cannot lead to uniform world productivity and social conditions.

In such circumstances, the universal law of value can only produce and reproduce polarization. In this sense integration into the world system is by its nature unfavorable and becomes increasingly so. I have argued this thesis on intuitive evidence: a few decades were enough to allow nineteenth-century Germany to "catch up" to England. How long would Brazil need to "catch up" to the United States?

Undoubtedly the forms and content of the polarization have evolved over time.[6] From the industrial revolution to the Second World War, it was a distinction between industrialized and nonindustrialized countries. Accelerated industrialization of some areas of the third world does not, in my view, raise a question mark over polarization as such, but merely over its forms. The mechanisms of the new polarization are founded on various forms of domination:

financial (new forms of global finance capital); technological (in relationship to the new scientific and technological revolution); cultural (with the growing influence of the media); and military. In this context the "newly industrialized countries" (the NICs) are not semi-peripheries on the way to becoming new centers, but the true peripheries of tomorrow.

By contrast, the countries of the so-called "fourth world" are not true peripheries, but are like the areas destroyed by capitalist expansion in its earlier forms. The perilous condition of the fourth world is not the outcome of a "refusal" to integrate within the international division of labour and a "failed" attempt to delink. In fact, the fourth world, which is talked of as something new, has been a consistent feature of capitalist expansion. A clear but lamentable example of this pervasive phenomenon is provided by the areas of slave labour in the Americas in the period of mercantilism: Northeast Brazil and the West Indies (including Haiti). These areas were regarded as prosperous in their day; they were the heart of the periphery corresponding to the system of the time. Later, new structures of capitalist development marginalized them, and they are today among the most grievously wretched parts of the third world. Is Africa not now on the road to exclusion from the world division of labour by a system that has consigned the continent to specialization in agriculture and mining until the soils are exhausted, and by a technological revolution that provides substitutes for some of its still-plentiful raw materials? Fourth world societies that have been rejected by the system cannot, by definition, solve their problems with open door policies.

From the standpoint of the various peoples of the earth, unification of the entire world system under the sway of the market is undesirable. It is not even the most likely outcome of the evolution now under way, so bitter are the conflicts provoked by the market in a world of "Darwinism." The ideological discourse of the West, which has chosen this strategy, aims to conceal the bitterness of these conflicts.

PART TWO

The values of socialism have scientific justification, not merely moral justification, in rejecting the three liberal theses—that economic rationality requires the market; that democracy requires capitalism; and that development requires free trade. All currents of socialist thought are primed to go beyond the philosophy of the Enlightenment, which sought to establish a "rational" basis that would serve society for all time. Socialism comes from an analysis of the historical limits of the "rationality" in question, namely its capitalist form. Socialism therefore offers the project of a qualitatively more advanced society, aiming at a more complete mastery over the human destiny. Here again, the Marxist theory of alienation returns to center stage: the scientific and social project of socialism is to liberate humanity from alienation in its bourgeois "economistic" form. The project cannot be defined more precisely in advance. Although it would be possible to be precise about what must be abolished (such as private ownership of the means of production), it would not be possible—in the absence of concrete social praxis—to delineate new methods of socialist management in advance. Any attempt to do so would militate against the liberative project itself, whereby the responsibility for shaping their destiny can lie only with the succeeding generations that will make their own history.

We are still faced with the fact that the so-called socialist societies of the East abolished private ownership and established self-styled socialist systems of economic and political management. *These systems, particularly those in Europe, have collapsed.* Must we conclude that the socialist project itself is hopelessly utopian?

If we want to provoke a fruitful debate on these experiences, we must turn to the character of the so-called socialist revolutions in the East and the historical limits of the capitalism from which they emerged. Two approaches are possible. One can focus on what defines capitalism at its highest level of abstraction—namely the contradiction between capital and labour—and define the historical limits of capitalist society by the boundaries imposed by its characteristic economism. This viewpoint inevitably leads to a "stagist" vision of the evolution of society: the backward (peripheral) capitalist societies must "catch up" with the advanced societies before they are in turn faced with the challenges of a possible (or perhaps necessary) supersession of the limits of those advanced societies. Or one may place more emphasis in the analysis on what really existing capitalism is, which in its actual worldwide expansion has given rise to a centres/peripheries polarization impossible to overcome within the framework of capitalism itself. Nearly all currents of socialist thought have underestimated this dimension of capitalism, as I have said.

A challenge to the capitalist order on the basis of revolts on its periphery requires a serious rethinking of the issue of the "transition to socialism" and the abolition of classes. The Marxist tradition, however subtly interpreted, is handicapped by an initial theoretical vision of *worker* revolutions, on the basis of advanced forces of production, initiating a fairly speedy transition, marked by democratic power for the mass of the people—a power that is more democratic in principle than that of the most democratic of the bourgeois states. By contrast, I would suggest that the profoundly unequal character inherent in capitalist expansion has brought onto history's agenda a revolution by peoples of the periphery. This revolution is anticapitalist in the sense that it stands up against really existing capitalist development that has become unbearable. But for all that, it is not socialist, even though it rises up against capital in its cruelest manifestation. It has by force of circumstance a complex character.

These postcapitalist societies are now faced with the demand for substantial development of the forces of production. It is illusory to imagine basing an "alternative development" on poverty, even if one rejects the consumer lifestyle of capitalism in its advanced centers, and takes into account its real waste and inhumanity.

A recognition of this does not mean accepting the thesis that an initial passage through a phase of capitalist accumulation is inevitable. Such a "bourgeois revolution" is a most unlikely outcome of a mass movement that is led by political parties with an openly anticapitalist ideology and view of the future. A capitalist expansion fostered by the local bourgeoisie but open to the world system will here be challenged by the mass of the people, for whom it could only be a form of oppression.

This specific and new contradiction, not envisaged in Marx's classic concept of the socialist transition, gives the postcapitalist regimes their real quality, of a national and popular construct in which there is a conflicting mix of aspirations and achievements of a socialist kind, and aspirations of a capitalist kind called for by the need to develop the forces of production.

This contradiction, inherent in the long transition imposed by the unequal development of capitalism, can obviously be defined by three fundamental elements, the inverse counterparts of the three liberal axioms criticized in Part I of this essay: bureaucratic planning (rationality without the market); antidemocratic political monopoly of a ruling party-State (no democracy to go with no capitalism); and total delinking from the capitalist world system, almost to the point of autarky (development with a closed door). This last axiom has been more an imposition by the West than a desire on the part of the East.

It is certainly significant that this so-called socialist construct worked through a nondemocratic political system and bureaucratic planning. The complex explanation includes social and cultural-historical determinants and the limits of the ideologies of the countries' revolutionary intelligentsia—Leninism and Maoism. I believe that national and popular hegemony could operate differently from the way they have operated in the past, that there is room for political democracy and market forces. These, after all, cannot operate in socialist societies, any more than in capitalist societies, outside the boundaries of the social base on which they rest. Indeed, I would go further and say that for this national and popular hegemony to progress it must move in these directions.

In these circumstances the magnitude of the crisis in societies of the East should come as no surprise to us, even if, like everyone else, we have been astounded by the suddenness with which it manifested itself. These societies now face a triad of options which I briefly summarize under three now familiar headings:

(i) Evolution toward a bourgeois democracy, or *progress beyond it* by strengthening the social power of the workers in the management of the economy?

(ii) Restoration of an out-and-out "market economy," or progress through carefully-controlled resort to market forces guided by democratic planning?

(iii) An unguarded door open wide to the exterior, or guarded relations with the surrounding world, albeit directed toward increased trade?

The confused theoretical debates and political disputes that are sending shudders down spines in the East arise in part because the ideological label "socialist" has imparted confusion about the status of the genuinely national and popular character of the revolutions that established some of the regimes in question. But more pertinent is the fact that the conflicting forces of capitalism and socialism are meeting within genuine national struggles. The forces anxious to restore capitalism propose unilateral acceptance of the market as a springboard for the restoration of private ownership, and of an "open door," with or without democracy in the Western sense, according to the tactical requirements of their project. If the socialist forces dither in their resistance to this project, if they find it difficult to articulate a coherent alternative along the lines sketched above, it is because the lack of democratic debate and the ideological confusion over the status of the present governments have proved to be major impediments to action. Need I add that the Western ideological offensive, orchestrated through powerful media, is massing entirely on the side of the procapitalist (and antidemocratic) forces?

A political response to the three questions posed above would lead to intensive internal class struggle, already (silently) under way. A significant minority in the East—perhaps twenty percent—might benefit from the restoration of capitalism. But in light of the inadequate levels of development and international competitiveness achieved by the socialist countries, this minority could never attain the Western standard of living which fuels their aspirations *without grinding down the mass of the people.*

In this struggle, the peoples of the various countries of the East start with unequal weapons. Intuitively, one can grasp why peoples who have by force of arms made their own socialist, nationalist, and popular revolutions (the USSR, China, Yugoslavia, etc.) have an ideological weapon that may enable them to put a progressive complexion on their struggles. By contrast, those of the East European countries with no comparable historical achievement run the risk of being bewitched by the attraction of annexing themselves to Western Europe.

In the current crisis, assertions such as "recourse to the market" and an "open door to the exterior" remain ambiguous because they unite those who seek a launching-pad to capitalism and those who seek a progressive social approach to the political and economic management of their society, and thus a genuine social advance. It is interesting to note that social surveys in the USSR show that the privileged classes prefer the "pluralist democracy and a market open to the exterior" formula, whereas the popular classes remain attached to the achievements of socialism (full employment, social services, national independence, and public ownership). The latter favour "planning" along with democratization of the political system. Gorbachev apparently straddled these antinomian currents, allied only in their opposition to the "conservatives," who always hoped for a standstill.

In China, Deng Xiaoping has opted for an open door to both internal and external capitalism; an option, it should be remembered, that is supported eagerly by the West.[7] The democracy movement has (remarkably) recruited forces both from the well-off classes who openly hope to restore capitalism and from the majority (some claiming to be Maoist) who complain that they have been harmed by capitalist developments during the Deng Xiaoping era![8] The Western media, by describing repression of the democracy movement as a return to "Maoism" mixed with "Stalinism," have certainly not contributed to clarity. They have played a leading role in supporting the reactionary option of restoring capitalism, even if it must be carried out to the total detriment of democracy.

The situation is quite different in the East European countries that have no revolutionary past. Here the social achievements, although real, *have not been won*, but were handed down in a paternalist manner by communist parties installed by the Soviet Union. It is quite "obvious" to an expert from the World Bank that the Polish problem is very simple: wages must be cut in half (without regard for the impact of this on productivity) and an unemployment level of two or three million accepted. The situation, remarkably similar to that of Argentina, is obscured by the illusions of the Polish people, to whom nobody has explained that in the world system they desire to join, that their place is closer to that of the NICs of the third world than to that of the Western societies whose advanced democracy they admire! One must also be wary of a drift from transitional democracy to an authoritarian regime (of the Pilsudski sort, based on the Catholic Church) as the only one capable of imposing the "discipline" that capitalism demands. Evolution of this kind is also to be feared in Hungary, for example. It is difficult at this moment to say more, especially about East Germany, where internal struggles are mixed up with the desires of the German people for unification, and with the initiatives that the Bonn government will take.

Generally speaking, one is struck by the incredible political naïveté that has grown up among the people of the nondemocratic regimes of Eastern Europe. Their attacks on the *nomenclatura*, which are intended as an indictment of "privilege" under actually existing socialism, ignore the fact that the class aspiring to form a bourgeoisie will inevitably be composed of just this *nomenclatura*; that the privileges it has enjoyed are nothing in comparison with the social inequalities under actually existing capitalism.

The initiative for change in the East was in fact taken by the ruling class itself. This was constituted on the basis of a "Statism" that has been the way of dealing with the capitalism/socialism contradiction within the national and popular construct. It hopes now to be rid of the constraints of the popular classes and to opt four-square for capitalism. The scuttling of the system to which it lends itself to a degree astonishing to Western commentators is not really surprising at all: it is the logical terminus of its evolution, and was perfectly foreseen by Mao. This class, in attacking its own system, repeats all the outworn prejudices of the critique of socialism by bourgeois ideology, but refrains from pointing out that the system which it is abandoning has been marvellously effective in making possible its own constitution as a bourgeoisie!

PART THREE

The question of the future of socialism is not limited to possible advances or retreats on the part of the countries of the East. One must look also at the countries of the third and fourth worlds—true peripheries and societies destroyed by capitalist expansion, where development that can meet the material needs of all social strata is impossible within the framework of capitalism, and where it becomes necessary to consider alternative development outside capital's bounds. This is the meaning of the expression *delinking*. It is not a recipe, but a fundamental and principled choice: that of divorcing the criteria of rationality in economic life from those that govern world capitalism, freeing oneself from the constraints of world-capitalist value and substituting a law of value of national popular reference.

If the bourgeoisie is incapable of delinking and if only a popular alliance must and can be persuaded that this is required for any development worthy of the name, the social dynamism must lead in a direction that we can only describe as socialist. It is understood that the socialism in question remains a prospect for society well in the future, and not a ready-made model that has merely to be copied.

The current changes in the world economy and in the political and cultural situation cannot alter the polarizing character of really existing capitalism, but can only heighten the contradictions through which it is expressed. The policies of surrender to world unification through the market—described as "adjustment" for the peripheries, although one speaks of "restructuring" when the centres are concerned—

do not in any way "neutralize" its effects. Such policies are not therefore acceptable alternatives to national and popular "breaking away," which is necessary now more than ever. The national bourgeoisies of the third world, who have co-opted national liberation to their own advantage, have already become compradors, under the laws of evolution of the world system. They are therefore incapable of mediating the new worldwide phenomena to the advantage of their own country. The popular classes are still confused and indecisive following the exhaustion of the former national liberation movements. Hence it is difficult to forecast the precise next step in an uninterrupted popular revolution that still threatens upheavals in the peripheries of the global system.[9]

In the short term, the responses of the peoples of the third world are generally inadequate, as in the past. The revival of fundamentalist religious movements here and there is itself a symptom of the crisis, and not an adequate response to its challenge.[10] But insufficient reflection has been given in the West to the significance of the failure of the Islamic fundamentalists in Afghanistan, presented in the media as "freedom fighters" (although they propose to close the schools opened by the "atheists in the pay of Moscow," beginning, of course, with the girls' schools). They were expected to make an undisputed entry into Kabul on the morrow of the withdrawal of Soviet troops.

There is no reason, of course, to exclude the West from the debate on the prospects for socialism. One must neither discount a labour movement that has made possible the achievements of social democracy, nor overlook the democratic victories of the West. But standing still means falling back. Socialist advance in the West requires that the people free themselves from alienation and idolatry as they appear in societies whose major means of communication are all in the hands of the dominant classes. The intense communication campaign that operates within really existing capitalism does nothing to contribute to liberation or democratization. Quite the contrary. People who are not permanent residents of the West on a day-to-day basis are always struck by the incredible saturation by the dominant media—a veritable carpet bombing of the public consciousness. From one country to another, from liberals and conservatives to socialists, an ideological consensus forces near-unanimity on many of the central issues. The pluralism that is so vaunted as synonymous with democracy is stripped of all real content, and minor, provincial differences among competitors of the political class are blown up in bizarre proportion. At a time when "the end of ideology" is being proclaimed, the West has never before been so subject to so exclusively ideological a discourse.

In a reference elsewhere to the remarkable breakthroughs in social consciousness exemplified by the women's movement, I did feel it necessary to express reservations on the real *extent* of these breakthroughs. They can be *absorbed* by a system that remains basically capitalist and imperialist in its relations with the periphery, or, to the contrary, be nodes of positive change. Everything, in the end, depends on how peoples of Western Europe, the United States and Japan see their competition with one another, and how they see East-West and North-South relations.

The intraWestern contradictions since 1945 have never gone beyond the limits of mercantile competition. The Japanese and the Europeans have never dared to take a stand that might really displease the United States. Will this necessarily be the case in the future? The question remains open. According to some views, these conflicts must worsen, and lead in the end to a breakup of the world market into spheres of influence around the dominant axes (the United States, Europe, and Japan). The strengthening of a détente in East-West relations should enhance this possibility, as the American military umbrella becomes meaningless. But one must be doubtful about the eventual consistency of a common neoimperialist policy for Europe, which is cornered between competition from the industrialized peripheries (the NICs) that are better placed relative to traditional industries from Japan and the United States, both of which may be better equipped in the fields of new technology. In this context could Europe possibly come to the fore? Furthermore, renewed German expansionism will weaken Bonn's solidarity with its European Economic Community (EEC) partners and further complicate intraWestern relations. In any event, one might ask whether the pursuit of the European construct, the EEC's single market, could withstand the absence of any common social policy. I doubt it. It seems to me that the social conflicts could become very severe.[11]

In fact the most likely scenario seems to be the following: either Europe presses on with the common capitalist market, with or without the East; or the more progressive forces in the West understand that an alternative Europe (that of the "common European home" envisioned by Gorbachev) would imply a greater social autonomy of all partners—Westerners, Germans, and Easterners.

The future of socialism in Western Europe will therefore depend heavily on the evolution of intraEuropean relations. Undoubtedly, the ideological polarization that has emerged from the socialist revolutions since 1917 would vanish if capitalism were to be restored to the countries in question. A change of this kind, unhappily desired by a high proportion of the anticommunist West, would have the consequence of a lasting retreat for Western socialist aspirations. It would rebound not to the benefit of social democracy, of course, but to that of the Right. In the event of greater national and popular evolution in the Eastern countries, everything would depend on the resonance of this for the peoples of the West. The change might leave things as they have been—cold war attitudes—if the workers of the West continue to think that with their higher living standards they have nothing to learn from their counterparts in the East. But it could also provoke a revival of socialist consciousness among workers in the West. This would be the most favorable outcome for the cause of socialism, and seems to me to be the implication of Gorbachev's "common home,"[12] an idea still worthy of mention.

But the crucial axis for the future of socialism in the West is the axis of North-South relations. I am not saying anything new here, as my main argument is based on the decisive part in history that is played by the polarization inherent in world capitalism. The bitterness of the East-West conflict had for a while obscured the more fundamental conflict arising from this polarization, just as the interimperialist conflict was in the forefront just before 1914. The lessening of intraWestern conflicts and of the East-West contradiction is accompanied by a renewal of hostility toward the peoples who are the prime victims of capitalism—those of Asia, Africa, and Latin America. There are many signs today of this regressive evolution: the recrudescence of racism and colonial arrogance, even in the detail of the "realignment" of the North Atlantic Treaty Organization (NATO) bases, whose guns are henceforth to be trained on the southern shore of the Mediterranean.[13]

PART FOUR

The contours of a new globalization of capital remain quite vague. The configuration that materializes will follow from conflicts which will inevitably occur despite the liberalism common to the nations of the capitalist center. Meanwhile, on the absurd hypothesis that the national and social forces in dispute will agree to sacrifice their several interests to the strict logic of "globalization by the market," the reshaped world will be formidable. Hence the future remains open to various possibilities and there is no justification for abandoning the thought and struggle to promote a better world project. This is no plea for "voluntarism," since the political options that delimit the possible futures are historically objective. Exploring these options calls for examining alternatives along three axes of evolution: (1) the centres/peripheries contradiction, governed by the logic of world capitalism; (2) West-East relations; and (3) intraWestern competition. I have attempted to do so briefly, from the starting point of unilateral unification by the market that constitutes the essence of the Western project.

More than ever, the forces of the Left have a duty to promote a credible alternative to this disastrous option. I shall not dwell here on the possible features of this alternative, some aspects of which I have discussed elsewhere.[14]

First: the only strategy that is meaningful for the progressive forces on a world scale, on the basis of which the peoples of the West, East, and South could together draw new breath, must envision a "polycentric" world. The various component areas must be articulated in a flexible way, allowing the implementation of specific measures required by their varying levels of development, and by other objective circumstances. It must be acknowledged at the outset that the problems that the peoples of the world must solve differ from one area to another. It is therefore essential that the world system permits people the autonomy to promote their own interests. There must be balance between general interdependence and this legitimate concern for autonomy. The logic of mutual and reciprocal adjustment must be substituted for unilateral "adjustment" by the weakest, and expansion for the exclusive benefit of the strongest.

Second: polycentrism means that the countries of the East and South pursue development policies that are delinked in the sense I have given to this word. This strategy looks to advances toward socialism (democratization and strengthening national and popular trends) and not to restoration of capitalism in the countries of the East, and to a refusal by the countries of the South to become compradors. It must likewise allow progressive advances in the countries of the West; through the opening of nonmarket social spaces; and through other reforms based on socialization of economic management.

Third: with particular reference to the third world, this strategy favours progress in the organization of the productive forces even to the detriment of "international competitiveness." It puts at the top of the agenda an agricultural revolution marked by the maximum of equality, and transformation of the informal sector into a popularly managed transitional economy. It calls for an effective combination of planning and market forces as the foundation for economic and social democracy. The vision of polycentrism it inspires gives the countries and regions of the third world a measure of autonomy that is denied them under world unification by the market.

Fourth: as regards international cooperation for interdependence, the strategy aims to encourage embryos of a democratic world government and, for example, a world tax to be spent on environmental measures. It also aims to reduce the arms race, notable by the superpowers. It aims finally to breathe new life into the democratic institutionalization of world management through the United Nations.

Let me say in conclusion that the construction of a polycentric world with new prospects for socialism implies acute awareness of the cultural universalism of humanity's project. On this point I have put forward elsewhere a critique of the eurocentrism and cultural nationalism that form the obverse image.[15]

NOTES

1. Translation from the original French by Michael Wolfers.
2. See Samir Amin, *Eurocentrism* (New York: Monthly Review Press; London: Zed Books, 1989); Samir Amin, *Unequal Development* (New York: Monthly Review Press; Hassocks: Harvester Press, 1976), chap., 2; Karl Polanyi, *La libertà in una società complessa* (Torino: Bollati Boringhieri, 1987); and the works of the Frankfurt School.
3. Science and technology is a major topic in the work of the Frankfurt School.
4. *Eurocentrism*, pp. 15-59.
5. See Samir Amin, "La question démocratique dans le tiers monde contemporaine," *African Development*, (1989). See in particular our critique of neoWeberian theses: Richard Sandbrook and Judith Baker, *The Politics of Africa's economic stagnation* (Cambridge: Cambridge University Press, l985). See also Giovanni Arrighi's theses on the world distribution of active and passive labour armies and my contribution, "The end of national liberation?"

in Samir Amin, et al., eds., *Transforming the Revolution: Social Movements and the World System* (New York: Monthly Review Press, 1990).

6. See Samir Amin, *Delinking: Towards a Polycentric World* (London: Zed Books, 1990).

7. The society to which this option logically leads would be South Korea or Taiwan.

8. Samir Amin, *The Future of Maoism* (New York: Monthly Review Press, 1983).

9. See *Delinking*, chapters 1 and 4; Samir Amin, *Maldevelopment: Anatomy of a Global Failure* (London: Zed Books, 1990; The Third World Forum), chap., 6; and our contribution in Samin et al, eds. *Transforming the Revolution: social movements and the world system* (NY: Monthly Review Press, 1990).

10. My writings on these movements are mainly in Arabic, but see "Existe-t-il une économie politique islamique?" *Peuples Méditerranéens* 21 (1982); *Eurocentrism*, pp. 124-135.

11. Samir Amin, "In favor of a polycentric world," *IFDA Dossier* 69 (1989).

12. Samir Amin, "La maison commune Europe," *IFDA Dossier* 73 (1989).

13. Observation by Alberto Santos of the CEDETIM study group, Paris. See Samir Amin, "Conditions for Autonomy in the Mediterranean Region," in Faysal Yachir, ed., *The Mediterranean: Between Autonomy and Dependency* (London: Zed Books; Tokyo: The United Nations University, 1989), pp. 1-24, esp. p. 11.

14. Samir Amin, "Une autre configuration des relations internationales Ouest-Est-Sud: est-elle souhaitable, probable, possible?" in *Forum de Delphes* (Paris: Harmattan, 1989); "L'Europe et les rapports Nord-Sud," *L évènement européen* 7 (1989).

15. *Eurocentrism*, pp. 124-152.

4.

SOCIALISM AS SOCIAL TRANSFORMATION[1]

Pat Devine

INTRODUCTION

Do the political revolutions and systemic changes in Eastern Europe and the former Soviet Union signal the end of Marxism as a theoretical tradition? Do they require us to give up the objective of socialism as a society qualitatively different from capitalism, and accept that the real choice is between different balances within a mixed or market economy? The answers to these two questions are interdependent. If the failure of the Soviet Statist model cannot be analyzed in terms of the Marxist tradition, then that tradition must be abandoned. If socialism is to survive as an objective, we must be able to offer an alternative analysis of the Soviet Statist model to that of the "end of history" school.

Existing Marxist analyses of the Soviet Statist model have, for the most part, attempted to force it into the space defined by a historical movement from capitalism to communism. This applies to the Trotskyist or Maoist concepts of a degenerate workers' State, a transitional society, and State capitalism. It also applies to the official

Soviet and orthodox communist positions which maintained, explicitly or implicitly, that while what has been called "actually existing socialism" might differ from what Marx had envisaged it was nevertheless socialism. Such analyses have never been convincing and must surely now be abandoned. The only alternative from within the Marxist tradition would be to characterize the democratic revolutions of 1989 and 1991 as counter-revolutions.

In fact, the end of history position is now dominant in the East as well as the West. Most of those in the East who until recently described themselves as "communists" or "Marxists" seem now to agree with those in the West who argue that the market economy has triumphed. Everyone visiting what were until recently the countries of actually existing socialism is struck by a near universal distaste for references to capitalism and socialism. In place of the mode of production and social formation as central analytic concepts, one constantly encounters references to "civilized," "humanistic," or just "modern" values, and an untheorized advocacy of a "market economy" and "privatization" as a sort of cargo cult.

From a socialist standpoint possibly the greatest long run indictment of the Soviet Statist model will turn out to be the effect it has had of bringing into disrepute the emancipating ideals of socialism and contributing to the postmodern disenchantment with the belief in the possibility of social progress. A Marxist analysis of these regimes and a restatement of socialist objectives in the light of such an analysis is probably a necessary condition for the rehabilitation of the socialist project, and the revival of a significant socialist movement. This paper is offered as a contribution to that process.

THE STATIST MODE OF PRODUCTION

Bahro and Horvat have argued that what was called actually existing socialism, or what I prefer to call "Statism," was not socialism at all, but rather a social formation *sui generis*, unforeseen by Marx, and an alternative to capitalism as a means of creating the preconditions for socialism and communism. Horvat states the argument clearly:

> Étatism is not a successor of capitalism, not a more
> advanced social system. It is an alternative mode of
> social organization that has to achieve essentially

the same task: the development of productive forces and socialist consciousness up to the point where socialism becomes possible.[2]

However, it is Bahro who has developed the argument most fully:

Actually existing socialism is the arrangement under which countries with a precapitalist formation work independently to produce the preconditions of socialism, and it is the pressure of the industrial productive forces created by capitalism that gives this process its decisive impulse. Its place in history is determined by the way that, just like capitalism, it brings the productive forces to the threshold of socialist restructuring, but in a completely different manner so far as the social formation is concerned.[3]

Although I have previously accepted this analysis,[4] it now seems wrong in one important respect. The process underway in Eastern Europe and the former Soviet Union before 1989 can certainly not be characterized as a transition from actually existing socialism, or Statism, to socialism. It will almost certainly turn out to be a transition to some form of capitalism. Nevertheless, the argument that the dominant mode of production in these countries has been neither capitalist nor socialist, but *sui generis* remains convincing.[5]

Bahro's analysis was that the interaction between the relatively stagnant Asiatic mode of production that was dominant in prerevolutionary Russia, and the dynamic impact of capitalism, in the form of imperialism, gave rise to a new, noncapitalist, industrializing mode of production. He thought that this new Statist mode of production was an alternative to capitalism for creating the conditions for socialism. However, his analysis can be reinterpreted, with Statism now seen as a distinctive precapitalist formation that emerged in countries whose Asiatic social formations had become dominated by imperialism.

The defining characteristic of the Statist mode of production can be briefly summarized as the dominance of the political, in the form of the party/State, and ultimately the party. Bahro identifies the polit bureaucracy in particular, and the apparatus or bureaucracy in general, as the leading or ruling group.[6] Nove considers those people on the *nomenclatura*, covering the leading positions in all officially recognized activities, to have made up the leading group.[7]

The relationship between the political and the economic in the Statist mode of production is set out by Bahro as follows:

> State property represents a relation of production *sui generis*. "For the good of the people"...the oligarchy at the top of the pyramid decides the goals for which the surplus product should be used, and subjects the entire reproduction process of economic, social and cultural life to its regulation. As in the case of all earlier systems of domination, the steady reproduction of its own monopoly, and when possible its expanded reproduction, goes into the overall calculation of social development and has to be paid for by the masses.[8]

The general relation of production in Statist societies, then, consisted of the power of disposal of the leading or ruling group over both economic activity and the "masses." Those who ran the society, in the sense that they performed a functional role of organizing and directing activities, also ran it in the sense of running, or rather directing, the subaltern masses. A functional or technical division of labour was fused with a social or traditional division of labour, with those at the top end of the fused hierarchy constituting the ruling group in society.

Members of the party/State apparatus controlled the means of production by virtue of their position in the apparatus. They did not hold their positions in the apparatus because they owned the means of production. All leading positions in the society were on the *nomenclatura*; all those who filled these positions were also on the *nomenclatura*. How did people come to fill leading positions and therefore to be included on the *nomenclatura*? Political reliability was always a key factor, and was often paramount in the early years of the Soviet Union. Increasingly, however, education and expertise became the dominant factors, with party membership frequently sought for careerist reasons as a necessary condition for progress up the hierarchy of the bureaucratic apparatus.

For those outside the ruling group, the absence of political and economic democracy in the Statist countries took the form, at its best, of totalitarian paternalism. In every aspect of their lives people were more or less dependent, typically more, on the bureaucratic apparatus—the enterprise, the State and ultimately the party. Not surprisingly, the most convincing accounts of the system came from those who had experienced it. Bahro's characterization is again striking:

> It regularly and inevitably reproduces precisely those barriers that block the way to the free development of self-conscious subjectivity and individual autonomy. It precisely embodies all the structural conditions of individual subalternity the mentality and behaviour of dependent "little people" alienated from the overall totality.[9]

This analysis, with the benefit of hindsight, suggests why the view that Statism was an alternative to capitalism as a means of developing the preconditions for socialism was unrealistic. All organized activity needs an administrative structure. The problem for socialism is to ensure that such structures are controlled by and accountable to society, rather than society being controlled by and accountable to the administrative bureaucracy. It should have been evident that dependent, passive, psychologically subaltern workers and citizens lack both the capacity, and to a large extent the desire, to participate effectively in decision-making. This is the most intractable problem inherent in a "revolution from above."

A precondition for socialism is the experience of democratic struggle and participatory processes, and the social and personal transformations associated with them. In the absence of such experience, the reaction against Statism becomes privatized rather than socialized. This is surely what underlies the naïve attitude to privatization and the market economy in societies emerging from Statism. The antithesis of the State is seen as the private, rather than the exercise of self-government by civil society. The antithesis of administrative command planning is seen as market forces, rather than participatory democratic planning.

TOWARDS A RECONCEPTUALIZATION OF SOCIALISM

If we reject the "end of history" position, with its assumption that competition between different social systems has resulted in a convergence on the liberal or social democratic market economy as the best form of social organization, what conclusions are we to draw from the historical exhaustion of Statism? First, the objective of human emancipation and empowerment cannot be achieved by leaders or vanguards acting on behalf of others, however well-meaning they may be. Second, and following on from this, the abolition of exploitation and oppression requires a society of autonomous, self-activating, self-governing people individually, and collectively in control of their lives.

Civil society, not the State and not the economic enterprise, is where self-government takes place. The process of achieving social control of the polity and the economy consists of ever more developed and extensive forms of self-government asserting themselves in relation to the State and to production. To argue this is in one sense merely to restate the classical Marxist position, interpreted as the State having a temporary and weakening role in relation to the polity and the economy during the process of transition to a classless society. In another sense, however, the argument could be interpreted as a socialist case for the creation of the conditions necessary for the full development of participatory political and economic democracy.

I have argued elsewhere that the socialization of the means of production, through various forms of social ownership and economic planning, is a necessary condition for developed participatory democracy.[10] However, as Williams has insisted: "change in a mode of production cannot occur only on the basis of a change in relations of production...but must also involve change in the forces of production."[11]

The forces of production he has in mind, of course, are people. This, then, suggests a second necessary condition for participatory democracy—the overcoming of the social division of labour; of the distinction between leaders and led.

Bahro is the principal theorist in modern times to have placed this objective at the top of the historical agenda. For the most part, however, the objective of overcoming the social division of labour has been regarded as a utopian hangover from Marx's vision of the disappearance of "the antithesis between intellectual and physical labour" under communism.[12] The prevailing view, as Nove puts it, is that "there is bound to be a division between governors and governed."[13]

Bahro's argument is based on a restatement of the classical historical materialist schema. He distinguishes between what he calls the primary, secondary and tertiary formations. The first corresponds to primitive communal society; the second to the social, or traditional division of labour, initially in the form of the State arising above and governing society, later generalized to a division between the directing and the directed in all human activity; the third formation corresponds to class society based on the private ownership of the means of production.[14] Only this tertiary formation is removed with the abolition of private property. The secondary formation remains with it and:

> the oldest historical layers of oppression and social inequality...the exploitation and oppression of women...the dominance of the town over the country ...the exploitation and oppression of the manual worker (whoever has to perform principally physical, schematic, executive work) by the mental worker (whoever performs predominantly intellectual, creative, planning and managerial activity).[15]

People who spend their lives performing partial tasks, determined for them by others who plan the activity as a whole, develop partial consciousness. People who spend all their time being told what to do, rather than learning how to decide what to do for themselves, develop subaltern consciousness. People with partial, subaltern consciousness cannot take an overall view and share the responsibility of running things. Thus, Bahro argues, the abolition of the social division of labour is a necessary condition for the full socialization of control over the means of production, and I would add also for developed participatory democracy. Turning Lenin's adage on its head, he refers to: "the inherently illusory demand that every cook should learn to govern the State, which she simply cannot learn in the normal case if she is to remain a cook."[16]

Bahro rejects any suggestion of social engineering to create a "new socialist man" overnight:

> It needs several generations to establish a new subjectivity as an average type [It is] simply impossible that an oppressed and alienated class of immediate

producers, subjected to the [social or traditional] division of labour, could "itself" become the ruling class and in this role exercise hegemony over the entire cultural process of its society.[17]

However, this is not a prescription for immobilism. On the contrary, it requires a transformatory perspective for achieving: "the overthrow of the traditional division of labour—not of course as a violation of living generations who have already internalized their confined character, but rather as a planned process to be executed in historical time."[18]

What is needed is realistic thought about what changes now will assist the process of the present generation's, of our own self-transformation, and therefore enable subsequent generations to start from a more emancipated consciousness.

Bahro's book appeared in English as *The Alternative in Eastern Europe*, but in the original German its title is *Die Alternative* (The Alternative). Although the analysis is primarily of Eastern Europe, his alternative is intended to apply to capitalism as much as to Statism. Many of the ideas contained in Bahro's alternative vision are, in my view, incompatible with participatory democracy, in particular his rejection of party political pluralism.[19] Nevertheless, his objective of a society in which the social or traditional division of labour has been overcome, in which there is no longer a division into a social group that directs, and a social group that is directed, seems to me central to any reconceptualization of the socialist project.

One conclusion that must be drawn from the collapse of the Statist system is the need for realism about what is possible. However, realism can be either conservative or revolutionary. Conservative realism starts from the way we are and assumes that that is how we will always be. Hence, Nove's construction of his model of feasible socialism on the assumption of "original sin."[20] Revolutionary realism starts from where we are but believes that we can change ourselves:

It all comes down to whether realism is presented fatalistically and apologetically, or alternatively in a critical and hence revolutionary way. Realism can only be critical and revolutionary if it neither sees the domination of the traditional division of labour

as an unalterable fact, nor leaves the task of overcoming it to future generations.[21]

ABOLITION OF THE SOCIAL DIVISION OF LABOUR

Bahro's guiding principle, which I share, is the belief that society
has now reached the level of development at which it is possible to
separate the functional hierarchy necessary for organizing central
aspects of social life from the hierarchical social structure with
which it has historically been associated. The essential distinction is
between the functional, or technical, and the social, or traditional,
division of labour. The argument is that it is now possible to abolish
the social division of labour while retaining the functional division of
labour, with people sharing between them the different levels of
functional activity that are necessary.[22]

The subversive and revolutionary twist that Bahro gives to the
classical Marxist precondition for socialism/communism is to conduct
the discussion not in terms of surplus labour or product, but of surplus consciousness. He insists that it is the characteristics of the
activities that we engage in, what we spend our time doing, that
retards or advances our development toward becoming self-activating subjects. That is why he describes the process of overcoming the
social division of labour as involving a transformation of consciousness, a cultural revolution.

The functional division of labour can be analyzed along two
dimensions, horizontal and vertical. Thus, at one horizontal level
there are many different types of, say, skilled manual labour, and at
another horizontal level many different types of, say, professional
skill. Yet in the vertical dimension the former skills are normally
thought of as being at a lower level than the latter. Within the vertical dimension, unskilled manual labour is typically considered to be
the lowest level of activity, and perhaps, planning and directing, or
possibly some professional or artistic activities, the highest level. The
actual vertical ranking of different horizontal levels of activity in
existing societies reflects both the intrinsic characteristics of different
sorts of activity and the values of the society, which in turn reflect
history and the distribution of social power in the society.

Both the horizontal and the vertical functional divisions of labour
are necessary. It is clearly impossible for people to perform every

type of task at every level. Within most horizontal levels, for example the level of skilled crafts, or of professional skills, we cannot be equally skilled at everything. With respect to the vertical dimension, in any organized activity of any complexity we cannot operate simultaneously at each vertical level at which tasks have to be undertaken. However, it is possible to envisage us all in the course of our lives performing at least one task, possibly more than one, at each level of functional activity. If the objective is to abolish the social division of labour, to share out the different tasks that have to be performed at each functional level, different sorts of activity need to be somehow classified according to their intrinsic characteristics; that is, the characteristics that determine their scope for contributing to personal development.

I have discussed in detail elsewhere what this might mean in terms of the five categories of social activity which seem to me desirable for everyone to participate in.[23] These categories are planning and running, creative activity, nurturing, skilled activity, and unskilled and repetitive activity. The first four categories, freed from the relationships of domination and subordination arising from the hierarchy of social power, are in different ways psychologically productive and contribute to the realization of human potentiality. The fifth category is in general psychologically unproductive, and an important social objective should be to reduce the amount of such activity that has to be undertaken. However, it is unlikely that unskilled and repetitive activity will ever be completely abolished and what remains should be shared.

Nothing turns on the particular categories I have chosen and I am certainly not suggesting that any particular task can be assigned unambiguously to any one category. For instance, much nurturing activity is both skilled and creative, as well as sometimes unskilled and repetitive. The categories actually found to be most meaningful will be determined democratically as the struggle for access to psychologically productive activities and an equal distribution of culture proceeds. Within each category there is a wide variety of different specific activities from which people would choose. There is no suggestion that everyone should do everything. Similarly, there is no suggestion that people would necessarily undertake activities from more than one category at the same time, although they might. What is being suggested is that there should be an expectation that, in the course of a lifetime, we would undertake activities within each category of social labour roughly corresponding to our share of the activities that are socially necessary, or available within each category.

By contrast with this approach, however, the prevailing consensus among socialists is that the social division of labour will always be with us. Rather than seeking to work toward the abolition of the social division of labour, emphasis is placed on ways of moving toward greater social equality within its framework and achieving greater control by the governed over their governors.

The strength of this approach is that it starts from present reality. Its concerns are an essential part of the process of moving toward the abolition of the social division of labour and the creation of a self-governing society. However, its potential weakness is that, by assuming a permanent division between people, and seeking to devise more humane ways of living with that division, it runs the danger of confirming and perpetuating inequality instead of confronting it and contributing to its erosion and eventual abolition.

Movement toward greater social equality within a framework of continuing social as well as functional division of labour is seen as having two aspects to it—the creation of real equality of opportunity to enter each category of social labour, and of real equality of status between the different categories.

Equality of opportunity could mean one of two things. It is usually taken to mean that people enter the race of life on equal terms with each other. Society's functional requirements determine the number of slots available in each functional role. People compete for one of the limited number of slots in their preferred functional role, with no handicaps due to their class or social background, ethnic status, sex, or gender formation. With equal life chances their success, or failure, would be entirely due to their individual characteristics. In the absence of any reason to suppose the existence of differential innate ability or preferences between groups, evidence that equality of opportunity had been achieved would be equal statistical representation of any definable group in each functional role. If there were such reasons, then the expected statistical distribution would have to be weighted accordingly.

Alternatively, equality of opportunity could mean that people had equal access to the resources required to develop their full potential. If these resources are not only material, but also and primarily cultural, and if their appropriation involves the active engagement by people learning by doing in activities within each category of social labour, then this interpretation of equality of opportunity is compatible with, possibly equivalent to, the abolition off labour. Its realization would require a society organized with the explicit objective of providing people with access to activities in each category—*all* people if they all turned out to have the ability and inclination. Instead of shaping people's education, training and work experience to fit the requirements of social labour, social labour would have to be shaped to fit the requirements of people's self-development.

The second aspect of movement toward greater social equality within a framework of continuing social division of labour is the achievement of greater equality of status between different categories of activity. The argument is that since all categories of activity, although not all activities within each category, are socially necessary, they should all be equally regarded and equally valued. What is needed on this view is a change in perceptions, perhaps assisted by an inverse relationship between pay, and the intrinsically rewarding characteristics of different jobs in order to equalize the combination of monetary and nonmonetary benefits from each activity.

Although there is something in this argument there is not much. It is true that what is regarded as women's work is systematically undervalued in most, if not all, societies. However, with this exception, the status that is attached to most activities in existing societies, the social valuation they enjoy, reflects to a significant extent their intrinsic characteristics and their potential for self-development. The reason why unskilled and repetitive activities have a low status is because they deserve it. There is nothing to be said for a life spent in drudgery, however socially necessary the work itself may be.

Within the skilled category the situation is more complicated. High-status-skilled manual or professional activities in existing societies reflect, as often as not, history and the social power of particular sectional interests, usually buttressed by trade union organization, or the influence of professional associations. Similar considerations apply within the creative, and the planning and running categories as they are defined in existing societies. Nevertheless, there clearly are differences in the intrinsic characteristics of different categories of activity, with different implications for personal development. It is unconvincing to suggest that the present distribution of people between different occupations reflects the personal preferences and real choices of autonomous, self-activating people, and that all that is needed is a change in social perceptions.

Policies to increase social equality by increasing equality of opportunity and altering the social evaluation of different sorts of work are likely to be contradictory. On the one hand, they subvert the existing distribution of resources and power. On the other hand, in the absence of a "transformatory" element, they are consistent with a conservative vision of a meritocratic society in which the monopolization of cultural resources, and the continued exercise of social power by the successful are obscured by a spurious ideology of equal worth. A transformatory element can be imparted by interpreting equality of opportunity, not as equal chances in a competition for limited places, but as equal access to the resources required for self-development. If the view that this involves access to all the different categories of social activity is correct, then this means consciously moving toward the abolition of the social division of labour.

A similar analysis holds in relation to the argument that the objective should be to devise ways of enabling the ruled to exercise more effective control over the rulers, rather than seeking to abolish the distinction between the two. Policies for more information and greater accountability are an essential part of the process of moving toward a self-governing society. However, their effectiveness is necessarily limited. In the context of a perspective of the permanent division of people into rulers and ruled, they are consistent with the perpetuation of political passivity and "subalternity" on the part of the ruled, and the continued exercise of social power by the rulers, obscured this time by an ideology of nonparticipatory, democratic control.

SOCIALISM AS SOCIAL TRANSFORMATION

My argument is that socialism should be reconceptualized as a society in which the social division of labour has been abolished. Since this is generally considered to be a utopian aspiration, it is as well to identify the major questions that have to be addressed if the project is to stand a chance of being taken seriously. First, are we all capable of functioning at each level of social activity? Second, even if, in principle, we could all perform functions at each level, is the skill and experience required for some activities such that they can only be acquired through a lifetime's specialization, with no time left over for other categories of social labour? Third, is society's productive potential sufficiently developed; is labour productivity high enough for all of us to be educated and trained to the level necessary for us to operate at each functional level, even if we were all capable of it? Fourth, even if we could all undertake tasks in each category of social labour, and resources were available to make this possible, perhaps we would be relatively better at some things than others, perhaps we would prefer to concentrate on what we are best at, or like best?

The case for consciously seeking to build into present policies, designed to deal with existing reality, a transformatory tension—one designed to change existing reality by moving toward the abolition of the social division of labour—does not require a definitive answer to all these questions. The way to discover whether everyone is capable of undertaking activities at each level of social labour is to ensure that everyone has the possibility of doing so. This means planning social activity in such a way that everyone has access to all categories of activity, without thereby depriving others of access to them.

The question of whether the skill and experience involved in some types of work, or in the highest levels of artistic excellence, require a lifetime of specialization is at first sight more difficult. Time, above all, is what is needed for all worthwhile activity, perhaps especially for creative activity. Is it impossible to achieve excellence in one activity and yet in the course of a lifetime also do a fair share of activities in other categories? I doubt it. I suspect that the crucial determinant is the social ethos. Given a social expectation that we should all undertake our share of each category of activity, in order to enable others to do the same, I would expect that in general people would find ways of doing so.

Resource availability is perhaps the most serious issue that has to be faced. However, in the more developed countries, at least, the problem is primarily one of cultural and not material resources. The question of material resource availability in these countries needs to be tackled primarily from the demand side. As long as the social division of labour, and the associated alienation and subaltern consciousness are justified on the grounds of scarcity, and therefore persist, the prophecy of limitless material wants will be self-fulfilling. Competition and alienation generate discontent and a demand for ever-more compensatory consumption. At issue are society's values, and in existing societies these are determined within a social structure in which some people have social power, and others do not.

Finally, there is the question of whether people might prefer to concentrate on the activities they are best at, or like best. Although frequently encountered, this argument is usually based on a misunderstanding. Within each category of activity there is plenty of scope for variety and choice—between different skilled work; between caring for the young and the old; between different forms of creative activity; between the planning and running of different social activities. Even unskilled and repetitive work is of different types between which people may not be indifferent; for instance, outdoor and indoor, manual and nonmanual. However, this should not be taken as an argument for specialization between categories. Such specialization is self-evidently bad for those confined to drudgery. It is also almost certainly bad for those who confine themselves to only one of the psychologically productive categories, since it seems unlikely that any individual's human potentialities are confined to only one category.

Socialism, then, may be thought of as the social transformation that is needed if people are to gain control over their lives, to be able to make informed and effective decisions about how they want to live. Self-determination has both an objective and a subjective aspect to it, or perhaps, more accurately, an external and an internal aspect. It involves the ability to make effective decisions about the external framework within which we live. It also involves our being aware of the determinants of our internal lives, our subjectivity, so that we can, collectively and individually, shape the external framework in ways that enable us to develop our human potentialities to the full.

In both capitalist and Statist societies the second of these considerations is typically ignored. Discussion of economic organization is concerned with the production of goods and services. Controversy takes place over which form of economic organization is most efficient at achieving macroeconomic stability, economic growth, innovation and consumer satisfaction. These are, of course, important questions but they are not the most important questions. In the end, what matters is the relationship between economic activity and the sort of people we are, or become. The production of goods and services is also, and more importantly, the production of people.

The principle of collective responsibility for ensuring that the resources people need for their self-development are available has long been accepted. The structure of education and training, provision for continuing education and retraining, the concept of career development, all reflect this. In existing societies, however, the principle and its application are bedeviled by unquestioned acceptance of the social division of labour. Social provision, and people, are shaped to the demands of the economy, rather than the economy and social provision being shaped to the needs of people. The economy is organized on the basis of coercion by market forces or State direction, with people treated as objects to be manipulated in the process of producing other objects—the goods and services comprising economic output.

A socialist society needs an economic system that promotes the self-activation and self-development of its citizens. I have elsewhere proposed a model of democratic planning which is consistent with this objective.[24] The model is constructed around the concept of negotiated coordination. Unlike coordination through the coercion of market forces or State direction, negotiated coordination requires people to engage consciously with their interdependence and the consequences of their actions for others. It encourages people to transcend their sectional interests and take account of the situations of others. It also, I believe, incorporates a dynamic that goes with the grain of abolishing the social division of labour. Indeed, its successful operation probably depends on it.

The argument of this paper has been that the classical Marxist concepts of the mode of production and social formation, as applied to the Statist system that developed in the Soviet Union and was imposed on Eastern Europe, can help us to reconceptualize socialism as the social transformation needed for the emergence of developed participatory political, and economic democracy. The fundamental transformation involved, I believe, is the abolition of the social division of labour; the creation of the conditions to enable the self-development of all. The experience of the Statist mode of production has brought Marxist analysis full circle. Advanced capitalism is the system in which the material and cultural preconditions for the abolition of the social division of labour have been most fully developed. It seems unlikely that historical evolution has come to an end.

NOTES

1. This paper is a shortened and updated version of my *Democracy and Economic Planning* (Cambridge: Polity Press, 1988), part III. I should like to thank Elena Lieven for comments on an earlier draft.
2. B. Horvat, T*he Political Economy of Socialism* (Oxford: Martin Robertson, 1982), p. 43.
3. R. Bahro, "The Alternative in Eastern Europe," *New Left Review* 106 (1977), pp. 9-10.
4. P. Devine, *Democracy and Economic Planning* (Cambridge: Polity Press, 1988), p. 116.
5. A. Nove, *Marxism and 'Really Existing Socialism'* (London: Harwood, 1986), chap. 4.
6. R. Bahro, *The Alternative in Eastern Europe* (London: New Left Books, 1978), chap. 9.
7. *Marxism and 'Really Existing Socialism,"* pp. 40-1.
8. *The Alternative in Eastern Europe*, p. 241.
9. *Ibid.*, p. 10.
10. *Democracy and Economic Planning*, chps. 5-6.
11. R. Williams, "Beyond Actually Existing Socialism," *New Left Review* 120 (1980), p. 7.
12. K. Marx, "Critique of the Gotha Programme," in *The First International and After* (Harmondsworth: Penguin; *New Left Review*, 1974), p. 347.
13. A. Nove, *The Economics of Feasible Socialism* (London: Allen & Unwin, 1983), p. 197.
14. "The Alternative in Eastern Europe," pp. 13-14.
15. *The Alternative in Eastern Europe*, pp. 46-7.
16. *Ibid.*, p. 152.
17. *Ibid.*, p. 199.
18. *Ibid.*, p. 278.
19. "The Alternative in Eastern Europe," p. 22; *The Alternative in Eastern Europe*, pp. 350-1.
20. *The Economics of Feasible Socialism*, p. 229.
21. *The Alternative in Eastern Europe*, p. 176.
22. *Ibid.*, pp. 436-7.
23. *Democracy and Economic Planning*, pp. 170-3.
24. *Ibid.*, section titled: "Abolition of the Social Division of Labour.

REFERENCES

Bahro, R. "The Alternative in Eastern Europe," *New Left Review*, 106 (1977).

———. *The Alternative in Eastern Europe* (London: New Left Books, 1978).

Devine, P. *Democracy and Economic Planning* (Cambridge: Polity Press, 1988).

Horvat, B. *The Political Economy of Socialism* (Oxford: Martin Robertson, 1982).

Marx, K. "Critique of the Gotha Programme," in *The First International and After* (Harmondsworth: Penguin in association with *New Left Review*, 1974).

Nove, A. *The Economics of Feasible Socialism* (London: Allen & Unwin, 1983).

———. *Marxism and 'Really Existing Socialism'* (London: Harwood, 1986).

Williams, R. "Beyond Actually Existing Socialism," *New Left Review*, 120 (1980).

II.

Economy and Politics in the Postwar Transformation

5.

TRANSFORMATION IN PROGRESS: The Labour Market and the World Monetary System in the Last Forty Years

Claus Thomasberger

INTRODUCTION

In my paper I shall try to analyze the development of Western economies in the last four decades, from the rise of Keynesianism to the neoliberal counter-revolution. This involves following a thought fundamental to Polanyi's classical investigation, *The Great Transformation*.[1] The roots of the great social transformations, positive or negative, in the last two centuries are to be sought in the utopian ideas of economic liberalism, i.e., in its attempt to set up a self-regulating market system. Such an approach implies a particular understanding of the prevailing liberal-economic presuppositions.

Liberal economic science considers the modern economic system basically in terms of a system of self-regulating markets. It is centered on isolated private individuals who, free of all traditional restraints, are guided only by egoistic interests. We are dealing with a very abstract model, an idealization, which leaves no room for many aspects of the "real world." Moreover it presupposes that the ideals of freedom and of equal opportunities in life can be realized, even if the people involved do not consciously take these values into consideration. Such a concept is indisputably utopian. However, the utopian character of this ideal is not an adequate reason for rejecting it. The idea that the market system should be self-regulating is the ideal of the modern economy, hence representative for the present market economy. In other words it is the ideal of the dominant approach. To this extent, the idea of the self-regulating market system is not only a theoretical construct but also presents the ideal according to which modern society organizes its economic sphere. As an organizing principle, the idea of the self-regulating market system is part of the real world.

The conviction that the idea of changing society into a system of self-regulating markets is, from the very start, utopian already occurs in Polanyi's research. As he shows, it is not only in line with the liberal ideal to subject social production to market laws, but also to transmute the substance of society itself—labour, nature, and money—into commodities. This involves no less than institutionally separating society into an economic and political sphere, and subordinating it to this venture.[2] Economic progress is taken as the single criterion of social progress; and not only economic liberalism, but also positivistic Marxism accepts that society is universally subordinated to the economy. It is only the reverse side of the dominance of the market over nature and society if, in the meantime, protecting nature and society from the consequences of a self-regulating market has become a dire necessity. However, its utopian character has not brought about the downfall of the liberal creed; quite the contrary. The unbridgeable gap between ideal and reality has always stimulated enthusiasm to further the market system. To put it another way: thanks only to its utopian character, the idea that a market system should be self-regulating has been able to dominate social development in the nineteenth and, as we shall show, the twentieth centuries.

In the following paper I consider under what conditions the Keynesian system has developed; what institutions it has established; what kind of relation between the economy and politics it entails; and, what inconsistencies point to its limits. As we shall see, Keynesianism and liberalism are not necessarily opposed. Keynes himself claimed his approach to be a contribution whose place was within the liberal fold. As regards basic aims, there are no principle differences: Keynesianism is concerned with nothing but upholding the market system. It does, however, stand apart from traditional liberalism insofar as Keynes accepted that certain conditions had changed, and so proposed a different combination of market organization and social protection: the market system itself needs to be protected by society. Keynesianism considers the intervention of institutions whose character is not mainly economic (i.e., the Nation States) as unavoidable for the stability of the market system. Liberalism itself had basically never prohibited State intervention, when the creation or preservation of the market system required it.[3] Keynesianism, however, in two decisive respects goes one step further: both the monetary system and effective demand (and thus the labour market) should be regulated by State institutions.

Perhaps the most convincing way of looking at Keynesianism is to interpret it as a variant of economic liberalism. This variant has specifically three characteristics:

1. The relation between the economy and politics is newly defined insofar as Nation States are given the task of continually regulating essential economic relations;

2. The self-regulation of the money market is replaced by a nationalized monetary sphere; the central banks become national institutions, and the national currency of the dominant power, the United States, takes over the function of international currency (less on the basis of gold than instead of it);

3. Active employment policies, designed to create full employment, take the place of the self-regulation of the labour market and become, together with stabilization of the currency, an independent aim of political intervention in their own right. The creation of full employment becomes the second objective of Nation States.[4]

My paper is structured accordingly. To begin, I shall try to set out some basic lines of development of the labour market. This will be followed by an analysis of world monetary relations as they evolved after the Second World War. In both cases the actual conflict and its theoretical dimensions will be laid bare. I shall try to show that the Keynesian system entails special ways of regulating the labour market and monetary relations—ways which have recently come up against their limits. The final section will be devoted to sketching some trends and key points of current institutional dynamics.

THE LABOUR MARKET AND EMPLOYMENT

Part A

The development of the West in the 1950s and 1960s was dominated by Keynesianism as an organizing principle. However, its origins go much further back. They are to be sought in the desperate and failed attempts to re-establish the international gold standard in the 1920s, following the world economic crisis, which lasted nearly a decade. These ideas were first formulated in Keynes' *The General Theory*, a fascinating work published in 1936. It had little immediate influence, and in spite of current interpretations, even Roosevelt's New Deal was not clearly Keynesian.[5] In the 1930s the objective was mainly direct social protection: protection of society, if not against the effects of the market system then against those of the system which no longer functioned. The State intervened by making jobs available, but all the initiatives taken were a long way from regulating the volume of employment, that is from eliminating the free play of supply and demand of labour. It took two events, both of which came from different directions, to implement Keynesianism.

The first of these was the Second World War. For the United States,[6] the rise in demand due to the war proved to be an extremely efficient way to overcome the economic recession.[7] In the 1930s, all attempts to reverse economic stagnation failed. In 1938, the crisis worsened. Only during the war did the economy improve.

But success and the knowledge that an instrument can be applied effectively may not be a sufficient argument if there are principles at stake. The contradiction between liberal ideals and social reality in the 1930s, given the collapse of the gold standard and the world economic crisis, was painfully apparent. But even a star reality cannot invalidate ideals. Indeed the latter seems more attractive if the former fails to conform. It needed a new confrontation—the partition of the globe into East and West, at first the cold war, then the hot war in Korea—to make the idea of extending the State and its regulatory functions acceptable, even within predominantly conservative circles. Keynesian policies and the increase in armaments were thus from the very start inseparable, and not only in the United States.

In the 1950s, the Keynesian system was more or less successful. The conflict betweem full employment and inflation could be kept under control. In the United States—on whose development (under the conditions of the system of Bretton Woods) the economic development of the Western world as a whole depended—the need for regulating nominal wages and price development was fully acknowledged. During the hot war phases, direct wage- and price-controls were viewed as legitimate.

In the following decade, President Kennedy's administration tried from the beginning to have increased influence over the development of nominal wage rates. Several Keynesians were quite aware that wage development was the Achilles heel of their system. The guideline set by the United States administration, and for a time accepted as the norm, was the following: "the general guide for noninflationary wage behavior is that the increase in wage rates (including fringe benefits) in each industry be equal to the trend rate of overall productivity increase."[8] There was some resistance to be overcome, as in the steel sector, but then the policy triumphed for several years. Even if quantitatively insignificant, it is worth noting, for instance, that in 1962 the United States Steel Corporation felt obliged, under pressure from the government and public, to hold price increases in connection with wage settlements within the given framework. Nominal wages developed for several years within the limits set by changes in productivity; the level of prices remained generally stable.

Nevertheless, wage and price movements continued to be the Achilles heel of the system. Due to initiatives by the Kennedy administration, the labour market had in practice been taken out of the framework of the self-regulating market system, but this step was never acknowledged in principle. Galbraith describes the conflict in the following terms:

> The control of wages and prices remained on the least secure footing. Partly this was because the divorce of ideology from action excluded any deliberate effort to devise a fully effective system of control. On occasions of public ceremony, businessmen and numerous union leaders still proclaim their commitment to the free market. And so did economists...To work on methods of wage and price control was not reputable. This absence of both ideological sanction and effective design left the mechanism of wage and price restraint subject to both misuse and nonuse.[9]

It did not take long for the informal wage controls to break down. Firstly, the tacit consensus broke down under President Johnson, who—faced by the rising costs of the hardly popular Vietnam War—preferred a rise in demand to an increase in taxation. Finally, at the end of the 1960s under President Nixon, the idea of the self-regulating labour market regained the upper hand completely. Paradoxically it was Nixon, who under public pressure in 1971, was very successful in applying wage and price controls. But from the start this step was taken without enthusiasm and came too late. As soon as Nixon had won the election it was abandoned.

The Keynesian State is unable to guarantee price stability, and this is its first limitation. But this is only the reverse side of the attempt to regulate the labour market without questioning the market's *raison d'être*. Keynes realized that changes in monetary wages do not necessarily tend to equalize supply and demand for labour without having any effect on prices.[10] This could not be denied by the neoclassical synthesis, which, accordingly, was forced to incorporate indirect effects via the real-balance effect into the theory, so as to reinstate the dominance of the labour market. At any rate, the stability of prices of commodities in the Keynesian system presupposes a development of wages which accepts the framework of the rise in labour productivity.

Full employment and stability of monetary value are thus mutually exclusive in a Keynesian system, as long as money wages are determined by the logic of self-regulating markets.[11] As soon as full employment is nearly reached, the forces of supply and demand enable workers to raise the nominal price of labour much faster than productivity.[12] So the wage-price spiral is an immanent conflict. The Keynesian form of regulation is caught in the paradox that in successfully creating full employment it produces the preconditions for eliminating itself. Indeed the State is able to regulate credit conditions and the volume of effective demand and employment, but it has no way of directly influencing supply. Without setting its liberal principles aside, it is in no position to question the tariff autonomy of employees and unions.

The end of Keynesianism is marked by a further fact. The Keynesian form of global economic regulation had in effect reduced the function of private property to that of a *rentier*, who, as A. Smith has put it, loves to reap where he has not sown. Through the government taxation of social demand on the one hand, and of credit conditions by means of the central banks on the other, the power and influence of the private owner and of his representative, the banks, had been very much reduced. The times in which haute finance pulled the threads seemed to have passed. The Keynesian system left no room for an N. M. Rothschild or J. P. Morgan. Galbraith already believed that he could proclaim the final domination of management over the now functionless entrepreneur and the birth of a new ruling class: the technostructure.[13] The conclusion was at least premature. The inflation which the Keynesian system left behind affected private owners not only directly as regarded their immediate interests, but also created a broad base for focusing social attention on the significance and rights of private property.

Part B

In fact, at the end of the 1960s and the beginning of the 1970s, there were two alternatives. Keynesianism was an answer to the failure of the self-regulating market system. It tried in practice to save the market system by means of State regulation of the labour market. The labour market had been withdrawn from the framework of the self-regulating markets *de facto*. Social recognition of this fact could have led to public questioning of the autonomy of the labour market and to its being taken back into the whole framework of social relations. Labour is not a commodity any more than earth and money are. The modern market economy, however, presupposes that all elements of industry—including labour, land, and money—be converted into commodities. A self-regulating market economy presupposes, no less than the separation of the economy from society, the removal of economic relations from the whole social framework of relations, and the institutional splitting up of society into an economic and a political sphere. This is an extraordinary division, a peculiarity which marks off the modern market economy from all earlier forms of social life.

Normally, economic institutions are nothing but one dimension of the social relations in which they are embedded.[14] Recognition of the fact that in the 1960s the labour market had been taken out of the market framework would have signified nothing less than recognizing that the economic sphere no longer needed to be split off from, and made independent of society; and that, in spite of the beliefs of economic liberalism, its integration into society might not have implied the end of our freedom but rather an extension of it. This was a possibility expressed by at least some of the social movements of the period.

The second alternative was naturally to develop the labour market into a real market, and to reintegrate it completely into the market system. This was the natural option of economic liberalism. And it was bound to be the path chosen, especially as—paradoxically— part of the Marxist-oriented Left were moving in the same direction. Marx's philosophy was concerned with the social as much as with the economic emancipation of mankind, and its ideal was to end the reign of economic relations over human ones. But this was not held to be crucial at this time. Marx followed Ricardo in defining social classes in economic terms, and economic exploitation was clearly one of the characteristics of capitalist society in which labour was a commodity. Marx frequently defended the right and indeed the duty of the working class to better its position, or at least to maintain it by struggling for higher wages. Though Marxists and liberals were nominally opposed, in practice they were all keen on re-establishing the labour market.

The only other possibility—more a compromise than a genuine alternative—was put forward by heterodox Keynesians concerned with the "real world." Their basic consideration was the following. In the 1960s, the labour market did not actually function as a market, so why not institutionalize this fact and control money wages by the State? A whole series of proposals for wage and price controls were developed, at first in the form of direct,[15] then later of more indirect controls (i.e., Wallich's and Weintraub's proposal of a sophisticated system of tax laws, which has become known as Tax-based Income Policy, or TIP).[16] The proposals were thought not to imply any disruption of the framework of economic liberalism, but in demanding the introduction of wage controls they also demanded the institutionalization of a principle—already put into practice but unrecognized— which economic liberalism would never be able to sanction: the withdrawal of the labour market from market relations. Within the framework of liberal logic, withdrawal of the labour market is illegitimate. The proposal of State regulation of wages was doomed from the start. If the pegging of wages is not (mis)understood as a market process, the State is not needed to control it; if, however, the liberal concept of the labour market as an integral part of the self-regulating market system prevails, where should the political consensus come from, to revoke the "game of supply and demand"?

Whatever the single factors may have been, the fact is that toward the end of Johnson's presidency the consensus which had been the basis of the wage and price guidelines in the period 1961 to 1968 had dissolved. The introduction of wage and price controls under President Nixon —which, beginning in August 1971, were to be applied for seventeen months—turned out to be a short intermezzo, unable to hinder the path of development. The vision of the labour market as part of a self-regulating market system was again fully accepted. The first consequence was a drastic rise in the price level.[17] After wage and price controls had been revoked, the rate of inflation rose above ten percent in 1974, and inflation became the most important problem of economic and monetary policy.

But if the labour market is viewed as being part of a self-regulating market system, economic policies have no path to follow but that of restrictive monetary policies, to gain influence indirectly—by lessening the demand for labour—over the development of nominal incomes and thus prices. Within the market logic, wage or income inflation can be brought under control only by producing a recession. As a result, economic policies in the United States in the 1970s were characterized by a continual stop and go. As soon as the rate of inflation rose, a restrictive line was chosen, but if recessionary tendencies prevailed, policies switched over to expansion.

> Between 1969 and 1980 each tight money episode increased unemployment rates to what were thought to be politically unacceptable levels. With congressional elections every two years and presidential elections every four years, most politicians lost the political stomach for the resulting unemployment, and deserted the conservative cause. As soon as the inflation problem began to abate, political pressure built up to restimulate the economy. Consequently the 1970s was a period of on-again-off-again restrictive monetary policies stringent enough to raise unemployment, but neither strong enough nor long enough to permanently subdue the inflationary struggle over the distribution of income.[18]

This phase of United States development came to an end only in

1979 with the abrupt change taken by the Federal Reserve under the new chairman, P. Volker.

THEORY I: REINTEGRATION OF THE LABOUR MARKET INTO THE SELF-REGULATING MARKET SYSTEM

Until a few years ago, the Keynesian State was generally thought to be an intrinsic part of social progress, a historical achievement from which there was no going back. We are all Keynesians now, was the cry in university auditoriums at the start of the 1970s, and even United States Republican presidents proclaimed Keynesianism as a pillar of their policies. The social climate in the 1980s fundamentally changed. The wind shifted. The Keynesians in politics and science have, save for one or two exceptions, gone into hiding and given free rein to a counter-revolution.

The claim of Keynesianism was, on the whole, conservative: the aim was never anything other than preserving the market system. But Keynesianism paradoxically reproduced the contradictions of State intervention in the name of liberalism on a higher level. The aim of intervention is to set up the self-regulating market system and, once intervention succeeds, it becomes superfluous. In effect intervention was supposed to make itself ultimately obsolete: "[If] our central controls succeed in establishing an aggregate volume of output corresponding to full employment as nearly as is practicable, the classical theory comes into its own again from this point onwards."[19] The rather astonishing fact that the successful creation of full employment through a form of Keynesian intervention produces the preconditions for abandoning intervention is supplemented by the paradox that the aim of State intervention is to make itself superfluous.

But this is only one side of the issue. Resistance to Keynesianism was rarely due to theoretical contradictions but rather to another factor: Keynesianism implied the use of extreme means. Firstly, the State, which is not mainly an economic institution, should regulate the international monetary and commodity markets and keep them under control. I shall later come back to this aspect. Secondly, in the Keynesian model, the labour market is taken out of the system of self-regulating markets—at least in principle, if not in practice. State regulation of effective demand, i.e., a policy which tries to guide the volume of employment by means of State intervention, is not at all in keeping with the idea of the self-regulating market. Instead of being self-regulating, supply and demand in the labour market are regulated by the State.

The labour market is anything but peripheral to liberal concerns. From the very start, the social and political opposition to setting up the labour market was considerable, and not until well into the nineteenth century did it come into being. As Polanyi has shown, a fully developed market economy did not exist in England until after the 1830s, when the Speenhamland Law was abolished and a competitive labour market set up. In the United States, liberalism was even willing to resort to armed intervention (as in the American Civil War between North and South) to create the preconditions for setting up a labour market. In view of these experiences, intervention in the labour market must seem to liberals to be an attack on cornerstones of liberal achievements. This is the actual reason why even among liberals Keynesianism is bound to seem potentially subversive.

Keynes must have sensed the resistance of his liberal colleagues. But this did not lead him to work out the critique of the concept of the labour market especially clearly. On the contrary, in *The General Theory* he chose to put this problem into a form which is certainly subtle but hardly clear. The attacks on the concept of the labour market in Keynes' "general theory" were therefore not immediately recognizable[20] but were clear enough not to be denied. According to liberal logic, there could normally be no "involuntary" unemployment in a market system. So the Keynesian approach could be generally acknowledged in the theoretical discussion only after this "weakness" had been corrected. A whole generation of economists had found an occupation: the task consisted in reintegrating the labour market into the economic system. The result is the neoclassical synthesis of Keynesian theory, or as J. Robinson called it, bastard Keynesianism.

Two main lines of argument were designed for this purpose. On the one hand the distinction between short-term and long-term theory was newly revived. The need for State intervention was said to be of only a temporary nature, as a reaction to disturbances and wrong external interference, etc. The long-term self-regulation of the market system was thought to be unquestionable. On the other hand an explanation had to be found for the existence of unemployed workers whom they described as only a deviation from the norm, not as the rule. Thousands of students were taught to regard the models from Hansen, Hicks or the IS-LM scheme as the quintessence of economic science.[21] Market rigidities, liquidity traps, money illusions and a whole series of further categories were developed, so as to explain what particular constellations obstructed the realization of the general tendency toward full employment. But only by introducing the "Patinkin resolution" did the neoclassical synthesis reach its theoretical peak and conclusion. It opened the way to re-establishing the dominance of the labour market over all restrictions.

So economic liberalism theoretically overcame its Keynesian trauma. The free market could be presented as the one royal road to human freedom, while *laissez-faire* limited State intervention not only in theory. The full dominance of self-regulating market relations seemed to be impaired only by State regulation of international economic relations.

THE LIMITS OF THE SYSTEM OF BRETTON WOODS

Part A

The system of Bretton Woods was the international economic system *par excellence*. It was international because national governments controlled the monetary parities. The policy of the central banks (transformed into national institutions) became the instrument with which the stability of the system was ensured. It was international, since it regulated the relations between the various national economies and currencies. The General Agreement on Tariffs and Trade (GATT) agreements, insofar as they were intended to enable the market logic to be extended onto an international level, and the system of Bretton Woods, which thought of monetary relations as being an international concern, made up a whole. It is the significance which national governments acquired in shaping international monetary relations that fundamentally distinguished the system of Bretton Woods from the gold standard of the nineteenth century and made it unequivocally into a Keynesian institution.

The currency of the hegemonic power, the dollar, had a special role within the system of Bretton Woods. The dollar was the central currency, which in practice took over the function of the international one. It was, at the same time, the international reserve currency, the international means of payment and the unit in which all other currencies found their expression and measure. A rise in the rate of inflation within the monetary sphere of the hegemonic power (i.e., a devaluation of the dollar) was bound to question the way in which the international system functioned. According to the logic of the system of Bretton Woods it was the first task of all other central banks to keep the rates of exchange of their respective currencies stable in relation to the dollar. The stabilization of the currencies with regard to the dollar implied the stability of the respective national monetary value, but only as long as the value of the dollar remained more or less stable.

Or, to put it in other words: inflation of the dollar signified for all other national banks a dilemma. Internal and external stability seemed no longer to be compatible. For the banks of the other countries, devaluation of the dollar implied that they would have to decide between two alternatives. They would have to defend either the rate of exchange or the value of their national currencies. In several countries of central importance for keeping the system of Bretton Woods together, especially—though not only—West Germany and Japan, the position was adopted of valuing the stability of the national currency more highly than the defence of the international monetary system.[22]

It was this dilemma which expressed a deep inconsistency in the Keynesian model: the tendency to globalize economic relations increasingly limited the scope of monetary regulation by the Nation States. Keynesianism had at first found a solution to this conflict: the fixing of rates of exchange within the framework of the system of Bretton Woods. The existence of a system of fixed rates of exchange ensured that any currency taking part in this scheme could be exchanged against any other and so find international acceptance. Or, to put it the other way around: for every national currency, the other currencies presented more or less perfect substitutes (according to the degree of faith in the stability of the parities). In the system of Bretton Woods, the dollar moreover did not only function as the national currency of the United States but also, due to its central position, as the international currency *per se*. So the conflict of globalizing economic relations and nationalizing the currencies remained latent, as long as the stability of the rates of exchange was unquestioned. It was first the decision in favour of stabilizing the national currencies which not only brought about the downfall of the system of Bretton Woods but also, in practice, nationalized the currencies. In the 1970s, battles against inflation and nationalization of currencies went hand in hand. It was monetarism which delivered the theoretical justification for nationalizing the currencies: on the one hand by maintaining that there was a direct connection between the amounts of money handled by the central bank and prices; and on the other hand, insofar as it claimed (in the form of monetary foreign trade theory) that the conflict between nationalizing the currency and internationalizing the trading area could be overcome by creating international money markets.

If one recalls what the guardians of the currencies of all relevant national banks said at the end of the 1960s, it is striking that, even while the debate about reforming the system of Bretton Woods was quickening, the existence of the system as such was beyond question. Toward the end of the 1960s, the United Kingdom deficit, which in previous years had given rise to some thought, seemed to be back under control. At this time, the whole system of Bretton Woods seemed to have lost nothing of its prevailing influence.

The situation changed dramatically at the beginning of the 1970s.[23] From having a surplus, the United States slipped into the red in 1970 with 10 billion dollars, and in 1971 with 30 billion dollars. In March 1971 speculation against the dollar set in. The deutsche mark (and to some degree the yen) grew increasingly interesting as alternatives. Between March third and fourth, the Deutsche Bundesbank bought more than a billion dollars, then in the first 40 minutes of March fifth, it had to intervene again with an additional billion. This triggered a withdrawal of federal German monetary guardians from the market: the deutsche mark began to fluctuate. It is interesting to note that it was not so much the direct difference in inflation between the United States and other member States of the system of Bretton Woods, as the worsening external balance of capital and the resulting loss in faith in the ability and willingness of the Federal Reserve Board to act which appeared to be crucial for the monetary turbulences.[24]

On 15 August, 1971, President Nixon concluded a packet of economic and monetary measures comprising the suspension of the gold convertibility of the dollar. In December of the same year, a new attempt was made (on the basis of a dollar which had been devalued against most other currencies) to reinstate the system of fixed rates of exchange. But even these efforts were short-lived. The turbulence from January until March, 1973, finally buried the system of Bretton Woods. On the first of March the Bundesbank had to issue nearly 8 billion deutsche marks. This was nearly as much as the increase in central bank money for a whole year in those days! At this point we applied the emergency brake. That was the funeral knell for the parity system of Bretton Woods.[25]

Part B

The collapse of the system of Bretton Woods can only be interpreted as a victory of liberal ideas, since transforming the relations between currencies into a market relationship subject to the logic of supply and demand is an immanent part of liberal strategy. So the immense dynamic of the development of the Euro- and Xenomarkets was a precondition and result of the collapse of the system of Bretton Woods. Naturally, the relationships between various currencies are not self-regulating market relations in terms of their functional logic, for a currency is not a commodity produced for the market and which the mechanism of supply and demand could explain something about. But the logic of economic liberalism naturally implies that monetary relationships too can be transformed into self-regulating market relationships. The 1970s were characterized by the fact that not only the labour market but also the monetary market was integrated into the system of self-regulating markets. Transforming the monetary market into a self-regulating market was to have decisive consequences.

After the collapse of the system of Bretton Woods, the United States behaved as if external relations could be left to themselves.[26] At first, fluctuations of the dollar as against the other relevant currencies did not disturb the United States government, or prompt it to change the direction of its relevant economic policies. The United States economic and monetary policies behaved as if the promises of monetarist theories—that by going over to market-regulated rates of exchange the individual nations would win back their economic and money-policy autonomy—were to be taken at face value. Subscribing to a system, generally described as one of "benign neglect," the United States monetary boards did not take any action to regulate the rates of exchange. Even as the dollar continually dropped in value compared to other nations' currencies, the United States boards restricted themselves to actions designed to smooth the daily fluctuations.

Only in the course of the late 1970s, as the balance of payments deficit again grew (1977: $14.5 billion, 1978: $15.5 billion) did

President Carter feel obliged to take cautious action. A decisive role was played not only by the increasing expenditure on natural oil imports, but above all by the unusually good market conditions. Whereas United States development was clearly showing expansive traits, West Germany and, to some extent, Japan were more concerned with stability. This was the background for the well-known controversy between Schmidt and Carter.

Initial United States measures to stabilize the foreign value of the dollar, like the International Emergency Economic Act passed by Congress in December 1977, showed no relevant effects. By threatening a further devaluation of the dollar, the United States then tried to induce the Bundesbank and the West German government to adopt a more expansive policy. But West Germany was not to be persuaded,[27] and the United States had no monetary instruments to enable it to get its own way. The opposite happened: in the second half of 1978 the dollar increasingly lost ground against the Mark and the Federal Reserve was obliged to change course. To save the international functions of the dollar within the system based on monetary competition, the United States switched over to restrictive monetary policy. The emergency program for supporting the dollar (November 1, 1978), followed barely a year later by the decision to switch over to the concept of controlling the quantity of money, meant no less than a change of American economic policy in the direction of stabilization. In this way the dithering between a financial policy oriented toward expansion and one oriented toward stability came to an end. Here, too, it was not so much the internal conflict of increasing inflation but the foreign economic weakness of the dollar[28] which forced the United States administration to adopt a policy more concerned with internal stability. This new orientation led to a fundamental change in global monetary relations in the 1980s.

It now becomes clear why the idea of a self-regulating currency market is not only utopian but also fails to match the practical behavior of the market participants. The owners of liquid assets, especially the banks, know perfectly well that a currency does not automatically follow the logic of some market law. For them it is of prime importance to maintain the control of a national central bank over the development of the foreign value of a currency. If a land loses this competence (or even if there is only the risk of the central bank's scope of action being seriously restricted), faith in the currency is lost and the capital flight intensifies.

The conflict which broke out in the Schmidt-Carter controversy points to the deep contradiction within which the world monetary system moved in the 1970s. On the one hand, the idea of a global, self-regulating monetary market was realized in practice; on the other hand the national currencies made up the building blocks of the whole system. The global character of markets and the national character of the currencies involve a contradiction. The conflict is not evident as long as either national or international institutions regulate the global market—as in the system of Bretton Woods—or if centrally regulated supranational markets guide national monetary policies, and if the national central banks, more or less, follow this logic—as under the gold standard.

To this extent, monetarism is still to be seen as an expression of the Keynesian system, since it finds its institutional point of reference in the policies of national State banks. Its intermediate success in the sphere of economic sciences has in fact appreciably contributed to escalating the conflict between globalizing the markets, and nationalizing the currencies.

THE THEORY II: FROM THE INTERNATIONAL MONETARY SYSTEM TO MONETARY COMPETITION

In his writings Keynes had been less worried about external economic instability than about internal imbalance, and had normally assumed that—where international relations, especially international movements of capital, restricted the scope of action of national economic policies—the national ability to act and govern should be maintained through capital movement and/or import controls. At the heart of post-Keynesian theory have been internal equilibrium and securing the scope of political action, in order to stabilize full employment. By regulating money and fiscal variables (especially rates of interest and national expenditure/taxes) the Nation States should be enabled to balance possible gaps in investment.

The logic of the IS-LM model was later extended through foreign economic dimensions into the so-called Mundell-Fleming Model. Not only the closed but also the open national economy was considered, seen generally from the point of view of the small country. The basic weakness of these approaches lay clearly in the fact that they had no instrument with which to draw attention to the problem of price development under the conditions of an underemployment situation.[29]

And it was this exposed flank which enabled monetarism in the 1970s—as inflation was increasingly recognized to be a real problem—to do away with approach based on the IS-LM model. As Johnson rightly remarked, the rise of monetarism went hand in hand with the growing significance of inflation as a politically central problem.

In retrospect this may seem to be a rather odd aspect of the development of theory. The monetarist theorists acted as theoretical vanguards in the fight for stable prices, although monetary theory, as it later grew increasingly clear, was not even able to explain why inflation was an economic problem at all, quite apart from being the "greatest evil" (Friedman). After monetary policy had initially been approved to be able to achieve short-term effects but to be neutral in the long run, the integration of rational expectations approaches led to the conclusion that the main problem might be false expectations of inflation rather than inflation as such. Leijonhuvud and others have rightly drawn attention to the paradox that a theoretical school which had come forward to highlight the significance of monetary policies ended by denying that monetary variables have any real influence.

But perhaps there is more than a superficial paradox. Monetarism advocated not only the importance of fighting inflation, not only the lack of a "trade-off" between unemployment and inflation, not only the advantages of a stable growth in the money supply and not only the validity of the quantity theory; above all it advocated that the system of Bretton Woods be abolished, together with international regulation of currency relations and that rates of exchange be self-adjusting via the market. And it is above all the foreign economic aspect which makes the priority of fighting inflation intelligible: not inflation but unemployment is consistent with market regulation of international monetary relations!

Monetarist attacks on the system of Bretton Woods were made easier by the increasing discrepancy between the Keynesian-liberal ideal and the actual functioning of the world economic system after the Second World War. What had theoretically been designated as a system of Nation States with (more or less) equal rights turned out in practice to be a hegemonic system dominated by the United States. Most member countries were obliged by the actual mechanism of Bretton Woods to orient their own monetary policies toward that of the United States, which seemed more and more to be an unjustified compulsion. National autonomy as regards monetary policy became a worthwhile aim, and monetarism claimed to know a way out: the self-regulation of rates of exchange through the market logic.

It was the foreign economic branch of monetarism that highlighted the problem of national autonomy as regards monetary policies. With fixed rates of exchange, monetary policy tailored to national requirements was said to be impossible. But if regulation of the rates of exchange were left to the self-regulation of the market logic, monetary policy should again be free to regulate the respective national price-levels in an autonomous way. Advocates of monetarist theory were among the first and most vehement advocates of deregulating the rates of exchange.

The strength of monetarism as against approaches based on the IS-LM model lay precisely—against the background of the dominant conflicts in the 1970s in delivering a theoretical explanation and justification of why—quite in accordance with the logic of economic liberalism—a whole bundle of apparently pressing domestic and foreign economic problems could be solved by cutting back State regulation of the international monetary market.

Monetarism remained marked by a characteristic paradox: it presented itself as being opposed to the Keynesian tradition, and advocated transforming monetary relations regulated by Nation States into self-regulating market relations. However, in its logic there always remained national currencies that were subjected to market regulation. To this extent monetarism had one leg firmly planted in the Keynesian tradition. Moreover as self-regulation of the monetary market proved to be illusory, abolition of the international monetary system failed to have quite the intended consequences: in practice it resulted in nationalizing the currencies. It is this fundamental contradiction in the monetary approach which Hayek's proposal[30] of denationalizing money aimed at overcoming. Only then was the reference to Keynesianism jettisoned.

Hayek's basic consideration is simple: if it is possible to transform relations between various currencies into self-regulating market relationships, why should it be left exclusively to the State central banks to create money? Just as the relationship of supply and demand fixes prices of various commodities, it could also regulate the price of money, the rates of exchange. Since faith in the stability of the value of money is essential, private suppliers of competing currencies must, much more than monopolistic suppliers, take over responsibility for the stability of the money they supply. The competitive mechanism between various privately "produced" kinds of money or currencies would automatically ensure that an adequate supply of money of stable value was always likely.

Hayek's idea of denationalizing money was, even if utopian, not a mere fancy. In fact, following the collapse of the system of Bretton Woods the various central banks were forced into the position of "producers" of competing currencies. Money is not in itself a commodity, nor does it become the product of private suppliers, but Hayek's idea of denationalization implied that national central banks had to behave as if they were competing suppliers of the commodity "money." Monetary movements were subject to the logic of self-regulating markets, and the central banks had to adapt themselves to their logic.

So the circle was closed. Not only the labour market but also the monetary market was reintegrated into the system of self-regulating markets.[31] The Keynesian State not only turned out to be superfluous, its intervention in the economic sphere seemed to be counterproductive, disturbing the self-regulation of the market system. The hard core of the liberal utopia—self-regulation of the economic sphere as a whole—seemed to be a real possibility. State regulation and intervention in the labour and monetary markets, which Keynesians had thought to be necessary, seemed to be pointless. In Hayek's vision, there was only one economic and political guideline: *laissez-faire*. Economic liberalism had thus returned to its origins.

THE LIMITS OF THE LIBERAL UTOPIA

Part A

In the 1970s, the Keynesian State had proven itself unable to overcome both the conflict between inflation and full employment and the contradiction between globalizing the markets and nationalizing currencies (or the macroeconomic regulation).[32] Was the Keynesian State only an episode, a wrong path of historical development, a dead end? Does its end mean a return to "normal" capitalism? And does the renewed transformation, as liberals maintain, really imply an increase in our freedom?

Above all, what is the alternative to the Keynesian State? Labour and money are not commodities. That does not mean that they cannot be subjected to market relations, but the markets for these fictitious commodities do not regulate themselves. And this is precisely where the weakness of economic liberalism reveals itself. Even under present conditions the monetary markets are anything but deregulated (quite apart from denationalized). One need only think of the various monetary snakes (with or without tunnels), the European monetary system, the so-called Plaza or Louvre agreements from September 1985 and February 1987, or the massive central bank interventions to stabilize exchange rates. And the "price of labour" continues to be regulated by unions and entrepreneurial associations, even if the power relations have shifted. At any rate the nature of regulation has basically changed.

The ideal of economic liberalism is, and remains, self-regulation of the market sphere, insofar as intervention is thought to be necessary. The collapse of forced attempts to constitute a self-regulating monetary market in the 1970s confirms this. It should stem from the economic sphere itself and not from political bodies. It is true that even in the Keynesian State the main aim was to uphold the market system. However, whereas the Keynesian State tried to stabilize markets by strengthening State intervention and social control over the economic sphere, economic liberalism tends to subject intervention to the logic of the economic system.

It is certainly not necessary to consider the regulation of markets of fictitious commodities as a task of Nation States. As the gold standard has shown, an institution which acts outside the Nation State sphere is quite able to fulfill this function successfully. But under present conditions there is no such alternative. Which institution, if not Nation States, should take over these regulatory functions? If no ready alternatives to the Keynesian State are available, are there at least developing trends which are leading to a new form of regulation or could at least be directed towards this goal? In fact, it is my conviction that there is not only one but several such trends, which partly supplement each other, partly contradict each other, and which—half-hidden by the liberal theoretical constructs dominating the economic discipline—are realized outside the range of attention of professional economic sciences.

During the period which we have characterized as "Keynesian," the process of—as Marx called it—"concentration and centralization of capital" continued. Concentration and centralization have, in fact, reached a point which might, in a certain sense, enable the market sector "to support itself."[33] It was one of the never-questioned articles of faith of the prevailing Keynesian system that no importance be attached to growing monopolization. Only a few theorists—belonging to heterodox schools—tried to analyze the matter seriously.[34] Keynes himself completely neglected to work on trends toward growing concentration and centralization.[35] But this neglect was taken as a further sign that monopolization would have no relevant influence on economic development.[36] Accordingly, the antitrust laws in the United States were formulated and implemented in a half-hearted way. It was easy to discount them later.

In fact, there are indications that in the 1980s, the key enterprises and banks, supported by the post-Keynesian State, have acted so as to make their influence felt, both to inhibit rises in the price level and to extend effective demand. There are no comprehensive academic studies of this question, since, as Galbraith put it, research into concentration and centralization does little for one's academic reputation. But there need be no doubt about the fact that the market sector's attempt to fill the vacuum left by the collapse of the Keynesian State is still a current concern.[36]

Such a form of regulation, which is due to the accumulation efforts of the banking system, is on the whole characterized by a fundamentally expansive outlook. Growth, extension of the scale of production, and a high level of investment activity are not only due to the market system's urge to expand, but are becoming more and more an existential necessity, a precondition of its existence. The stability of the banking system presupposes that the great majority of enterprises are able to pay their interest, which is obviously the case only if they make enough profit. Considered from a macroeconomic point of view, profits are a result of investment activity. So growth and expansion of the volume of investment is not an aim which enterprises pursue, but rather is becoming a precondition for the stable development of such a regulation model.

This does not imply that a new power center is emerging which—led mainly by profit interests—controls society. Certainly, every macroeconomic institution that governs relevant markets has appreciable power and should be democratically legitimate. But even here, the fate of various more or less powerful groups is governed far more by the "needs" of society than the fate of society is governed by the interests of the dominant social classes.

The barriers to the formation of such an institution are not technical but a matter of principle. The above solution may be wholly in the interest of several key enterprises and banks but is no more necessary than the need to pursue a strategy of increasing money wages in relation to productivity growth within the Keynesian model. Recognition that it is not the markets which regulate the decisions of the enterprises but the strategies of several key enterprises which regulate the markets (and not only several single markets but the market system as a whole) is impossible within the framework laid down by economic liberalism so far. Economic liberalism in its present form cannot legitimize regulation of the price level and effective demand through a complex of enterprises and banks.

Part B

A second trend toward overcoming the limits of regulation by Nation States depends less on big enterprises and banks than on institutions which reach beyond national borders. One could speak in a certain sense of the creation of supranational institutions. Naturally, I am mainly thinking of trends in Europe, the former cradle of Nation States; of the growing significance of attempts to shift economically relevant responsibilities from the national to the community level; of efforts toward harmonizing economic and monetary policies; and the formation of new institutions of economic regulation. Such perspectives are not limited to Europe. Even outside the European continent there is a need for, and a trend toward, growing coordination, which is expressed by supranational institutions. Since the debate has been concentrated on the problem of debts, it has been easy to overlook the fact that the function of many traditional international organizations has fundamentally changed in the last few years, and that their task has been newly defined. For instance, the International Monetary Fund (IMF) and the World Bank have taken over a new and decisive role in coordinating economic and monetary policies, especially among countries of Latin America and the United States.

It is true that there have been a number of approaches which have been aimed at creating supernational organizations on a global level. Hankel's proposals for a world central bank is one of them. Nonetheless, under present circumstances such a perspective seems rather unrealistic. Developments are tending toward setting up supranational organizations with authority over regional areas. Graziani distinguishes between three economic areas within the western hemisphere: the American continent, Western Europe and the Pacific region. At present, this is more a trend than a reality, but his description of the development is apt.[38]

Such a model of supranational economic regulation overcomes, at least tendentiously, the Keynesian conflict between globalizing economic relations while at the same time nationalizing monetary and market regulation. Regulation of currencies and the market system tends to be taken out of the sphere of national responsibility. Such a model seems to be weaker regarding the conflict between unemployment and inflation. Just as the Keynesian State had no direct instrument for controlling inflation, supranational institutions will hardly be able to influence conditions of supply, money wages and the level of commodity prices. Only an income policy which regulates the development of nominal wages could be of use here. But so long as this supplementary element is lacking, the problem of inflation will remain critical. This is one reason why, on the basis of such a form of regulation, a restrictive bias prevails.

The model of supranational institutions of economic regulation is to be distinguished in one essential point from Keynesian institutions of international regulation. The system of Bretton Woods was a typical Keynesian institution insofar as the responsibility for decision-making remained in all essential aspects at the national level. In contrast to a whole series of theoretical models, which at that time had already been worked out, international institutions had only subsidiary significance in the system of Bretton Woods. Power rested in the hands of national governments, and, in practice, the United States dominated Bretton Woods institutions.

The outlook in Europe today seems to be different. In the 1980s, the political dimension of European integration clearly receded into the background and attention was focused unequivocally on economic and monetary integration. This aspect is especially clear in the debate about monetary harmonization, the allocation of tasks to and the structuring of a possible European central bank, and the significance which should be given to the autonomy of the incipient monetary institutions regarding all political influences.

The trend toward self-organization of the market sector and the creation of supranational autonomous institutions of economic regulation do indeed contradict each other to some extent, but are not to be thought of as simple opposites. Certainly a trend toward the latter form of regulation may predominate in Europe, whereas in America the former seems to do so. Even though a coordination of economic, financial, credit, and monetary policies are irreplaceable in the relationship between the United States and Latin America, it is still notable that European economic integration is to be brought about by opening markets to create a European common market.

So far there have only been trends. At the end of the 1980s the institutional vacuum was still the central problem facing the Western world. The resulting instability and increasing insecurity affect all aspects of social life. But the limits of the liberal utopia are more fundamental. Both multinational firms and supranational institutions can only take over the functions of the Keynesian State in part. Their separation from democratic political influences and their subordination to the functional logic of the economic sphere prevent them from fulfilling the role of social protection. The competence of regulation is one-sidedly shifted toward stabilization of the economic sphere. Economic liberalism is unable to produce institutions that are able to take over the protective role of Nation States in the Keynesian system.

Ensuring stability of the economic system seems to be the fundamental aim of regulation. Whether there are problems on the stock exchange, fluctuations in the rates of exchange or inflation, all intervention is directed to recreating stable market conditions. But the liberal economic forms of stabilization not only involve contradictions and insecurities as regards the actual effects, they also involve enormous social costs.

Stabilization of the value of money succeeded only by accepting sudden rises in the level of unemployment. The efforts to implement expansive employment policies collapsed in the face of increased inflationary tendencies. The price of stabilizing the world monetary system is the growing poverty of the masses in many countries in the third world. In practice, industrial nations have managed to shift social costs disproportionately onto the shoulders of people in less developed areas. To the extent that the intervention of Nation States has been held back, social protection has been weakened. Or, to put it the other way around: social protection did and does depend on the instrument of State intervention. Economic liberalism is unable to offer an alternative.

Today, as in the nineteenth century, it is utopian to believe that the market is automatically the institution able to guarantee freedom and equal opportunities to everyone. Moreover, the concentration of efforts on stabilizing the market system is again endangering the social content, the cultural achievements of modern societies, and freedom and self-determination on an individual as well as on a national level.

The Keynesian system has come up against its limits. But this does not mean that it can be relegated to the past. Economic liberalism is even unable to reflect on the actual conflicts and the need for social protection against the consequences of a self-regulating market system. It stands apart from the real problems; the rediscovery of the ideal of the self-regulating market system (which characterizes the current theoretical discussion) is not a sign that the market system of the nineteenth century is being revived, but an expression of the unbroken dominance of basic liberal beliefs, and of their influence over the institutional structuring of the economic sphere. In other words, the crisis in the field of economics is no coincidence, but an expression of the real conflicts within the market economies of the Western world following the collapse of the system of Bretton Woods.

NOTES

1. K. Polanyi, *The Great Transformation* (New York: 1944).
2. *Ibid* ., chap. 6.
3. But it is just as true that liberalism has never been able to integrate State intervention in a consistent way into its structure. Means and ends contradict one another. Basically *laissez-faire* is the only method which economic liberalism can apply without contradiction.
4. Attempts to describe Keynesianism in terms of a class conflict remain superficial. The fixation on "interests" seems to remain wholly caught up in the world of liberal ideas. Class interests offer only a very limited explanation of long-term social developments. The fate of classes seems to be much more determined by the "needs" of society than the fate of society is determined by class interests (*The Great Transformation*, p.152). The economic crisis in the 1930s meant not only that workers were out of work but also that firms stagnated and collapsed. Did State regulation of effective demand lie more in the interest of the workers or of capitalists? The question cannot be answered in such terms. Of course the Keynesian policy of stabilizing demand, as Minsky put it, was never anything other than a safeguarding of profits, so as to eliminate unemployment. In this case the category of the compromise has little explanatory power. (It should not be overlooked that Keynes too was rather skeptical about the explanatory power of interests.

Cf. J. M. Keynes, *The General Theory of Employment, Interest and Money*, Collected writings, Vol. VII (London: Macmillan, 1936), p. 383.

5. H. P. Minsky, *Stabilizing an Unstable Economy* (New York: n.p., 1986), p. 7.

6. For our purposes it is sufficient to follow the lines of development from the standpoint of the United States, since its influence was crucial for the Western world as a whole.

7. J. K. Galbraith, *The New Industrial State*. 3d ed. (Boston: n.p., 1978 [1967]), pp. 259-261.

8. "Economic Report of the President" 1962, cited in *The New Industrial State*, p. 265.

9. *The New Industrial State*, p. 266.

10. *The General Theory*, chap. 19.

11. C. Thomasberger, *Löhne, Profite, Inflation - Theorie der Monetären Wirtschaft* (München: n.p., 1987).

12. *The New Industrial State*, p. 256.

13. J. K. Galbraith, *The Affluent Society*. 4th ed. (Boston: n.p., 1984 [1958]), ch. 23; *The New Industrial State*, chaps. 5-8.

14. *The Great Transformation*, chap. 4; K. Polanyi, *The Livelihood of Man*, edited by H. W. Pearson (New York: Academic Press, 1977).

15. *The Affluent Society*, chps. 21-23.

16. Cf. S. Weintraub, *Our Stagflation Malaise* (Westport/London: n.p., 1982), chaps. 12-13.

17. G. Davidson, and P. Davidson, *Economics for a Civilized Society* (Basingstoke and London: n.p., 1988), p. 138.

18. *Ibid* ., p. 138.

19. *The General Theory*, p. 378.

20. *The General Theory*, chap. 2, esp., the "Two Postulates of the Classical Theory."

21. This refers to the equilibrium model of investment in macroeconomic theory.

22. In the Federal Republic of Germany the setting of priorities in favour of internal stability was represented by the president of the Bundesbank, Emminger, who in this respect took a different line to his predecessor.

23. B. Tew, *The Evolution of the International Monetary System* (London: n.p., 1982), chap. 14.

24. From 1971 to 1973 the rates of inflation in the United States were not—at least in no relevant sense—higher than those in other countries, not even than those in the Federal Republic.

25. O. Emminger, *D-Mark, Dollar Währungskrisen* (Stuttgart: n.p., 1986), p. 240.

26. *Ibid.*, chap. 20.

27. *Ibid.*, p. 374.

28. *Ibid.*, p. 397.

29. The proposal from the theorists arguing from the point of view of the Mundell-Fleming model, to apply under conditions of flexible exchange rates a policy of easy money to achieve full employment, proved to be especially fatal. In most cases devaluation had the same significance as a rise in import prices, the average price level and—with given wage rates—a lowering of their actual value. Efforts made to balance real income by raising the nominal wages accordingly encouraged the rise in inflation. The result was

a superimposition of a devaluation-inflation and a wage-price spiral.

30. F. A. Hayek, *Denationalization of Money—The Argument Refined* (London: n.p., 1978).

31. The so-called BHF School (Black, Hall, Fama) or the "New Monetary Economics" school, as they sometimes denote themselves, go somewhat beyond Hayek with regard to the quantity theory of money. However, they share Hayek's advocacy of denationalization.

32. A further weakness of the Keynesian State, to which we can only refer, has become even more evident in recent years: nature is not a commodity, either, although this does not prevent its being converted into a fictitious one. The difficulties in establishing market regulation in the field of agriculture are well known. Subjecting natural conditions to the logic of the self-regulating market system has, in the last few decades, not only led to wholly arbitrary oscillations of raw material prices, which, since the markets are not limited to single countries, cannot be kept under control by the national States; it has also become clear—and this is perhaps a much more fundamental aspect—that treating nature as a commodity even threatens our living conditions, and that the possibilities of State control are far less than sufficient.

33. The following considerations naturally apply mainly to the United States. But they are of interest to the Western world as a whole, not only because of the position of hegemony which the United States still has but also because there are similar, though weaker trends, in most European countries.

34. It may suffice to recall the classical investigations by Robinson and Chamberlain.

35. So in *The General Theory* he viewed the degree of monopoly as given. Cf. *The General Theory*, p. 245.

36. Even in the discussion involving Keynesianism in the 1970s, the fact that about 25 percent of world oil production, not including East Bloc countries, was in the hands of a single joint-venture was virtually overlooked, in spite of the attention given to the two so-called oil-price shocks.

37. It is sufficient to bring together findings from post-Keynesian and institutional approaches to see that there is no technical reason why the economic sphere—i.e., several multinational concerns and banks—should not be able together to achieve what the Keynesian State did: to support social demand and thus employment by extending credit. From the technical point of view such a strategy would have two clear advantages over the Keynesian form of intervention. Firstly key enterprises play a weighty and direct role in the process of wage bargaining. They have immediate influence on wage increases and thus on the conditions of supply. Second, the concerns are not bound by national borders. Still more, creating the world market is very much their affair. In fact, several multinational concerns are greatly interested in renouncing allegiance to any particular nation. Not only the choice of names (International Business Machines, etc.) points to this trend. The production itself is internationalized. Ford's Escort model, for example, was the first really international car, since it was not only produced in various countries, but its very creation was due to cooperation between various Ford centres all over the world.

38. A. Graziani, ed. *Il dollaro e l'economia italiana* (Bologna: 1987).

REFERENCES

Davidson, G., P. Davidson, *Economics for a Civilized Society* (NY: Norton, 1988).

Emminger, O. *D-Mark, Dollar Währungskrisen* (Stuttgart: n.p., 1986).

Galbraith, J. K. *The Affluent Society*, 4th ed. (Boston: Houghton Mifflin, 1984 [1958]).

———. *The New Industrial State*, 3d ed. (Boston: Houghton Mifflin, 1978 [1967]).

Graziani, A. (ed.) *Il dollaro e l economia italiana* (Bologna: n.p., 1987).

Hankel, W. "Die Finanzkrise zwischen Nord und Süd. Gründe, Lehren, Schlußfolgerungen," in *Entwicklungsländer in der Finanzkrise, Probleme und Perspektiven*, edited by U.E. Simonis (Berlin: n.p., 1983).

Hayek, F. A. *Denationalisation of Money—The Argument Refined* (London: Institute of Economic Affairs, 1978).

Keynes, J. M. *The General Theory of Employment, Interest and Money*, Collected Writings, Vol. VII, (London: Macmillan, 1936).

Minsky, H. P. *Stabilizing an Unstable Economy* (New Haven N.J.: Yale University Press, 1986).

Mundell, R. A. *International Economics*, (NY: Macmillan, 1968).

Munkirs, R. M. *The Transformation of American Capitalism* (London: n.p., 1985).

Polanyi, K. *The Great Transformation* (New York: Farrar & Rinehart, 1944).

———. *The Livelihood of Man*, edited by H. W. Pearson (New York: Academic Press, 1977).

Tew, B. *The Evolution of the International Monetary System* (London: Hutchinson, 1982).

Thomasberger, C. *Löhne, Profite, Inflation - Theorie der monetären Wirtschaft* (München: n.p., 1987).

———. "Globalisierung der Märkte und Nationalisierung der Währungen," in *Marktwirtschaft und Formen politischer Regulierung. Beiträge zur Wirtschafts- und Gesellschaftsgeschichte der Bundesrepublik Deutschland*, edited by K. Voy, W. Polster, and C. Thomasberger (Marburg: n.p., 1990).

Voy, K., W. Polster, and C. Thomasberger, eds. *Marktwirtschaft und Formen politischer Regulierung. Beiträge zur Wirtschafts- und*

Gesellschaftsgeschichte der Bundesrepublik Deutschland (Marburg: 1990).

Weintraub, S. *Our Stagflation Malaise* (Westport: Quorum Books, 1982).

6.

IDEOLOGICAL AND POLITICAL CONTRADICTIONS OF CAPITALISM IN THE LATE INDUSTRIALIZING COUNTRIES

Ayse Bugra

Karl Polanyi concludes *The Great Transformation* with reflections on the possibilities for postmarket societies. In spite of Polanyi's deep-rooted conviction as to the incompatibility of a self-regulating market with human nature, these reflections show a burning concern for the place of freedom within the new system of values, which would emerge after the dismantling of the institutional separation of politics and economics—the separation being a crucial feature of market society. Polanyi writes:

> Yet there are freedoms the maintenance of which is of paramount importance. They were, like peace, a by-product of nineteenth-century economy, and we have come to cherish them for their own sake. The institutional separation of politics and economics, which proved a deadly danger to the substance of the economy, almost automatically produced freedom at

the cost of justice and security. Civic liberties, private enterprise and the wage system fused into a pattern of life which favored moral freedom and independence of mind. Here again, juridical and actual freedoms merged into a common fund, the elements of which cannot be neatly separated. Some were the corollary of evils like unemployment and speculators' profits; some belonged to the most precious traditions of the Renaissance and the Reformation. We must try to maintain by all means in our power these high values inherited from the market economy which collapsed.[1]

The purpose of this paper is both to emphasize that when we turn to the nonWestern, late-industrializing countries we observe that the separation of politics and economics has never been an integral part of the institutional structure, and to discuss the implications of the absence of this separation for democracy and freedom in these countries. We will argue that although in late-industrializing, nonWestern countries the economy is not organized around self-regulating markets this does not imply the subordination of the economic to the social, but rather the emergence of State structures which shape and mould the society in conformity with national objectives of an economic nature. We follow, in other words, Jacques Godbout's idea of the "self-regulating State"[2] and maintain that, through the action of developmentalist states, social objectives are defined in economic terms reflecting the requirements of the capitalist world economy. Although this process largely excludes inputs from societal actors, the relations between the State and different social groups reflect major asymmetry whereby big business enjoys a special position in policy formulation and implementation. We find that this special position acquires central significance especially in countries seeking to implement outward-looking development strategies through trade liberalization policies. In these countries the nature of State-big business relations appears to be a crucial factor in determining the economic and social coordinates of a situation where market autonomy is replaced by the autonomy of the State. It is this relationship between big business groups and developmentalist States that forms the central focus of the analysis presented in this paper.

It is necessary to begin this discussion with a word of caution in order to clarify the specificity of State-business relations in the context of late industrialization. This relationship must be discussed without placing it in contradistinction to the theoretical construct of a pure market economy where we see a clear dichotomy between the market as the realm of private interest, and the State as the realm of public policy. In other words, Polanyi's thorough questioning of the relevance of this theoretical construct must be kept in the background of the analysis. It should also be remembered that Polanyi's warning "against relying too much on the economic interests of given classes in the explanation of history,"[3] which has a special significance in the context of late industrialization, is nevertheless also applicable to past history and the current situation of developed, Western countries.

In fact, many social scientists have recently stressed that economic development and interest representation is increasingly becoming a matter of "political design" in developed, Western countries in today's world of more intense and uncertain international competition. This observation defines "State-centered approaches"[4] as well as "coalition models of State-society relations."[5] The political determination of the content and form of private interest and the ways in which it is reflected in State-business relations is also the central point in the neocorporatist literature of the 1980s.[6] In Claus Offe's work, for example, we find a distinction between two types of political rationality, one associated with "conjunctural" and the other with "structural" policies. The first type of rationality aims at optimal satisfaction of interests manifested by societal actors. In periods of institutional or economic crisis situations, however, parameters of production and interest representation become subject to redesign. Offe argues that in the domestic and international conjuncture prevailing since the 1960s, the second type of rationality and policy orientation has become prevalent in advanced capitalist nations, making the organization of production, the nature of interest, and interest representation dependent variables shaped by the political system.[7]

We believe that political rationality associated with structural policies becomes naturally more relevant in the context of late industrialization where the imperative of economic development and structural change dictates the rules governing the policy process. We also believe that there are some fundamental, qualitative differences between early and late-industrializing countries with regard to the social position of the haute bourgeoisie and the democratic implications of State-business relations. In other words, we share Amsden's view that "late industrialization...is a new paradigm, in terms of the operation of the market mechanism and the role of the State. It is not merely an extension of advanced country capitalism."[8]

At the risk of oversimplified generalization, which should of course be dispensed with in detailed country case studies, we may analyze the factors accounting for the differences in the type of interaction between the State and the social actors in early and late-industrializing countries by referring to the historical conditions of the emergence of a modern bourgeoisie in the latter. In this regard, we can state that in late industrialization, industrial development and nation building take place simultaneously in a process which generally involves a certain rupture with the past. The nature of this process often excludes the possibility of the gradual development of a bourgeoisie as in the West, but leads to the rather rapid emergence of a business class formed with considerable government support. It would not be mistaken to affirm that these businessmen often form a class which appears as an integral part of a State-undertaken project.

Since class formation takes place in such a setting, members of society appear as "citizens" rather than as belonging to different classes or professional groups.[9] The legitimacy of organized pursuit of sectional interest is denied through the emphasis on citizens' duties toward the fulfillment of national goals. What is of crucial significance here is that these national goals are defined in an environment of very intense "growth consciousness." Economic development appears as the most important social objective shaping the content of sectional interests and the forms of interest articulation. The analyses that highlight the economic successes of third world authoritarianism often refer to this type of subordination of class interests to national goals.[10]

The ideology of developmentalism thus excludes the elements of the liberal creed which accompanied the development of the modern bourgeoisie in the West. We are therefore faced with a situation where the bourgeoisie develops without the parallel emergence of a bourgeois culture in which the mechanisms of legitimation of business activity, and the ethical foundations of business behavior are rooted.

Most studies on entrepreneurial history in nonWestern countries refer to the lack of legitimacy of private interests in the traditional value system, and emphasize the culturally downgraded status of business activity. Statements such as the following abound in this literature: "within the traditional Japanese value system the private interests of any group are not considered to be legitimate. Therefore it is relatively difficult for any group to articulate its own interests. At the very least, these groups have to find some way to legitimize their own interest as an aspect of the broader public interest"; "In Turkey the notion of the business leader is misunderstood. Often, he is viewed as a speculator, if not a thief. Business for a long time was downgraded and looked upon as an occupation which no respectable Turk would enter"; (in India) "the basic attitudes of the political culture are strongly antibusiness"; (in traditional Korean Confucianism) "trade and commerce, without being esteemed, even nominally, had been regarded as the meanest sort of work...Such ideas of traditional Korean Confucianism should be thoroughly eliminated to make way for the ideological bases for democratic and liberalistic modernization."[11]

The fact such observations are made in societies with totally dissimilar cultural systems seems to suggest that what is at issue is not an attitude specific to a particular culture. It seems to reflect, rather, a universal trait of most human societies where one observes a conscious effort to protect the social fabric from the disruptive effects of market interest as the legitimate basis of an economic system organized around self-regulating markets. In late-industrializing countries, on the other hand, the market has come to be accepted as a "useful" institution without the acceptance of liberalism as "the organizing principle of a society engaged in creating a market system."[12] In this setting, the legitimacy of business activity does not derive from the ideological principles which appear in the same package as individual freedom and political democracy, but from the State-delegated position of entrepreneurs as agents of development.

To different degrees in different contexts, depending on the previous class structure in the country, businessmen's state-delegated role may be determined by their previously acquired wealth or social status.[13] Otherwise, actual circumstances, such as the importance of foreign direct investment or the strength of other social groups, render it possible for businessmen to enter into alliances which can modify the nature of their relations with the State.[14] But their social position as well as the norms of conduct that govern their activities remain based on their partnership with the developmentalist State.

In late-industrializing countries, institution building, such as class formation, takes place simultaneously with industrial development and is shaped by the requirements of economic development objectives. Hence, the legal and bureaucratic framework of entrepreneurship appears to be much less designed to serve the needs of a good and just social order, than to serve the goal of economic development. The relationship between businessmen and the State is often not mediated by an autonomous, rule-bound bureaucracy or a politically neutral legal system, but is pervaded by an overwhelming pragmatism. Discretionary moves of policy makers thus become very important in determining the social coordinates of business activity which, as we have argued, lacks the legitimating support of liberal ideology. In this framework where discretionary measures taken by self-regulating States tend to replace institutional rules and societal norms, businessmen find themselves in a degree of dependency incomparably more severe than that of Western businessmen on the State in a neocorporatist framework. Yet, by virtue of the often arbitrary and particularist nature of State-business relations in late- industrializing countries, the support that businessmen can obtain from their governments generally exceeds what businessmen in developed countries can ever hope to get. As we will argue in more detail below, the dependent position of the bourgeoisie in late-industrializing countries is often accompanied by considerable privileges mostly obtained at the expense of third parties such as labour and small business.

The fact that the entrepreneurs of late-industrializing countries function in a different environment than do their developed country counterparts should also be related to another fundamental characteristic of late industrialization. Late-industrializing countries can be defined as countries where the process of development takes place with the aid of imported technology. Hence, unlike the Schumpeterian entrepreneur, the main prerogative of the entrepreneur in these countries does not appear as innovation.[15] What appears more significant is the ability to successfully manipulate relations with government authorities in order to benefit from the development policy process. In Cardoso's words, "the typical entrepreneur in underdeveloped countries is no longer merely an industrialist striving to introduce new manufacturing and marketing methods so as to increase profits, but a man with the ability to steer his activity in such a way that he can benefit from the social and economic changes. Therefore, industrial activity is taking on political dimensions."[16]

The fact that the late-industrializing country entrepreneur does not appear as an innovator is only natural in an environment where industrialization is not based on the creation of an indigenous technology-producing capability. This technological dependence also plays a role in limiting the gradual development of small enterprises into modern business firms, since the economies of scale associated with modern technology often entail the requirement of "starting big" from the outset.

However, the fact that the degree of concentration in late-industrializing countries often far exceeds that observed in developed western economies should also be explained with reference to the role the State plays in restricting the realm of competition. The attempts of the governments of late industrializing countries to encourage the development and strengthening of an indigenous business class can be interpreted as the sign of a probusiness policy orientation. But this policy orientation can hardly be described as promarket and procompetition. In the context of late industrialization, the policy of "creating businessmen" reflects a desire to make sure that industrial tasks are performed by those people who are likely to be successful without actually allowing market competition to determine this success. While political favors and corrupt deals often play a role in this particularist process through which government encourages certain individuals to enter into designated fields of activity, such practices at least partly reflect a deep-rooted belief in the wastefulness of competition.[17]

The governments of most underdeveloped countries have a strong distaste for small competitive enterprises for the same reason. This distaste for small business also seems to reflect other concerns which might be qualified as "political" and "aesthetic." Political concerns have to do with the difficulty of controlling a large number of small enterprises and making them subservient to national goals set by the political authority. As to aesthetic concerns, these stem from the fact that such enterprises do not conform to the ideal of modern, large-scale industry as found in developed Western countries.[18] Hence, there are a whole set of measures—ranging from the lack of incentives provided to small business,[19] through the active encouragement of small enterprises to combine,[20] to the political manipulation of business associations to promote the interests of big business against those of small enterprises[21]—serving to enhance economic concentration in these countries. Paradoxically, outward-looking development strategies, in which the merits of increased competition via import liberalization is emphasized, often lead to the strengthening of big enterprises, and increase the degree of economic concentration.[22]

The phenomenon of economic concentration has two dimensions. One is the market share of a given number of enterprises in a particular industry; the other has to do with the control exercised by certain groups of affiliated industries in different markets. The significance of the role played by multiactivity firms in some developing countries makes this latter aspect of economic concentration especially significant in the context of late industrialization.[23] Where scarcity of entrepreneurial resources is emphasized, it is not surprising that the multiactivity firm (or the "group") appeals to pragmatically oriented governments and also to some social scientists.[24] These latter not only favor multiactivity firms as institutions "permitting pure Schumpeterian entrepreneurship to become effective,"[25] but also praise the role they play in the planning process. It is argued that "the coordination of investment and production decisions by the group has both reduced the need for, and lessened the burden on government planning of the modern sector in developing countries."[26]

The groups of large enterprises are also represented as interest organizations which, unlike associations representative of narrow sectional interests, pursue policies conducive to the public good. For example, in a study based on Mancur Olson's distinction between narrow interest groups and broad-based encompassing organizations, multiactivity firms are qualified as "cellular encompassing organizations" which present a "mirror image of the society."[27] Since the interests of these firms are spread over a large number of sectors, and hence are closely affected by the global development of the economy, it is argued that "the public good becomes the self-interest of the diversified conglomerate." Such arguments attempt to show that multiactivity firms in developing countries are well placed to assume a quasi-governmental role in the planning process, and consequently present to highlight the merits of a certain degree of privatization of the planning process.

These views in fact reflect actual trends in societies that have a pragmatic developmentalist policy orientation, and serve to justify them. The social implications of this particular association between the State and big business are far from being unambiguous. Even from a purely economic perspective, it is not clear that the multiactivity character of big business firms provides an incentive to take into account more than sectoral interests. Nor does the intersectoral character of these companies imply that all these sectors are equally important for the central management. It is likely that there could be priorities at times leading to less favorable treatment of certain activities. The preferences and priorities of groups can be highly different from those of society. Consequently, there is no *a priori* reason for which the company would act in such a way as to minimize the divergences between private and public benefits and costs.

What seems to be clear is that this particular State-business relationship, where big companies are accorded a quasi-governmental planning function, increasingly reinforces informal and particularist ties between the State and big business and increasingly excludes other social groups from the policy-making process. Discretion, rather than rule-based policy formation and implementation, becomes the central characteristic of the policy process, while legal and bureaucratic mechanisms through which State-business relations are mediated become further undermined. Moreover, the size and scope of the activities of multiactivity firms reduce the need for *organized* contact with government authorities. These big business firms have little difficulty in gaining access to government authorities to present their demands and to influence policy changes. The role of association-based pursuit of interest becomes increasingly less important.[28]

One implication of this particular state of affairs is accentuation of the problems of legitimacy concerning the social status of business activity and businessmen. Where informal, one-to-one contact with government authorities replaces association-based relations through legal and bureaucratic mechanisms of intermediation, a certain lack of transparency in business practices seems to set in. The direct relationship between big business firms and government is such that it eliminates certain checks and balances that formal relations— through the intermediation of the legal system, bureaucracy and business associations—would entail. Hence there is additional room for special favors, arbitrary decisions and simply corrupt dealings where there are no formal mechanisms for the imposition of professional ethics. In societies where the social legitimacy of business is far from well-established, it becomes increasingly difficult to find justification for commercial activities according to socially and professionally set norms. The State increasingly becomes, in other words, the main source of social legitimacy. Somewhat paradoxically, the increasing strength of big business firms and the consolidation of their position in the policy process do not lead to a parallel strengthening of the bourgeoisie as a social class, and serve instead to reinforce the "self-regulating" character of the State.

Another aspect of the difficulties attending the formation of a self-confident bourgeois class organized around a coherent system of professional norms of behavior has to do with the conditions of access to the position of business manager. Cardoso's research in the Latin American context, for example, documents how effective control is exercised mainly on a family basis and through the selection of individuals who enjoy the confidence of shareholders in the light of nonprofessional criteria and relationships.[29] Cardoso explains this through reference to the general uncertainty that marks the business environment in underdeveloped countries, and emphasizes the government-policy-induced nature of this uncertainty. According to him, in this uncertain environment flexibility in decision making and implementing becomes very important, and family firms enjoy important advantages over professionally managed ones in this respect. It seems natural that the dominance of discretionary over rule-based and legally-bound policy processes would enhance this type of uncertainty and present an obstacle to effective professionalization of management. Moreover the lack of transparency in business operations fostered by the informal particularist relations between big business and the State is also likely to render difficult the delegation of management responsibility on professional grounds. The legally and bureaucratically ambiguous nature of business activity consequently enhances the importance of the confidence factor. Besides, in such an environment where particularism is dominant, it becomes highly important for owners to be in charge of the relationships with government authorities which set the rules and determine the conditions for the success of business ventures. Our research on the business environment in Turkey suggests that these factors are significant in hampering the professionalization of management. Similar factors perhaps explain why large South Korean enterprises remain family-run businesses.

This aspect of capitalism in late-industrializing countries considerably modifies those ethical arguments in favor of capitalism that are based on the separation of ownership and management.

While this argument urges that the possibility of success is contingent upon professional merit and not upon status by birth, the significance of family ties among other nonprofessional personal relations in determining access to managerial positions casts significant doubt as to the scope of social mobility in late-industrializing countries. Similarly, the role of market relations in dismantling the ties of kinship and other traditional bonds, which is stressed not only by liberal thinkers but by Karl Marx himself, appears in a totally different light. Instead of the revolutionary transformation of tradition-bound social relations in market societies, we might find in developing countries a mere modification of these relations in ways which conform to developmentalist policy orientation. In the context of late industrialization, where separation between economics and politics is absent, market relations can easily work in ways which merely modify traditional relations without actually diminishing their importance.

The most significant implication of the special status of big business in its relations with the developmentalist State is in connection with third parties such as labour, small business and consumer groups. The privileged position enjoyed by big business by virtue of its State-assigned role in the development process is accompanied by social inequalities stemming from the denial of social legitimacy to the organized pursuit of interest. While the subordination of sectional interests to the national objective of economic development often appears as a general principle affecting all social groups equally, its implications are highly different for big business and other groups. Some observations made by Claus Offe are relevant with regard to this problem.[30] For as he suggests, business and labour are affected very differently by the corporatist transformation of society, because both the articulation of interest and its imposition by economic obstruction are more difficult for unorganized labour than for unorganized capital. For labour, small businessmen and consumer groups alike, unorganized articulation and pursuit of interest are much more difficult than they are for big businessmen. Hence obstacles to the formation and strengthening of interest groups tend to reinforce the privileged association of big business with the State in the formation of social policy.

The economic implication of this process for nonbusiness groups differs according to the type of development policy implementation. In South East Asia, for example, authoritarian governments seem to have been quite successful in assuring a certain trickle-down of progress to the masses. As C. Johnson writes in his analysis of the industrialization experience of Japan, Taiwan and South Korea, "all three nations compensate labour for its decreased political role through policies of comparatively equitable distribution and automatic wage increases tied to increases in productivity."[31] Apart from the fact that this is far from being the case in a large number of other countries where authoritarian States seek to implement similar developmentalist policies, the presence of a degree of economic compensation could hardly be said to offset the politically undesirable nature of a situation in which the masses passively remain at the mercy of the State-big business partnership for any improvement in their economic position. Politically, this presents a situation little resembling our ideal of democracy.

NOTES

1. K. Polanyi, *The Great Transformation* (Boston: Beacon Press, 1957), pp. 254-5.
2. J. Godbout, "L'état auto-regulé," *Revue du Mauss*, no. 8 (1990).
3. *The Great Transformation*, pp. 155-6.
4. See, for example, P. B. Evans, D. Rueschemeyer, T. Skocpol, eds., *Bringing the State Back In* (Cambridge: Cambridge University Press), 1985.
5. See in particular P. Katzenstein, "Domestic and International Structures and Strategies of Foreign Economic Policy," *International Organization* XXXI (1977), pp. 587-606 and 879-919. See also C. Jo Martin, "Business Influence and State Power: The Case of U.S. Corporate Tax Policy," *Politics and Society* XVII (1989).
6. See, among others, W. Grant, ed., *Introduction to the Political Economy of Corporatism* (London: Macmillan, 1985); W. Streeck and P. C. Schimitter, "Community, Market, State and Associations? The Prospective Contribution of Interest Governance to Social Order," in W. Streeck and P. Schimitter, eds., *Private Interest Government* (London: Sage Series in New Corporatism, 1985); W. Streeck, "Between Pluralism and Corporatism: German Business Associations and the State," *Journal of Public Policy* III (August 1983).
7. C. Offe, "The Attribution of Public Status to Interest Groups: Observations on the West German Case," in S. Berger et al., eds., *Organizing Interests in Western Europe: Pluralism, Corporatism, and the Transformation of Politics* (Cambridge: Cambridge University Press, 1981).
8. A. H. Amsden, "Third World Industrialization: 'Global Fordism' or A New Model?" *New Left Review,* no. 182 (July/August 1990), p. 131.
9. For this distinction see A. Insel, "De la démocratie inachevée," *Revue du Mauss*, no. 8 (1990).

10. See in particular the recent literature on South East Asian industrialization. For example, L. P. Jones and I. Sakong, *Government, Business, and Entrepreneurship in Economic Development: The Korean Case* (Cambridge, Mass.: Harvard University, Council on East Asian Studies, 1980); and the essays in F. C. Deyo, ed., *The Political Economy of the New Asian Industrialism* (Ithaca, N.Y.: Cornell University Press, 1987). See also G. Ranis and J. C. H. Fei, "Development Economics: What Next?" and R. Findlay, "Trade, Development and the State," in G. Ranis and T. P. Schultz, eds., *The State of Development Economics: Progress and Perspectives* (Oxford: Basil Blackwell, 1990).

11. T. Ishida, "The Development of Interest Groups and the Pattern of Political Modernization in Japan," in R.E. Ward, ed., *Political Development in Modern Japan* (Princeton N.J.: Princeton University Press, 1968) p. 300; G.G. Alpender, "Big Business and Big Business Leaders in Turkey" (P.h. D. diss., Michigan State University, 1966), p. 1; S. A. Kochanek, "The Federation of Indian Chambers of Commerce and Industry and Indian Politics," *Asian Survey* XI (Sept. 1971), p. 866; Jai Hi Choi, "Traditional Values of Korea and Problems of Modernization," in *Report of the International Conference on the Problems of Modernization in Asia* (Seoul: n.p., 1966), p. 82.

12. *The Great Transformation*, p.135.

13. It is argued, for example, that in the "Japan, inc." big business and the State appear as equal partners due to the strength of the position of the big bourgeoisie while the "Korea, inc." is a partnership where the State is unambiguously the dominant partner. See, for example, R. Boyd, "Government-Industry Relations in Japan: Access, Communication, and Competitive Collaboration," in S. Wilks and M. Wright, eds., *Comparative Government-Industry Relations* (Oxford: Clarendon Press, 1987). We also see references to the relative weakness of the South Korean bourgeoisie in comparison to the less-State-dependent bourgeoisies of Latin American countries. See, for example, B. Cumings, "The Abortive Abertura: South Korea in the Light of Latin American Experience," *New Left Review*, no. 173 (February 1989).

14. It is maintained, for example, that in Latin America the significance of joint ventures with foreign capital as well as the traditional differentiation of the society along class lines enables big business to enter into alliances with other groups and to improve its position *vis-à-vis* the State. See F. H. Cardoso, "The Industrial Elite," in M. Lipset and A. Solari, eds., *Elites in Latin America* (New York: Oxford University Press, 1967); J. A. Kahl, Fernando Henrique Cardoso, in J. A. Kahl, ed., *Modernization, Exploitation and Dependence in Latin America* (New Brunswick: Transaction Books, 1976; P. Evans, "Class, State, and Dependence in East Asia: Lessons for Latin Americanists," in F. C. Deyo, ed., *The Political Economy of the New Asian Industrialism*; and also P. Schmitter, *Interest Conflict and Political Change in Brazil* (Stanford, California: Stanford University Press, 1971), chap. 2. Further comparisons of State-business relations in South Korea and Latin America can be found in Ranis and in Findlay, in G. Ranis and T. P. Schultz, eds., *The State of Developmental Economics*.

15. A general survey of studies on third world entrepreneurs which highlight the differences with the Schumpeterian model can be found in E. W. Nafziger, *Entrepreneurship, Equity and Economic Development* (London: Jai Press Inc., 1986).

16. "The Industrial Elite."

17. *Government, Business, and Entrepreneurship*, chap. 8.

18. The significance of this esthetic concern is largely documented in the literature on appropriate technology. See, among others, F. Steuard, *Technology and Underdevelopment* (Boulder, Colorado: Westview Press, 1977).

19. Our research highlights the policy bias against small business through an analysis of policy discourse under different governments as well as through a survey of plan documents prepared by the State Planning Organization.

20. Silin mentions that the Taiwanese government actively encourages the combination of smaller firms, and trade associations with compulsory membership play an active role in this process. R. H. Silin, *Leadership and Values* (Cambridge, Mass.: Harvard East Asian Monographs, no. 62, 1976), pp. 14 and 21.

21. See D. McNamara, "Origins of Concentration in Korean Private Enterprise." Paper presented at the conference of the International Sociological Association Research Committee on Economy and Society, Milan, 1989.

22. See A. Kohli, "Politics of Economic Liberalization in India," *World Development* XVII, no. 3 (1989).

23. The extent of economic concentration in developing countries is documented in C. H. Kirkpatrick et al., eds., *Industrial Structure and Policy in Less Developed Countries* (London: George Allen & Unwin, 1984).

24. An early study on the Indian managing agency firms highlights the significance of these types of organizational structures, where a centralized managerial control is exercised over the activities of firms operating in different areas, in an environment of scarce entrepreneurial resources: F. Brimmer, "The Setting of Entrepreneurship in India," The Quarterly Journal of Economics LXIX (Nov. 1955). For a general study of the role of groups in underdeveloped countries, see N. Leff, "Industrial Organization and Entrepreneurship in Developing Countries: The Economic Groups," *Economic Development and Cultural Change*, XXVIII (July 1978).

25. "Industrial Organization and Entrepreneurship," p. 668.

26. *Ibid.*, p. 670.

27. R. Jankowski, "Preference Aggregation in Firms and Cellular Encompassing Organizations: The Enterprise Group as a Cellular Encompassing Organization," *American Journal of Political Science* XXXIII (November 1983).

28. This is clearly demonstrated by our interviews with big business leaders in Turkey. The relative insignificance of association-based relations between the State and big business is also documented by studies on different countries such as India and South Korea. See Kochanek, "The Federation of Indian Chambers of Commerce" and Jones and Sakong, *Government, Business, and Entrepreneurship*.

29. See Cardoso, "The Industrial Elite" and Kahl, "Fernando Enrique Cardoso."

30. "The Attribution of Public Status to Interest Groups."

31. C. Johnson, "Political Institutions and Economic Performance: The Government-Business Relations in Japan, South Korea and Taiwan," in F.C. Deyo, ed., *The Political Economy of the New Asian Industrialism*, p. 151.

7.

THE NEXT TRANSFORMATION

Alain Lipietz

With the breakdown of so-called socialism, the world is now entering the twenty-first century ten years in advance. The great hope of the twentieth century, that is the transition from capitalism to a more progressive mode of production, or, as Karl Polanyi would have put it, a more "Christian" organization of society,[1] has collapsed. It is now clear that the October 1917 Revolution led to nothing more than a form of authoritarian State capitalism, which proved to be less efficient and socially fair than many market-capitalisms. A new international order is now developing, with its first geopolitical crisis: the Kuwaiti war. At the same time, it has proved by now impossible to resolve the last major economic crisis of the twentieth century, which started at the beginning of the 1970s, the market-capitalist countries experienced tremendous transformations in the 1980s. The breakdown of the "socialist camp" does not appear as a victory of the former Western leaders, but as the claim to hegemony of Japan in the Pacific Rim, and Western Germany in the Atlantic one.

In other words, capitalist societies are now experiencing a "great transformation," in the meaning explained in Karl Polanyi's pathbreaking book. Undeniably, Karl Polanyi overestimated the originality of the 1930-1940 period, and underestimated the transformations

112

which capitalism had already undergone. The model he proposed then now looks a bit oversimplified. Yet his approach brilliantly enlightens our times, as it did his.

We shall first look back to this approach, to its insights and to the limits that could be formulated from the point of view of the so called "French regulation approach." Then we shall reinterpret *what* the "great transformation" of Karl Polanyi's time was, and then ask why there is a need for a new transformation, a transformation which is not predetermined. In fact, a first attempt was made in the 1980s which looked much like a reversal of the "great transformation." Yet other possibilities remain, seductive for "workers, citizens and lovers."[2] The possibilities for this "next transformation" will be the content of the last sections.

KARL POLANYI, THE "REGULATION APPROACH," AND THE CONCEPT OF TRANSFORMATION

It is well known that, while dedicated to the explanation of the "transformation" of the 1930s, *The Great Transformation* is mainly concerned with a *former* transformation, the one that led from feudalism to the "self-regulating market." Karl Polanyi's thesis could be summarized as following:

a. Before this "former transformation," market relations existed and productive activity existed, but were embedded in the more general frame of social life.[3]

b. The outburst of the industrial revolution within the frame of a market economy led to the destruction of any social regulation that could oppose the growth of a "self-regulating market."[4]

c. This destruction was carried on by the State.[5]

d. The autonomization and domination of market relations over any social relation implied that labour, land and money would be considered mere commodities.[6]

e. This was a utopia, leading to the self-destruction of society.[7]

    i. To consider human beings as mere "manpower" would lead to the exhaustion of the majority of population.

    ii. To consider nature as a spot of soil dedicated to feeding the industrial population would lead to the exhaustion of nature and ecological crises such as erosion, dust bowls, etc.

    iii. To limit the movement of the productive apparatus by the "sound" reproduction of commodity-money would lead to a recession of productive activity.

f. As a result, antimarket countertendencies developed in an uncoordinated way all through the nineteenth century and up to the 1920s: labour legislation, tenure and environmental legislation, credit money and central banking, protectionism. For the "liberal creed," this was no less than a "collectivist conspiracy."[8]

g. While the breakdown of the international order triggered off the crisis of the 1930s, this crisis expressed the fact that the contradiction between the laws of a free market and the needs of society had become incompatible. The New Deal (i.e., social-democracy), socialism (of a Stalinist type) and fascism are the three solutions for this crisis. Polanyi's choice is the first one, in the name of a correctly conceived freedom.

Though connected to the old Austro-Marxist tradition, Polanyi's book was surely a great leap forward. Too often, Marxist theorists of his time had considered capitalism as a well-defined mode of production, with its immutable social relations, subject to some variations and which could be substituted by socialism only through a general revolution.

The history of capitalism is much more complex. Capitalist socio-economic relations experienced more dramatic changes from 1848 to the present than any socialist of the early times would ever have thought possible. In that process, major social tensions and economic problems are a constant trigger of crisis, political struggles, and sometimes...revolutions. Yet, for fairly long periods, capitalism works. A general framework, rules for the game, must be more or less reluctantly acknowledged. Three times since 1848, a major, long crisis occurred: first, at the end of the nineteenth century; second, in the 1930s; and, finally at the end of the 1960s.[9] But between these major crises, a great compromise seems to have been accepted "by workers, citizens, and lovers." This compromise includes the acceptance of a "pattern of development" as the economic basis for what could be considered as the best thing humankind may expect from economic activity. A large spectre of political tendencies, from the Right to the Left, battle about marginal improvements that could be implemented within the same compromise, but the model itself is not questioned.

We are now, as in the 1930s and 1940s, in one of these periods of struggle, not about "how to carry out an (already given) economic design," but about what should be the new compromise, hence what should be the *next* transformation. We are not only in an economic crisis, but in a "great compromise crisis," or, in the words of the Italian Marxist sociologist Gramsci, a "crisis of hegemony."

At least, this is how the "French regulation approach" would put it nowadays.[10] Both similarities and differences with Polanyi are striking. "Regulationists" would fully accept to embed economic relations in a more general social framework (point (*a*)). They acknowledge that "competitive capitalism" was not natural but imposed by politics (point (*c*)). They insist that wage relations, land ownership relations, and the reproduction of the currency are *not* commodity-relations, despite their form in competitive capitalism.[11] They show that contradictions should emerge between these different social relations, which cannot be regulated by the market (point (*e*)). They maintain that social movements (not only class movements) develop reactions against these shortcomings, eventually merging into the making of new modes of regulation (point (*g*)).

Yet they mitigate the singularity of the "great transformation" of the 1930s, while acknowledging that Polanyi grasped the kernel of it. Other major transformations happened at the end of the nineteenth century. And the "great transformation" just led to a new model of development, which in turn collapsed during the 1970s.

Moreover, while they share the point of view of Polanyi on the open-ended nature of history (Stalinism, Rooseveltism or social-democracy and fascism were equal candidates in front of the breaking-down liberal conservatism in the 1930s), they do not accept the technological determinism of point (*b*). "Industrial revolution," in its material form, was also an effect of social relations. Changes in labour organization from the late 1890s to the 1930s (the "Taylorist revolution") are also the material form of a social conflict. Some scholars, making reference to regulation approach, such as Piore and Sabel (1984), are now ready to say that the "next transformation" (which they call, precisely, the "second industrial divide"), will be determined by a shift from "mass production" to "flexible production," but most French regulationists think that even this point is still open-ended.[12]

As may be seen, the regulation approach is not an assault against Polanyi's approach. On the contrary, it may be considered as an enlargement, an *"aufhebung"* of Polanyi's work. So let us now "re-read" *The Great Transformation* (in the real world), and then come back to the next one.

THE "FORDIST" TRANSFORMATION

In order to understand the present world crisis, we have to understand the logics of the post-World War Two period. That period of economic boom expressed the hegemony of a peculiar "pattern of development" within the main advanced capitalist countries, and the stability of a "world configuration" between these countries.

A *pattern of development* can and must be analyzed from three different angles at the national level:

• As a *model of industrialization* (or a *technological paradigm*): the general principles which govern the evolution of the organization of labour during the period of supremacy of this model;

• As a *regime of accumulation*: the macroeconomic principle which describes the compatibility over a prolonged period between the transformations in production conditions, and in the types of usage of social output (household consumption, investment, public expenditure, international trade);

• As a *mode of regulation*: the combination of forms of adjustment of the expectations and contradictory behaviour by individual agents to the collective principles of the regime of accumulation. These forms of adjustment may include cultural habits as well as institutional features such as laws, agreements etc.[13]

The regime of accumulation therefore appears as the macroeconomic result of the workings of the mode of regulation, *based* on a model of industrialization. Using a term first proposed by Gramsci but also by Henri de Man (a Belgian theorist who moved from socialism to fascism: a trajectory that Polanyi makes understandable), some French and Italian economists labeled the post-World War Two hegemonic pattern of development as "Fordism."

Its *industrial paradigm* included the Taylorist principles of rationalization, plus constant mechanization. That "rationalization" was based on separation of the intellectual and manual aspects of labour, this did not mean that there was no longer intellectual involvement of the manual workers. This involvement had to remain "informal," the social knowledge being systematized from the top, and incorporated within machinery by designers. When Taylor and the Taylorian engineers first introduced those principles at the beginning of the twentieth century, their explicit aim was to enforce the control of management on the workers. The first three decades of the twentieth century saw a resistance of the skilled workers, and their evolution (including amongst communists) toward a new compromise: acceptance of the Taylorist forms of control, against the sharing out of the gains in productivity.

This sharing-out was at first rejected by the great majority of bosses, except a few like Henry Ford and some economists like J. M. Keynes. Yet Keynes and Ford were preaching in the desert until the dramatic confirmation of their prophecy: the Great Depression of the 1930s. As Polanyi rightly noted, "capitalist production itself had to be sheltered from the devastating effects of a self-regulating market."[14] The conservative liberalism of Hoover, Lloyd George or Laval was unable to deal with the problem. Three alternatives were competing: a fascist organization of social demand, a Stalinist-type revolution toward some State-capitalism, and a new "social-democratic" compromise between management and workers. Fortunately, the coalition of other forces defeated the first (fascist) solution during World War Two. And within ten years, the competition between the Stalinist-type and the Fordist compromises within the advanced industrialized world had turned to the advantage of the latter. This compromise materialized as a new regime of accumulation warranted by a new mode of regulation.

This *regime of accumulation* was characterized as follows:
• Mass production with polarization of skills, high productivity growth, growing capital-output ratio (in volume, but not in value);
• A constant sharing-out of value-added, hence real income of wage earners growing parallel to productivity;
• Thus the rate of profit remained rather stable, with full employment of productive capacity and the labour force.

In other words, the "Fordist compromise" consisted of matching mass production and mass consumption. It was accepted all over the world as "the American way of life": a productivist and hedonist model which was only contested by a few radical intellectuals like Herbert Marcuse, and considered as a goal by political forces ranging from Christian Democracy to Western communist parties, with conservative political forces supporting it in spite of the initial prejudices of a majority of bosses.

But which forces could finally induce individual bosses to accept that compromise, which was in conformity with their middle-term interests ? That was the task of the mode of regulation.

The *mode of regulation* included more or less (according to countries):
• Social legislation of growing minimum wages, and a strong

collective bargaining mechanism, inducing *all* bosses to grant annual improvements in real wages parallel to gains in national productivity;
• A developed Welfare State granting nearly all the population the possibility to consume, even in case of temporary or indefinite incapacity to earn money from one's work: illness, unemployment, retirement, and so on;
• A credit money supply regulated by central banks, issued by private banks according to the needs of the economy (and not according to a stock of gold).

All these institutions provided new structural "rules of the game." These rules granted the State an active responsibility in the "fine-tuning" of expansion (the so-called "Keynesian policy").

As may be noted, the main "transformation" within the mode of regulation consisted in withdrawing two of the three "pseudo-commodities" (point (*d*)) from the "self-regulating market": labour and money. And what about land? Certainly, huge reforms were carried out from the 1930s to the 1950s, in the United States, Europe, and Japan, as far as farming and food markets were concerned. In some cases, environmental issues were mixed with these new regulations (in the English meaning of the term!). But in general, nature was the great loser in the "great transformation," in the "great compromise" between the requirements of capitalist production and the needs of society. Karl Polanyi may have been correct in writing: "The congenital weakness of nineteenth-century society was not that it was industrial, but that it was a market society."[15] This statement should be revised as far as the Fordist model is concerned. The dramatic world industrial growth allowed for by the "great transformation" would eventually lead to the most dreadful ecological crisis since the Great Plague crisis of the fourteenth century. Among the congenital weaknesses of Fordism, we have to note first its *productivism*.[16]

Moreover, at the international level, the world economy never reached such a degree of macroeconomic organization. The Fordist model was hegemonic only in OECD countries. This regime excluded most of the third world from international trade in manufactured goods, and the world currency was *de facto* the credit money issued by the United States. There was a semi-free trade between mainly auto-centered industrial countries, with fine-tuning of trade balance through changes of parity and slight cooling of inner markets.

That was possible because the superiority of the United States in the industrial production paradigm was such that its capital goods were both necessary and competitive. So the other countries were induced to accept the dollar as the international general equivalent. At the time, the trade balance of the United States was structurally positive and its capital balance structurally negative. The United States gave Europe and Japan both the technical and financial means to "catch-up."

It may be useful to emphasize the similarity of this United States international attitude, stemming from a real hegemonic leadership position in the context of competition with the USSR, with the domestic, "Fordist" compromise. After 1947, the United States administration rejected the temptation to "crush" possible competitors by enforcing complete free trade. On the contrary, as Spiro has pointed out,

> The United States encouraged European and Japanese trade protectionism and discrimination against the dollar. And it promoted European and Japanese exports to the United States...To encourage long-term adjustment, the United States promoted European and Japanese trade competitiveness. Aid to Europe and Japan was designed to rebuild productive and export capacity. In the long run it was expected that such European and Japanese recovery would benefit the United States by widening markets for American exports.[17]

As far as the third world was concerned, a similar attempt was Kennedy's "alliance for progress." But then, shortsighted neocolonial interests prevailed most often, except in countries exposed to communist competition such as South Korea and Taiwan where the United States fostered land reform, import-substitution and national capitalist development.

THE END OF THE GOLDEN AGE

This regime began to weaken for two different sets of reasons. Some are "internal," that is, they stemmed from the very development of the Fordist regime in each individual country. The second set is "international" in that it stemmed from the linkage of national economies. The concrete development of the crisis, roughly from the second half of the 1960s, may be explained only through the inter-weaving of these two sets of reasons.[18] Yet, for the purpose of this text, it is sufficient to acknowledge the two-sided explanation of the crisis. Let us start with *internal reasons*.

Basically, all advanced capitalist countries experienced, from the end of the 1960s, a slowing-down in the growth of productivity, in contrast with ever-growing real wages (including welfare), and an acceleration in the rise of the capital-output ratio in volume, engendering also its rise in value. The combination of these trends led to a fall in the share of profits in annual value added, and in the ratio of capital-revenues (profits) to the capital advanced: the rate of profit.

The reasons for these developments can be found in a latent weakness of the very pattern of the organization of labour: the crisis of "informal involvement." That weakness may have been triggered by the outbreak of workers' militancy due to the full employment sit-uation at the end of the 1960s. More precisely, the incorporation within the active population of young people, women, immigrants from countryside and the third world had facilitated at first the implementation of Taylorist principles. But, in the late 1960s, the increase in education and in social consciousness, in the desire for self-development and dignity at work, led to a growing revolt against the denial of any human responsibility within the crudest forms of separation between "conceptors" and "operators." And this separa-tion was still largely responsible for the exhaustion of the sources of productivity gains (because only a minority within the labour process was in charge of improving collective efficiency) and for the increase in fixed capital per worker (because that minority could improve the productivity of the majority only by increasing the complexity of machinery).

The resulting fall in the profitability of firms led them to react by reducing real wages, thus leading to a sectorial and general under-consumptionist crisis, and spreading and socializing their losses through mark-up policies, entailing a "cost-pushed" inflation allowed by the nature of credit money.[19]

But the main result of this complex process was growing pressure on the social compromise. In fact, declining profitability, hence a declining rate of investment, combined with a declining number of new jobs created by each investment, and later with the shrinking of inner markets, led to growing unemployment. In the early 1970s, both the economic and social logics of Fordism induced governments to raise transfer payments for unemployed people (dole, social programs). This effectively limited the social and economic risks of cumulative depression (a great contrast with the 1930s). But eventually these transfers were felt as too heavy a burden on the productive economy, further reducing the profitability of firms. It led to a fiscal crisis of the Welfare State, and kept the legitimacy of State social policies at bay. Hence, from inner tendencies alone, the Fordist compromise had become economically unsustainable in the 1970s. And this root of the crisis was on the supply side: a "crisis of labour" inducing a crisis in profitability, and not on the "society side," *à la* Polanyi.

International factors were also responsible for that erosion. In the 1960s, and even more in the 1970s, the search for a higher scale of production and for regions with lower wages led to an international interweaving of productive processes, contrasting with the national nature of economic regulation. Thus, the competition of "newly industrializing countries" (NICs) became disruptive for old industries, replacing well-paid workers by poorly paid workers, hence leading to a "negative-sum game" on world effective demand. On the other hand, the quest for equilibrium in trade balance within increasingly free trade led each country to recessive policy, either in the name of "price-effect" (lowering the per-unit labour cost) or in the name of "volume-effect" (lowering of domestic demand). Here, the "self-regulating market" was vindicated, and began to act again as a "satanic mill" against world society.[20]

It may be argued that, at the world level, the crisis was directly of the Marxist "underconsumptionist" type (or, in Keynesian terminology: lack of effective demand), due to this negative-sum game. On the other hand, from the internal point of view, and as far as the regime of accumulation is concerned, the "Keynesian" character of the crisis (underconsumption) is only a by-product of a more fundamental "classical" crisis (fall in profitability).[21]

Of course, the reactions of firms, trade unions, and States shifted several times during the crisis from one policy to another, thus leading to various world configurations.[22] The major tendency during the 1970s, within the OECD, was demand-side Keynesian-type policies. Incentives were given to growth through development of the Welfare State, easy money, including risky recycling of Eurodollars toward

NICs. That led to an opportunity for the acceleration of a real industrial revolution in several countries of the third world. But, due to the inefficiency of this policy in advanced capitalist countries, a shift towards "monetarist" policies occurred in the late 1970s. The inflation of the 1970s led key States into restrictive issuing of credit money and high rates of interest. This "monetarist shock" restricted the possibilities for the firms to invest and triggered off a debt crisis in the NICs, thus adding an unnecessary Keynesian (demand-side) component to an unsolved, classical, crisis of profitability. After 1982, a more lax policy from the FED and from the United States Treasury induced a deficit, Keynesian based expansion in the United States. All the rest of the world, including the NICs, benefitted from this "world social demand." But different types of countries appeared, according to the form of their adaptation to world competition and to the "supply-side" of the crisis.

Indeed, some attempts were made as early as the 1970s to attack directly the "inner" roots of the crisis (too much capital-intensive technologies, inadequate gains in productivity, and too many people on the shoulders of the Welfare State). The "new technological revolution" was supposed to provide solutions. Yet, the discovery of new productive social relations is not purely a matter of technology, as we are about to see.

A ROLL-BACK OF THE GREAT TRANSFORMATION

Just like in the 1930s, the question of the ways out of the crisis is a political one. There is no such thing as "the solution" that could be dictated by the knowledge of the "actual" economic laws. Nor is it true that the crisis is an inevitable calamity. And, like in the early 1930s, the main competitors for a solution may not include the next winner. Moreover, I must say that "socialism" is not a competitor either, if by "socialism" one understands a ready-made model of a new mode of production. After the present crisis of capitalism, that is at the beginning of twenty-first century, there will exist all over the world market relations between productive units and wage relations between management and the labour force: hence capitalism. The question is: *what sort of capitalism is it to be?* How good for people and how promising for further steps will it be?

With all these *caveats*, we shall begin with an examination of the first competing model for the title of "the way out of the crisis": *liberal productivism.*

I give this name to the ideology expressed by the Reagan and Thatcher administrations, and more or less accepted in the mid-1980s by most West-European governments and the main international economic institutions (IMF, OECD, but not the UNCTAD). The great strength of this ideology stems from the breakdown of the Fordist compromise (let alone the disaster of "socialisms"). Hence there was a great temptation to simply assess that a restoration of the old "self-regulating market" would be "the" solution: just rewind the "great transformation."

The story seems to be as follows. There is a "technological revolution." But the "rigidities" imposed by the State (social and environmental legislation, social security, etc.) block the way. So let us get rid of rigidities, and the laws of free competition will automatically impose the new model of development consistent with the new technologies. This is very similar to the nineteenth-century confidence in technical progress that could be limited only by inefficient social relations: the "former transformation" in Polanyi. However, there are some constrasts with the utilitarian liberalism of the eighteenth and nineteenth centuries. That was "utilitarian" and "hedonistic" liberalism. The aim of technical progress and free enterprise was the enrichment of economic agents. Of course, that possibility still exists within the new liberalism. But more and more often technical change and deregulation are presented as a *necessity* stemming from international competition: "modernize or perish," "lower wages or perish," "be flexible or perish." But the results are the same: we are back to the central chapters of *The Great Transformation.*

First of all, this trend leads to a polarization of society: "Brazilianization" looks like the future of the model.[23] At the top, the "winners in competition" will benefit from the advantages of the technological revolution (such as there are). In the middle, one group of permanent skilled or semi-skilled workers will benefit from regular employment, but with no more prospect of permanent improvement in real wages (contrary to the Fordist compromise). At the bottom, a crowd of "job seekers" will float between cheap employment and unemployment, without the benefits of the Welfare State. The political consequence is obvious: it is the comeback of the nineteenth century "dangerous classes problem," with the possibility of their disruptive collective action (the most positive result, in my view), or the generalization of individual delinquency and social diseases (drugs, etc.).

Second problem: this solution does not solve the crisis in Taylorist industrial relations. On the contrary, there is a risk of an evergrowing gap between the workers and their firm. So the noninvolvement of manual workers in the battle for quality and productivity remains a problem. Of course, "technology" is supposed to solve that problem. But "technology" is nothing but the embodiment of skilled activity into machinery. If direct workers are not involved in technical change, the implementation of highly sophisticated technologies requires a great deal of work at the design and maintenance levels. Hence new growth in the capital/labour ratio and no clear recovery in direct labour productivity.

The alternative is obviously the choice of less sophisticated technical systems, involving machine-worker interaction during the production process. This involvement (or "responsible autonomy," as opposed to Taylorist "direct control" of the workers as Friedman (1977) suggests) could not remain "informal" any more. The gamble lies in inducing the working teams not only to involve themselves willingly in the permanent tuning and maintenance of the plants, but to do so in such a manner that the improvements they make can be systematically embodied in the hardware and the software. The "know-how" acquired through learning-by-doing within the day-to-day maintenance of the labour process should be capable of formalization and assimilation by the methods, design, and engineering staff. In fact, the problem is *to reconnect what Taylorism had disconnected*: the manual and intellectual aspects of labour.

Nowadays this latter kind of industrial relations looks more "rational" than the former.[24] In fact, the 1980s may now be read as a great economic war between two solutions to the "supply-side" of the crisis of Fordism. On the one hand, the "flexible-liberal-productivist countries"—United States, Great Britain, France, Spain, Brazil—try to relax the "rigid" aspect of Fordist industrial relations. On the other hand, the "involving-the-workers" models—Japan, Scandinavia, West-Germany, and partly South Korea—try to relax the Taylorist direct control of the workers. And the great news is the following: the second group is winning that war! I will come back later to the important differences within the second group, but the fact is that "Taylorist direct control plus flexibility in the wage contract" (neo-Taylorism) was not such a good solution, even from the capitalist point of view.

The third problem with the liberal-productivist model is macro-economic: the great comeback of business cycles. Since there is no longer explicit expression of collective prospects, individual expectations have no other guideline than an evaluation of other's expectations. If the "animal spirits" of the other capitalists are understood to be turned toward investment, there will be investments, leading to a growth that will justify these investments until...some industrialists, merchants, or bankers will notice that there is not sufficient effective demand for the products of past investments. Hence, panic, crashes... The classical solution to this old problem is State expenditure. But "classical State expenditure," excluding welfare, is *warfare* expenditure. Militarism reappears as the major tool of macroeconomic policy, i.e., the United States post-1983 boom. But, by the end of the 1980s, the United States deficit (due to its less competitive industrial paradigm) became so important that this macroeconomic policy reached its limits.

Anyway, the "free trade" spirit of productivist liberalism is in itself a source of international instability, and it is the fourth problem. As we have already noticed, the "golden age" did not follow the path of ultra-free-tradism which was the primary ambition of the United States administration in 1945. Difficulties eventually stemmed from the lack of a more complex world organization when the conditions of global competition became more intense. To these new difficulties, liberalism's answer is: still less organization. Free trade was supposed to provide mutual adjustment to multilateral balance in trade and capital flows. In fact (and apart from the problem of OPEC surplus in the 1970 structural imbalances appear. In a free-trade situation, the only solution for a deficit country is to organize domestic deflation. Of course, if all the deficit countries organize deflation (and, first of all, the United States), the external markets of surplus countries are contracted in the same proportion, with a deflationist effect in these surplus countries. The aggregate result of this "beggar-my-neighbour" game is stagnation. A very clear case is the European Community, a free trade zone without coordination in policies.[25]

But the situation is far more serious in the case of the third world, since here trade problems are connected with credit problems, with dramatic consequences for welfare and even for ordinary lives.

The "miracles" of the NICs in the 1970s were made possible by a peculiar world configuration: there were still prospects of growth in industrial countries (due to Keynesian policies); there was great purchasing power in the OPEC countries, and the lax United States monetary policy induced private transnational banks to grant easy credit to the NICs. When the United States reversed their policy with the "monetarist shock" of 1981, the NICs were trapped: their prospects of exportation worsened, and credit was becoming extraordinarily expensive. Once again (but with terrible social consequences) the only solution was domestic recession. Today, only Korea is able to "pay for its debt" while allowing for a growth of the purchasing power of its working class. Even the leading country (both the most powerful and the herald of liberalism), the United States, experienced the shortcomings of *"laissez-faire,"* when their trade deficit became overwhelming in the middle of the 1980s.

Besides the story of the battle between two ways out of the "supply-side crisis," the 1980s may thus be read as the long result of an initial monetarist shock. Not so far from the 1920s, as described by Polanyi:

> Stabilization of currencies became the focal point in the political thought of peoples and governments; the restoration of the gold standard became the supreme aim of all organized effort in the economic field. The repayment of foreign loans and the return to stable currencies were recognized as the touchstones of rationality in politics; and no private suffering, no infringement of sovereignty, was deemed too great a sacrifice for the recovery of monetary integrity. The privations of the unemployed made jobless by deflation; the destitution of public servants dismissed without a pittance; even the relinquishment of national rights and the loss of constitutional liberties were judged a fair price to pay for the fulfillment of the requirement of sound budgets and sound currencies, these *a priori* of economic liberalism.[26]

Last but not least, this economic war is leading to the most dramatic ecological crisis that humankind has ever faced.[27] In fact, capitalism had multiplied by fifty the industrial world product within one century. But four-fifths of this growth were obtained in the Fordist period, after the Second World War. And liberal-productivism fosters a completely insensitive use of the "natural" environment. This ecological debt of past and present generations to the future ones (destruction of the ozone layer, the greenhouse effect, etc.) has to be paid in the next forty years.

FOR A NEW DESIGN WITHIN THE LABOUR PROCESS, AND A NEW WAGE-CONTRACT[28]

Whereas liberal-productivism appears to be a backlash from the "great transformation," its flaws could be cured by a new progress of society (but, this time, world society) against the "self-regulating market." The "supply-side" of the crisis of Fordism, on the other hand, escapes from Polanyi's paradigm. We have now to take as a political issue what Polanyi considered as an exogenous *primum mobile*: the form of industrial activity. For a "next transformation" alternative to liberal-productivism, we are to start with this point.

At the root of the current economic crisis, there is the crisis of labour, a crisis of Taylorism. I think that the labour movement and all democratic movements should challenge and even promote an anti-Taylorist revolution. Not only as a compromise, but as a first step toward their historical goals: a more and more democratic, self-managed society, a step toward the humanization of humankind.

The crux of the matter is the following. When management tries to reconnect what Taylorism has separated, this increases the shop-level bargaining power of the workers. So, how could a compromise between the new involved and multiskilled collective producer, and the management be regulated? Obviously, in the pure "flexible" version of the wage-contract consistent with the liberal ideology, this is impossible. "Involved workers" must feel that their interest is linked to the firm's interest! But there may be different forms of bargaining. One form could be a nonmarket agreement (on employment, careers) between management and skilled or semiskilled workers at the *firm* level, like in Japan. In this case, there is a compromise between capital and a part of the waged population, with growing competition inside the "privileged" segment of the labour force (the workers aristocracy) and an overexploitation of the other components (women, ethnic minorities). Another solution is bargaining at the *sectorial* level, like in Germany. Here, the advantages for workers are certainly greater than in firm-level bargaining, but some sectors (especially in services) are once again neglected (and once again, women and ethnic minorities). Taking it one step further, bargaining could be settled at the *society* level, like in Sweden. This is certainly the better solution for workers, though with some problems for capitalist profitability and competition.[29]

Summarizing a long debate,[30] one may assess that, while being economically and (at least in the privileged segment of its labour force) socially superior to Thatcherism and Reaganism, Japanese industrial relations do not avoid some of the shortcomings of liberal productivism. One reason is that, since the compromise is negotiated firm by firm, it allows for a deep segmentation and competition in society, solidarity being restricted to the family in a way that isolates women at home or in neo-Taylorist sectors at work. This is partly true also in Germany.

Yet, what Japan (and Germany, and Sweden) showed to the rest of the world is that the supply-side of the crisis of Fordism could be solved through the negotiated involvement of workers. This is the productive basis for a progressive alternative, but it is only a basis.

It should *also* be a compromise. Of course any boss would welcome workers enthusiastically working, with all their intellectual capacities, for the greatest glory of their firm. If the Taylorist movement chose to cancel those capacities, it was for political reasons, which were both micropolitical, shop-floor, and macropolitical, State level. The Taylorist revolution was not only directed against the "dawdling" of skilled workers in the shop, but also against the political capacities of a proud, self-conscious working class, against the dangerous idea, widespread in Europe from 1917 to 1936 as Polanyi reminds us, that "those who can rule the factories can rule society." And that was a success: with the loss of the knowledge of productive process, the working class lost any ambition toward self-management. In exchange, and after the 1930-1945 crisis, workers acceded to the Welfare State and "consumerism."

If we are to reunify what Taylorism has divided, what could the bargain be? What could the working class (men *and* women, citizens *and* migrants) get *at once* in exchange? In exchange, the first bargain is obviously *more stability in employment*. No worker would exercise his or her cooperative spirit in search of gains in productivity entailing his or her own redundancy. The problem is that most single firms cannot warrant a job on the same task for a while. So job guarantee should be a dynamic guarantee, involving both intrafirm and social aspects. That raises the issue of "mobility." Most workers are not ready to accept any mobility, in job and in space. They are right. Labour is but a part of human individual and social life. As Polanyi noticed,[31] friendship and love relations are the main part of happiness, a strong basis for social mobilization, and they depend on material conditions: existence of stable groups, linked to territories. So the compromise should not entail "employment anywhere" but the "right to live and work in a homeland." This implies a collective concern of unions about the dynamic creation of new jobs, as and when old jobs become redundant. Workers' involvement in "how do we work?" entails involvement in "what should we do?"

Another major point of the compromise should be settled. What about the *sharing-out of the gains in productivity*? Assuming that the new industrial relations entail a comeback to the high rates of growth in productivity of the Golden Age, who should benefit from these? At least, the workers as much as the firms. If it were not the case, sluggish social demand contrasting with roaring productivity would lead to overproduction and unemployment or to an export war (with its losers). But the new regime of accumulation could solve that problem either through higher wages per worker, or through less labour-time per worker. In my opinion (and this is my major point), *the compromise should be based on more and more free time*. The reasons for that choice are many.

First, a majority of people in advanced capitalist countries are reaching sufficient quantitative conditions of living (the situation being different in the third world). The "right to the search of happiness" is at present constrained, not by a lack of "having," but by a lack of "being." *Second*, a dramatic reduction in labour time is the only efficient solution to quickly reduce unemployment. *Third*, logics suggests that, in the long term, an active, involved worker inside production-time should be a citizen active in democratic life, with free time for cultural life and permanent increase in his or her degree of education. *Fourth*, such a regime of accumulation, where full employment is based on slower growth of market relations and expansion of free, nonmarket social relations, is less subject to economic disturbance stemming from international competition. *Fifth*, the global and local ecological constraints are now weighing heavily against any increase in the production of material goods (with the consumption of raw materials and energy that any production implies). Since a large part of the third world population *has* to increase its material welfare, Northern populations should prefer a form of progress based upon the growth of *free time*.

SOLVING THE CRISIS OF THE WELFARE STATE: SPEENHAMLAND VINDICATED

As emerges from a century of union militancy, the Welfare State is a powerful but very peculiar form of social solidarity. Basically, it consists in a compromise between capital and labour in the form of a compromise between citizens. A part of direct revenue is subtracted from individual purchasing power and directed to a pool. That pool provides with money-revenues people who, unwillingly, cannot, or can no longer, earn their living through a direct wage. The active sector provides the taxes that feed the pool of the Welfare State. When this burden becomes too heavy, the active sector begins to protest: it pays for "lazy" people, people who do not work. Actually, these people would like to work, but they are not allowed to work while receiving welfare transfers. They bear the burden of this inconsistency.

The reason for this inconsistency is well exposed in Polanyi's critique of the Speenhamland experiment. At the time (1795), a "generous" form of Welfare State consisted in warranting a total minimum revenue whatever be the amount of the wage. As a result, this "social minimum wage" induced workers not to work, and employers to pay very low wages. Indiscriminate subsidies to workers were from this time considered as a bonus to laziness, or an indirect subsidy to employers.

In addition to the generally unjust and stupid accusation of laziness, the Welfare State is now attacked by conservative liberalism as being economically counterproductive in one microeconomic argument. "If there were no (or less) tax on the active sector for the Welfare State, then the total cost of labour would be less. Then a lot of new workers could be hired." That may be true at a microeconomic level, but it is a fallacy of composition. If there were no tax for the Welfare State, there would be no welfare transfer, with all the entailed dangers for macroeconomic stability.

Some proponents of the reduction of the Welfare State outline the alternative possibility of "family welfare," including housewives cares and private insurance. It should be pointed out that, from a macroeconomic point of view, any transfer at a definite period is financed by the production of the same period, so any system of social security is based on redistribution. As for family solidarity, it is too often based on the patriarchal oppression of women.

However, there is a way to eschew the two-sided schizophrenic argument against the Welfare State, taking into account the "Speenhamland" argument—the microeconomic argument—but avoiding its composition fallacy and the feminist attack on sexual division of labour. It is the creation of a *new sector of activity*, limited in size, whose workers (or more precisely the agencies paying for them) would receive from the Welfare State the normal dole. The workers would not have to pay any more tax for the welfare than if they were unemployed, though they would receive a net normal wage for their activity. This activity should be dedicated to socially useful tasks, the kind of tasks that are expensively covered by the Welfare State (care for old people or convalescents), or covered by women's free labour, or not covered (improving the environment, such as poor neighbourhoods, and so on).

The development of this sector would eliminate many problems of the Fordist Welfare State. Active taxpayers would know what they are paying for: useful social services. Workers of that sector would have a useful job from which they can receive more social and self-esteem than from "moonlighting" or from part-time jobs such as in fast food or shoe-polishing. The microeconomic argument will be acknowledged to develop a new sector of activity with stable revenues and which does not compete with others, hence with no composition fallacy or "Speenhamland" effect.

But there is more. With that new economic sector, new social relations may be experienced. First, within the sector. It could be organized in self-managed small agencies; with the help of psycho-sociologists, it could mix labour and professional retraining. In its relations with the "customers," it could innovate in nonmarket, non-patriarchal forms of contract, with constant democratic control from the contractor (a local community, an agency of protection of the environment, etc.) on the permanent social usefulness of activities of the self-managed group.

Thus, this new "alternative" sector could be a school for self-management, gender equality, and democracy in the social definition of tasks. Though it would be immersed in market, wage relations (but protected by its connection with the Welfare State), it could be another step toward the humanization of economic relations.

A NONAGGRESSIVE INTERNATIONAL ECONOMIC ORDER

Let us assume that the reader likes the above design for a "next transformation." She or he will certainly object: "Well, it is all right if some nation chooses that design, but this nation will be in trouble in the context of international competition. How could a worker working thirty hours a week compete with a Korean? On the other hand, a democratic Korea might choose to work hard and improve his popular standard of living." That is right. The problem with the present international economic order is that the burden of balance adjustments usually falls on the shoulders of the most expansionist country, even if economic expansion is a vital necessity for its citizens.

At first, protectionism looks like the easiest way to solve the problem, and it was the most obvious feature of the 1930s "great transformation." If one country agrees on one "good" inner compromise, and if this compromise is formulated so that the capacities of citizens answer to the necessities of the community, why should such an agreement be disturbed by the arbitrary law of free trade? Now, protectionism has its counterparts. The spread of new products and processes may be slowed down, economies of scale are lost, heavy investments are uselessly engaged in what could be complementary countries. Those were the reasons for the creation of the European Common Market. It was all right as long as the European countries, all together, were seeking the speediest growth. Once some of them had to deal with trade imbalance, and when they did so through competitive deflation, problems arose. And that remained the only solution when competitive devaluations were forbidden with the European Monetary System.

Let us take the European Economic Community (EEC) example as a reduced model to study the problems of international trade between advanced countries. The European community is a multinational economic space with an explicit mode of regulation, with rules of the game. These rules penalize too fast growth, or too fast labour-time reduction. One solution could be precisely an explicit agreement on coordinated faster growth, or labour-time reduction. But such an agreement supposes that the rules of democracy lead *at the same time* to coalitions supporting such a design in all the separate countries of Europe. That appears unlikely, and an institutional "putsch" of the European Parliament against national governments is also unlikely.

So we have to look for a "second best." Not an international agreement for the same design, but an agreement not to penalize the best designs. One rule could be the following. If a country experiences a trade-deficit with a higher rate of creation of jobs than the European average (either through growth, or labour-time reduction, or development of an alternative sector) then, after six months, that country has the right to improve its trade balance through nondeflationist protectionist devices (devaluation, quota, import taxes). These privileges are suppressed when its situation is matched by the average. The adjustments are induced at the top and not at the bottom.[32]

Such a settlement is more difficult at the international level: the best one can hope for is a gentleman's agreement. When the United States administration started anxiously to beg Japan and Germany to increase their growth in 1986, because "if they did not, it would be impossible to hold back United States Congressmen from adopting protectionism," was it not a good demonstration of the sensibleness of a new set of rules of the kind I propose?

Let us consider now the implementation of this new multilateralist spirit in the case of trade between newly industrializing countries and advanced capitalist countries. At first (in the early 1970s) the latter benefitted highly and willingly from the misery wages of the former. Then the low labour-costs of NICs appeared as "unfair conditions of competition," entailing unemployment in the North, and justifying protectionist reactions in the 1980s (including against Korea). This is the clearest consequence of the fallacy of composition in the free-tradist belief that all countries could develop by becoming net exporters at the same time. If a new industrial revolution is to spread to the third world, then the third world will have to create new markets for its new products. This implies the possibility for third world countries to protect their young industries. But on the other hand, the exports from the NICs should not be too disruptive for employment in the North. A rule could be the following. The North could be protectionist versus countries whose competitiveness is based on dictatorship, and low wage imposed through terror. On the contrary, the North should be open to exports from countries engaged in rapid increase of the standard of living of their population, with full union liberties. The referee could be the International Labour Organization at Geneva.

Such a rule would protect the new democracies in the third

world against savage competition, and it would be an incentive for the ruling classes of dictatorships to shift toward democracy, ecological and social policies. It would secure a better consistency between growth in the North and faster growth in the South. In a word, it would induce a positive-sum game for the world economy and employment. But there is a rub: debt crisis.

The weight of past debts induces the NICs to "adjust" toward export-led growth, which is exactly in the opposite direction of that needed by a more stable world economic order. The best solution would be the cancellation of debt. This is neither a foolish, nor a "generous" idea. It is in the macroeconomic middle term interest of the North. The problem is that debt cancellation could entail lenders' bankruptcy. Hence we reach the problem of the "lender of last resort." If the South does not pay, the losses in the international banking system should be fed with some money. Up to 1979, the world lender in the last resort was the United States Federal Reserve. After its conversion to monetarism, the world monetary situation became too tightened for the requirements of world economic expansion (another reason for the negative-sum game of the early 1980s, and for the crash of October 1987). At present, there is no other candidate among national central banks to be the lender of last resort, issuing the world key currency according to the needs of international trade. A national currency could be the world currency if the bills of that nation are accepted as a means of payment, and that is possible only if these bills are secured by the uncontested economic leadership of the issuing nation. There is no longer such a nation. On the other hand, private multinational banks, no matter how big, cannot be lender of last resort. They cannot issue more credits when they are nearly sure that old ones will never be repaid. That is the reason for the relative failure of the Baker Plan, and later of the Brady Plan.

An international institution should be in charge of issuing fresh credit money. A renewed International Monetary Fund, for instance, could issue some kind of special drawing rights, with international legal tender, according to the needs of world recovery.[33]

CONCLUSION

In this text I have proposed a new design, according to an analysis of the shortcomings of the post-World War Two hegemonic model of development, Fordism. The problems of these shortcomings are on the agenda of all the competing designs. That is the reason why similar proposals could appear both in the "liberal-productivist" project I criticized, and in the alternative project I proposed. In the same way, in the 1930s the idea of "corporatism" (explicit cooperation of State, firms and unions in the regulation of economic life) was on the agenda of fascism, social-democracy and Stalinism, and Karl Polanyi gave the correct reason for it: the main problem appeared to be over-production stemming from anarchy in the market.

The "next transformation," I propose, is only one possible transformation. So the differences between the projects could not emerge from comparisons between partial solutions. It is the completeness of the design that makes the difference. The alternative design I propose includes:

• New social industrial relations based on conscious involvement of direct workers in exchange of their right to control the implementation of technical progress, the right to live and work in one's homeland, and more free time;
• Preservation of the degree of socialization of revenues so as to maintain social security, but a thorough reform of the Welfare State so as to develop a new self-managed sector contracting for socially useful services with communities;
• New international relations based on multilateralism and international credit money, but rejecting systematic free trade in favour of a new set of rules making room for faster social progress in separate democratic nations.

This alternative design is aimed at the social and intellectual promotion of everybody; at more freedom and welfare for everybody; at more democracy and peaceful international relations; and at an ecologically sustainable development. It accepts wage and market relations, the existence of a hierarchy of management. It is not a revolutionary project, not "the *last* transformation." It is only one step forward, a compromise for the next decades.

As may have been noted, the "next transformation" shares two targets with the "great transformation": it tends to remove from both labour and money the status of "commodity." More generally, it is clearly an "anti-*laissez-faire*" option, especially at the international level. And it adds two issues to those of Polanyi's: the organization of labour and the creation of a new sector of activity.

But one could say again: "And what about land?" My answer is clear: today, it is impossible to consider environmental issues as only soil issues. Ecology (the interaction between humankind and nature) involves all aspects of social life. The setting-up of a really "sustainable" model of development is the great challenge of the twenty-first century. Environmental regulation will be important. Growth of free time instead of purchasing power will be more important.

Ecological issues are much more than a question of economy. They are a matter for cultural revolution, breaking with a tradition that established itself long before the "former transformation." And that may not be a new transformation but, really, *the great transformation*.

NOTES

1. K. Polanyi, *The Great Transformation* (Boston: Beacon Press, 1957), p. 258A.
2. *Ibid.*, p. 154.
3. *Ibid.*, pp. 56-57.
4. *Ibid.*, p. 40.
5. *Ibid.*, p. 35.
6. *Ibid.*, chap. 6
7. *Ibid.*, chap. 11.
8. *Ibid.*, chap. 12.
9. On the differences between these crises, and on the core economic and political problems which they expressed, see A. Lipietz, *Le Monde enchanté. De la valeur à l envol inflationniste* (Paris: La Découverte-Maspéro, 1983).
10. This methodology was progressively elaborated by M. Aglietta, *Régulation et crises du capitalisme* (Paris: Calmann-Lévy, 1976); R. Boyer, and J. Mistral, *Accumulation, inflation, crises* (Paris: P.U.F., 1978); B. Coriat, *L'atelier et le chronomètre* (Paris: C. Bourgeois, 1979); A. Lipietz, *Crise et inflation: pourquoi?* (Paris: F. Maspero, 1979); A. Lipietz, *Le Monde enchanté.*; A. Lipietz, *Mirages et miracles. Problèmes de l industrialisation dans le Tiers Monde* (Paris: La Découverte, 1985b). Here I follow the presentation in A. Glyn, A. Hugues, A. Lipietz, and A. Singh, *The Rise and Fall of the Golden Age: an Historical Analysis of Post War Capitalism in the Developed Market Economies* (Helsinki: United Nations University/WIDER, 1986). For a longer presentation of the main concepts of the "regulation approach" and their connection with a broader approach to social theory, see A. Lipietz, "Réflexions autour d une fable. Pour un statut marxiste des concepts de régulation et d accumulation," *Couverture Orange* CEPREMAP, no. 8530 (1985c), and A. Lipietz, "La trame, la chaine et la régulation: outils pour les sciences sociales" (paper presented at the Congrès International sur la théorie de la Régulation, Barcelona, June 16-18, 1988).
11. Point (*d*). Contrary to what Karl Polanyi says (*The Great Transformation*, chp. 6, p. 72, footnote 3), this idea is fully enlightened by K. Marx (Vol. III) under the heading of "the enchanted world." See A. Lipietz, *Le Monde enchanté*.

12. D. Leborgne, A. Lipietz, "Avoiding two-tiers Europe," *Labour and Society* XV, no. 2 (1990a).
13. The word "régulation" in French connotes this adjustment of contradictory tendencies. It belongs to the vocabulary of biology and cybernetics. In English, "regulation" mainly connotes the legislative and administrative action of the State (in French: "règlementation"). Of course, legal rules are part of social self-control, but the latter must not be reduced to the former. In this text, we shall use the word "regulation" in its more general French meaning.
14. *The Great Transformation*, p. 132.
15. *Ibid.*, p. 250.
16. More on this in A. Lipietz, *Choisir l'audace. Une alternative pour le XXIè siècle* (Paris: La Découverte, 1989), p. 93.
17. J. E. Spiro, *The Politics of International Economic Relations* (London: G. Allen and Unwin, 1977).
18. *Mirages et miracles*; *The Rise and Fall of the Golden Age*.
19. *Le Monde enchanté*.
20. *The Great Transformation*, p. 73.
21. This distinction between two different dimensions of crisis was popularized by E. Malinvaud, *The Theory of Employment Reconsidered* (Oxford: Oxford University Press, 1977). But it was well known among Marxists since *Das Kapital*, Volume III. (For an application of the twosided explanation of crisis in Marx to the present crisis, see, for instance, A. Lipietz, *Le Monde enchanté*.)
22. *Mirages et miracles*; *Choisir l'audace*.
23. *Mirages et miracles*.
24. M. Aoki, *Intrafirm Mechanism, Sharing, and Employment: Implications of Japanese experience* (Helsinki: United Nations University/WIDER, 1987).
25. "Avoiding two-tiers Europe."
26. *The Great Transformation*, p. 142.
27. See the United Nation report, *Our Common Future*.
28. All the following is deeply influenced by numerous discussions among economists and activists, about the failure of the attempt of Mitterrand's two first governments (1981-1984) to get out of crisis through a radicalization of social-democracy (See A. Lipietz, *L'audace ou l'enlisement* (Paris: La Découverte, 1984)). It is more developed in my last books: *Choisir l'audace*, and *Vert-espérance* (Paris: La Découverte, 1993).
29. Mahon, "Crises, Transition and Chance Discoveries: Solidaristic Work as an Historically Progressive Strategy for the Shaping of Post-Fordism?" (paper presented at the 7th International Conference of Europeanists, Washington, March 23-25th, 1990).
30. See "Avoiding two-tiers Europe"; A. Lipietz, "Capital-Labour relations at the dawn of twenty-first Century." United Nations University/WIDER Project on Capital-labour Relations, 1990.
31. *The Great Transformation*, p. 154.
32. "Avoiding two-tiers Europe."
33. On "fair" trade and debt issues, see A. Lipietz, "Trois crises," Colloque La crise actuelle par rapport aux crises antérieures, Binghamton, November, 1985a; and *Choisir l'audace*.

REFERENCES

Aglietta, M. *Régulation et crises du capitalisme* (Paris: Calmann-Lévy, 1976). English translation: *A Theory of Capitalist Regulation* (London: Verso, 1979).

Aoki, M. "Intrafirm mechanism, sharing, and employment: implications of Japanese experience," Marglin and Schor, eds., *The Golden Age of Capitalism* (Oxford: Oxford University Press, 1990) Originally published as a mimeograph (Helsinki: United Nations University/WIDER, 1987).

Boyer, R., and J. Mistral, *Accumulation, inflation, crises* (Paris: P.U.F., 1978;1983).

Coriat, B. *L'atelier et le chronomètre* (Paris: C. Bourgeois, 1979).

Friedman, A. *Industry and Labour* (London: MacMillan, 1977).

Glyn, A., A. Hugues, A. Lipietz, and A. Singh, "The Rise and Fall of the Golden Age: an Historical Analysis of Post War Capitalism in the Developed Market Economies," Marglin & Schor, eds., *The Golden Age of Capitalism* (Oxford: Oxford University Press, 1990). Originally published as a mimeograph (Helsinki: United Nations University/WIDER, 1986).

Itoh, M. "The Japanese Model of Post-Fordism." Paper presented at UCLA conference: Pathways to Industrialization and Regional Development in the 90s, Lake Arrowhead, March 14-18, 1990; edited by M. Storper and A. Scott, *Pathways to industrialization and regional development* (New York: Routledge, 1992).

Leborgne, D., A. Lipietz, "New Technologies, New Modes of Regulation: Some Spatial Implications," Paper presented at Dubrovnik Seminar, June 1987; and Samos Seminar, September 1987; published in *Space and Society* VI, no. 3 (1988).

———. "Avoiding two-tiers Europe," *Labour and Society* XV, no. 2 (1990a).

———. "Fallacies and Open Issues about Post-Fordism." Paper presented at the UCLA conference, Pathways to Industrialization and Regional Development in the 90s, Lake Arrowhead, March 14-18, 1990b; published in *Pathways to industrialization and regional development*, edited by M. Storper and A. Scott (New York: Routledge, 1992).

Lipietz, A. *Crise et inflation: pourquoi?* (Paris: F. Maspero, 1979).

———. Le Monde enchanté. De la valeur à l'envol inflationniste (Paris: La Découverte-Maspéro, 1983). English translation, *The*

Enchanted World (London: Verso, 1985).

————. *L'audace ou l'enlisement* (Paris: La Découverte, 1984).

————. "Trois crises," Colloque: La crise actuelle par rapport aux crises antérieures, Binghamton, United States, November 1985a. English translation, "Three Crises: Capitalism and Labour Movement," in Gottdiener and Komninos, eds., *Modern Capitalism and Crisis Theory* (New York: Macmillan-St. Martin Press, 1989).

————. *Mirages et miracles. Problèmes de l'industrialisation dans le Tiers Monde* (Paris: La Découverte, 1985b). English translation, *Mirages and Miracles: Crises in Global Fordism* (London: Verso, 1987).

————. "Réflexions autour d'une fable. Pour un statut marxiste des concepts de régulation et d'accumulation," *Couverture Orange* CEPREMAP no. 8530 (1985c). English translation, "Reflections on a tale: The Marxist Foundation of the Concepts of Regulation and Accumulation," in *Studies in Political Economy*, no. 26 (1988), pp. 7-36.

————. "La trame, la chaine et la régulation: outils pour les sciences sociales." Paper presented at theCongrès international sur la théorie de la régulation, Barcelona, June 16-18, 1988. English translation in Benko, ed., *Space and Social Theory.* (Ottawa: University of Ottawa Press, 1988).

————. *Choisir l'audace. Une alternative pour le XXIè siècle* (Paris: La Découverte, 1989). English translation, *Towards a New Economic Order: Postfordism, Ecology and Democracy* (Cambridge: Polity Press, 1992).

————. "Capital-Labour relations at the dawn of twenty-first Century," United Nations University/WIDER Project on Capital-labour Relations, 1990. Mimeograph. Also published in Schor and You, eds., *Changing Production Relations: A Global Perspective* (London: Edward Elgar, forthcoming).

————. *Vert-espérance* (Paris: La Découverte, 1993). English translation, Green Hopes (Cambridge: Polity Press, 1995).

Malinvaud, E. *The Theory of Employment Reconsidered* (Oxford: Oxford University Press, 1977).

Mahon, "Crises, Transition and Chance Discoveries: Solidaristic Work as an Historically Progressive Strategy for the Shaping of Post-Fordism?" Paper presented at the 7th International Conference of Europeanists, Washington, March 23-25, 1990.

Piore, M. J., and C.F. Sabel, *The Second Industrial Divide: Possibilities for Prosperity* (New York: Basic Books, 1984).

Polanyi, K. *The Great Transformation: The Political and Economic Origin of Our Time* (Boston: Beacon Press, 1957 [1944]).

Spiro, J. E. *The Politics of International Economic Relations* (London: G. Allen and Unwin, 1977).

III.

CRITICAL PERSPECTIVES AND ALTERNATIVE PATHS

8.

THE SILENT CONSTRUCTION OF A NEW ECONOMIC PARADIGM

Alfredo L. de Romaña

INTRODUCTION

For many years now much of the world—the Americas, Europe, Africa and a major part of Asia—has been confronted with various impasses whose persistence raises serious doubts about future prospects.[1] In the industrialized countries irremediable unemployment, together with a new feeling of uncertainty and vague apprehension of serious disruption underlie the relative prosperity and visions of a "global economy." Less-industrialized nations, especially those with economies mortgaged through past indebtedness, frustration, and impoverishment, have been closing in ever since the debt crisis erupted in the early 1980s. Indeed, beneath today's poverty-blind "culture of contentment" lay historically unprecedented hunger, continued ecological destruction, pervading corrosion of the social fabric, growing insecurity, and poverty, even in industrial societies. Yet these everyday realities are barely reflected in routine economic indicators, and soothing mass media entertainment.

None of this is really new. Increasing unemployment and poverty (even in contexts of "good" economic performance), the incapacity of governments to act cohesively, and the exhaustion of ideas have presided over deteriorating living conditions for quite some time. The very persistence of this predicament, the prospects of its exacerbation and its presence in even the most diverse nations—together with a general diffusion of conflict, ungovernability and lack of either credible political leadership or alternatives—reflect a crisis much deeper than anything our cultural elites today are equipped to deal with.

For decades, economic science had served political leaderships quite successfully in the construction of flourishing industrial societies, although its results in "developing" countries are questionable. But now economics seems to be running out of responses capable of addressing the growing social ills. Indeed, its prescriptions are often no more than common sense crisis-management responses—for instance, fiscal equilibrium—such as any reasonable layman might urge. Such therapies may correct financial imbalances, according to the "post-Keynesian consensus" of the profession, but they conspicuously fail to address the social disruptions that will be triggered by such adjustments.

Among other ills—not least of which is an endemic poverty that seems to be beyond remedy—economics has proved incapable of addressing the worsening unemployment problem. Average unemployment in Organization for Economic Cooperation and Development (OECD) countries has increased from 3.1 percent during the 1960s, to 4.7 in the 1970s; from 7.3 percent in the 1980s to 8.2 in 1991-92.[2] Its prospects for the late 1990s are even grimmer, given the underlying fiscal, trade, and financial imbalances incurred during the last decade or two, and the new global context of exacerbated competition. By now it has become clear that any politician or economist who continues to promise that "job creation" will significantly reverse the tendency is either lying, or stupid.

The continuing inability to remedy these ills—indeed, their positive aggravation for the majority of people—is typical of a theoretical system that has exhausted its capacity to explain what is happening or to devise solutions.

THE CONTEXT OF TODAY'S PROBLEMS

Historical Evolution of the crisis

During the "thirty glorious years" following World War Two, society attained its full splendour. More than a century of convulsions and social disequilibrium inaugurated by the industrial revolution culminated in the brilliant performance of the nations around the North Atlantic. This golden age of modern industrial society occurred just when systematic development began in the "third world." A new type of economic organization was replacing centuries-old subsistence and *rentier* economies. Modernity was introducing industrialization and consumption, the development of Nation States and worldwide communications networks. At the same time, it was causing peasants to leave the countryside, thus fostering rapid growth of cities with their shanty towns of the marginalized and the excluded. The material benefits first introduced into Europe by the modern era's organization of life had begun to spread globally on a massive scale—as had the social costs accompanying economic progress from its beginnings.

But humanity as a whole looked to a future symbolized by the splendour of the industrial powers of the time; amid the general optimism of those days the new social ills, many of them unprecedented, were viewed as the temporary "price of progress." A new project called "development" was launched by United States President Harry Truman in the famous "Point Four" of his inauguration speech: one that was spontaneously adopted by virtually all nations. For years this project had unified all political persuasions in a tacit consensus with the promise of prosperity for all. The notion that the type of society flourishing around the North Atlantic could be replicated worldwide, that it was sustainable and desirable, had been established and indeed still lives on in today's leaders who grew up when industrial society had reached its apogee.

By the early 1970s, however, fissures had appeared in the economies of the North, and a series of sectoral impasses shook the world-Centre: the energy crisis; the dissolution of the international monetary system established at Bretton Woods at the end of World War Two; the spread of unemployment especially in Europe and North America; and the slow decline in real wages (generally obscured by misleading indicators, as we shall see).

In the early 1980s the debt crisis erupted in large portions of the developing world. Taking everyone by surprise, it erased much of the improvement made during the 1960s-1970s period of debt-led economic growth; for most people everyday life would become harder, and for many it became a nightmare. Despite acute sacrifices and the transfer of massive resources to creditors in service charges, in most countries the debt remained largely intact, thus generating what amounted to a perpetual rent collected by creditors. Though debt servitude has now lost its journalistic prominence, it remains as the backdrop to misery and frustration.

After a tumultuous decade, the 1980s ended with the spectacular collapse of Marxist regimes, already ossified for quite some time. In even more unexpected fashion, the Promethean project which promised to correct the ills of capitalism and to implement a harmonious industrial society also disintegrated.

In short, the decade that started with the foundering of "third world" economies ended with the collapse of those of the "second world." Both events were unexpected, for a social system rarely dies progressively and according to a predictable schedule; rather, it rots slowly from within until the malady affects the entire body, attaining its central organs, and suddenly manifesting itself. First, it was the dependent capitalism adopted by a wide variety of third world regimes that suddenly foundered. Then came the collapse of State capitalism, i.e., the communist regimes that took "command" economies to the point of caricature. The "managed capitalism" of first world economies remains the foremost political expression of modern society: indeed, the organizational paradigm of industrial civilization. As we shall see, "managed" is the proper term, not "market" capitalism, for its massive markets are coordinated, sustained *and fostered* by a policy framework in which command (i.e., the State) plays a key role.

While the unfolding of history has attracted attention amid the politics of the day, few have noticed a less spectacular but more significant phenomenon: while the periphery crumbles, the fissures that had unobtrusively appeared at the centre have become serious cracks. In the early 1970s, the major industrial powers, until then confident and optimistic, were confronted by the various difficulties regarded as "conjunctural," or cyclic at the time. The French president declared that "he already sees the light at the end of the tunnel." But problems are now different: they can no longer be resolved with the Keynesian macroeconomic instruments that had ensured prosperity since the 1950s. A series of sectoral crises have followed each other, or are camouflaged, diverted, postponed.

This is how, during the 1980s, the United States entered a unique cycle of growth ushering in a period of consumption that indirectly fueled the economies of Japan and Europe. Though packaged with the conservative rhetoric of the Reagan years, it is actually neo-Keynesian policies that sustained the economy with growing deficits and debt. Official indicators and televised entertainment informed the United States public that prosperity reigned. Few paid any attention to the ugly sores of poverty and homelessness that even appeared on TV screens along with the so-called "erosion of the middle class." After the "great communicator" retired at the end of the decade, everybody realized that the prosperity of the few, televised for the consumption of a frustrated majority, had been fueled by unprecedented budget, debt, and trade deficits. This is what was most significant: for most people conditions were stagnating, if not slowly deteriorating, while massive imbalances were being incurred to keep the economy rolling.

The situation of the United States is particularly significant. For the United States has been, beyond all countries, *the* protagonist of modernity: inventor of modern democracy; embodiment of the American way of life imitated everywhere; first exporter of culture; and now, with its triumph over the USSR, its only philosophical and military challenger, the ultimate arbitrator of world order, sponsor of a political philosophy that has spread spontaneously across the planet. At the same time, once the imperatives of the United State's geopolitical duel no longer impeded analysis and debate, the disequilibrium that had continued to increase since the early 1970s became more apparent. At the same time the United States entered a phase of decline as its internal strength became exhausted.

The problems of the paragon of modernity, however, not only mortgage its own future, they also throw the world capitalist system into a state of disequilibrium. For in a world economy, integrated to an unprecedented degree through economic "interdependence," serious disruption at the centre cannot but cause equally unprecedented repercussions. It does not much matter whether this originates in the United States or in another country such as Japan: in conditions of disequilibrium a critical triggering event can override the key levers of control, and precipitate unforeseen dislocation of the precarious order. Such a crisis is not only possible but also probable;

although its exact circumstances are obviously unpredictable, the likelihood of human shortcoming in a context of unprecedented complexity is high. Otherwise, the system will continue to function, prolonging slow agony as "the economy" performs well enough—while poverty, erosion of the social fabric, and conflict in various forms worsen.

STRUCTURAL AND SYSTEMIC IMPASSE

Nobody believes any longer that present economic dysfunctions are merely "conjunctural." Now they are widely regarded as being "structural." That is, their correction is deemed to require major reorganization, or essentially new strategies to achieve the growth needed to provide jobs and further economic prosperity. These strategies may be market liberalization and free trade on a worldwide basis, or, at the other end of the ideological spectrum, investment in infrastructure or human "capital" (through job retraining and the like). More often, they consist of various compromises and dubious combinations thereof.

The problem is that the crisis seems to go much deeper. Indeed, the spirit of the times has begun manifesting what scholars for long had omitted to record and interpret. The unusual nature and scope of the impasse started making headlines and unobtrusively appearing in significant data. In October 1993, for example, a special issue of *Le Monde* devoted to political debates concluded that the "durable nature of crisis" reflects "the end of a world."[3] Shortly after, the annual meeting at Davos (Switzerland), which brings together some 1,300 of the most powerful men on the planet, opened under the official rubric "Redefining the Basic Assumptions of the World Economy." For problems now appear in a peculiarly troubling manner which does not fit our usual interpretation of data, and, thus, contravenes conventional views of problems and solutions. Unemployment, for instance, is usually attributed to insufficient growth. But the number of jobs in North America had doubled between 1960 and 1990.[4] That is, job creation was outstripping population growth. Yet unemployment kept growing, and even the relatively "low" rates in the U.S. have been recognized as grossly inexact; up to only half the real level according to data from the U.S. Bureau of Labour itself.[5] Besides, since the last recession, growth has not been creating jobs. Quite significantly, as the *Wall Street Journal* observed,[6] this "jobless growth" has meant that the conventional goal of improving productivity was being achieved: output per worker was increasing precisely because techno-economic accumulation permits greater output with fewer workers. Thus "productivity," a cornerstone of "competitiveness," appears to be part of the problem rather than the solution. Of course such jobless growth—particularly visible at one point at the end of the 1992 recession—has been precisely the overall tendency in OECD countries during the last two decades.[7] And according to all predictions, that tendency will become more pronounced in the next decade, thanks to the new practices of "re-engineering" now being adopted to make firms more efficient. As the *Wall Street Journal* noted in another article, "the price of progress" means that in the near future re-engineering may well eliminate twenty-five million of the ninety million jobs in the United States private sector (in Germany the estimate is nine million out of thirty-three million).[8]

An even more interesting observation was made at the height of the 1980s boom by French Canada's elite daily in a full front page headline: "The Economy is Faring well but Canadians are Getting Poorer."[9] Real wages, which are the main if not the only source of income for the majority, were declining just as the gross national product (GNP) was going up.

In 1992, English Canada's elite daily noted, in another full front page headline, the distress of families who were overworked and lacked time for family life and leisure.[10] For decades, official statistics had been announcing a "slow rise" in "household income," ignoring the fact that two paychecks were becoming indispensable for families to make ends meet. Thus the average household's sphere of "free time" was cut virtually in half; or, put another way, people had to double the effort necessary for subsistence. In other words, high income consumption levels in industrialized lifestyles reflect a high cost of living rather than a high *standard* of living. In short, income levels can be interpreted to mean neither greater freedom nor increased well-being. For increased consumption requires increased production, and the many stresses associated with it. Thus, a cover story of *Time* magazine entitled "The Rat Race: How America is Running Itself Ragged," pointed to the disquieting effects of employment on family and social life.[11]

In short, economic growth is no longer delivering the jobs, jobs are no longer delivering the incomes, and incomes are no longer delivering the good life they were supposed to foster.

Very similar problems also affect the industrializing countries. During the Brazilian "miracle" of the 1970s, a president observed that the "Brazilian economy is strong but Brazilians are starving." Not only did the economic miracle mean nothing for the majority, like most other miracles (such as Spain's and Mexico's in the late 1980s and early 1990s) it turned out to be a mirage. The boom invariably came to an end amid serious crises, leaving the country with longlasting problems and impasses. As elsewhere, modernity did not eliminate poverty: it simply modernized it. And this means that people who previously lived under the poor, but comparatively decent and secure conditions of subsistence economies sink further into misery amid a daily struggle for survival. The age-old subsistence poverty that at least provided the material basics and ample time for leisure and socializing—not to mention other amenities lost with industrialization, such as diversified and satisfying work, set in convivial living patterns and a hospitable environment—is often transformed into destitute deprivation and daily frustration. The modern mind, of course, sees the past as beset by infinite "poverty and ignorance" which progress will slowly cure. But as the "losers" in the modernization process have been at pains to document—for whenever the winners may care to observe—such degradation of life is the consequence of change introduced in the name of "development," a goal that is never attained.

The GNP and other such statistics do not of course reflect deterioration, although they conventionally purport to show that a people's overall situation has improved. Whatever the case may be, it is the most confusing of measures. "The unemployed man in a Caracas shantytown is stupefied to learn that according to GNP statistics his standard of living is actually enviable compared to that of others. At the same time, the Samoan fisherman, who lives rather comfortably in a subsistence economy, is no less flabbergasted to discover that he is among the poorest inhabitants of the planet."[12] However, since GNP growth is not only an *indicator* but also a *guide* for policy, the suspicion grows that it may actually foster many of the ills inherent in the modernization of poverty. It is not a question of adequate redistribution of the "benefits of modernity," indeed, maldistribution attendant upon economic growth is more easily criticized than corrected.

In short, it is becoming increasingly apparent that the GNP, regarded as the key indicator of modern society's well-being, indicates nothing that is at all relevant. Not surprisingly, this has led to serious attempts to re-evaluate and redefine the concept, given its importance as a policy-shaping goal. But nothing better has emerged to replace it, so that growth of the GNP still remains the axis of policy. The problem is that if such growth does little to improve social conditions, decrease in the GNP translates into a recession which in present circumstances can only make matters worse. This only confirms our disquieting predicament of living in a lose-lose situation.

What we are witnessing, yet can hardly interpret with sufficient cogency, are problems that are less "structural" and more deeply "systemic." That is, they do not result from the wrong *strategies* being applied to achieve a given set of *goals*. Rather, it is this very set of goals, according to which socioeconomic policy is shaped, that are no longer conducive to realizing the human purposes they were meant to fulfill; indeed, they may be actively working against them. To become effective, the macroeconomic sector will have to define quite different goals.

What GNP Actually Reflects

The central assumption of economics today is the notion of scarcity; it marks the most widely accepted definitions of the discipline, and either tacitly or explicitly underlies its analyses. Its conception of the world as made up of *scarce* rather than *limited* resources is itself the result of the axiomatic (though usually tacit) "postulate of non-satiety," according to which man's material needs are insatiable. If men's material needs were *limited*, then resources would not be *scarce*. A direct consequence of this diagnosis is that "economic growth" becomes necessary to address this condition of insatiability or scarcity. Indeed, a central idea in current thought is that industrial growth, with the increased consumption it enables, reflects an increase in "wealth" which improves social well-being.

GNP, however, does not measure human welfare—not even "wealth," as we shall see. If anything, it is a measure of a society's degree of industrialization: GNP merely measures the *output* and consumption of a society, and by implication its level of techno-economic accumulation required to sustain this output.

The "Qualitative" Dimensions of Welfare

GNP does not reflect a society's welfare because it does not and cannot measure important phenomena.

It does not measure the many forms of production-for-use that lay outside the market and the State. They therefore involve no monetary transactions—such as domestic activities, various forms of useful unemployment (do it yourself building, gardening and so on), as well as many activities and forms of social life (including care of the young, old or sick) that take place during time usually classified as "leisure." These forms of activity still constitute a massive part of people's lives, but remain largely invisible in social and economic analysis due to the lack of appropriate theoretical categories. They can be readily identified in so-called subsistence economies, or in the "domestic" sphere of "reproduction" as opposed to "production." Neither does GNP appropriately account for the natural "capital" that the open environment constitutes, nor does it account for the "nonproductive" accumulation that underlies nonmarket activity in all its forms. The value of these activities has nonetheless become obvious when their erosion requires replacement in the form of commodities and services that have to be paid, and worked for.

At the same time, techno-economic accumulation underlying the GNP generates a variety of *human* costs that range from everyday alienation (in meaningless, depersonalized, or repetitive work often associated with materially-efficient production methods) to unemployment, to the pollution of free time (in traffic jams, stress, and the like), as well as the so-called "erosion of the social fabric." (These "human" costs of industrialization, which in one way or another affect everyone, are not to be confused with the "social" costs of "economic" progress, the poverty, insecurity and inequality that affect mostly the weak in a society). Many of these costs have reached truly alarming levels, but since they are computed in monetary terms the corresponding deterioration in the quality of life associated with high GNP levels goes unmeasured. As with the erosion of the nonmaterial positive aspects of life, increases in these ills engenders the need for replacement commodities.

These two nonmaterial aspects of life (the nonmaterial positive benefits outside of production and consumption, and the human and ecological costs of industrialization) affect human welfare decisively, yet are not reflected in the GNP. They have already been recognized as basic shortcomings, and have led economists of repute, such as Paul Samuelson, to attempt to factor them into calculations of welfare. But the fact that these nonmaterial features are qualitative in nature, or at least cashless, renders such attempts at quantification at best dubious. In any case, they have singly failed to generate clear alternatives to reorient action.

Social Duality

A second key problem with GNP, one that has often been denounced, is that it tells us nothing about the distribution of useful output. It is obvious, however, that increasing material output is irrelevant for the majority (and hence to society as a whole) if it is not well distributed. For the existing form of techno-economic accumulation (the level of industrialization) seems to result in a high degree of *socioeconomic* accumulation, with the concomitant perpetuation of poverty, marginalization, and exclusion which beset the losers in the process. The incapacity of most governments during the past fifteen years—even many with socialist sensibilities—to reverse the widening gap between rich and poor, strongly suggests that exclusion and impoverishment are positively correlated with economic growth.[13] At any rate, this explains why the recurrent calls for "economic development with social justice," or "ethics in economics," usually end up as empty rhetoric as did the call for "full employment."

The social-democratic experience has long suggested that growth in output is compatible with social redistribution mechanisms. But with the erosion of the Welfare State, widely distributed growth in output increasingly appears as a geopolitically—and historically—circumscribed exception. Indeed, much impressionistic evidence indicates that harmoniously distributed economic growth is the exception rather than the rule, given the accompanying social costs: people losing their jobs precisely when more competitive enterprises displace the less productive ones, be it at a national or international level; when automation and restructuring result in massive layoffs; when peasants are expelled from their lands as agro-industry takes over, etc. As unemployment worsens, as it has over the past twenty years, wages are subject to downward pressure. And what has now been happening for years will become more intense in the years to come: nowadays, virtually all governments are chanting, almost in chorus, the imperative of international competitiveness as a key to ensure continued economic growth. Indeed, this probably will lead to increased productivity and output. But we all know that in practice competitiveness translates as more layoffs in the name of efficiency, as further reductions in wages, as continued erosion of social security mechanisms—all of which will accentuate unemployment and poverty. In short, the majority of the population has to get poorer in order to become richer.

Growth is not only irrelevant but positively harmful if it concentrates economic power in such a way as to engender exclusion or pauperization. There is much evidence to show that the gap between rich and poor widens not only because the "winners" in the system become wealthier without the poor also benefiting from the overall increase in wealth, but also because conditions worsen for the poor within growing economies, as has been documented in numerous cases, thus characterizing the modernization of poverty. For instance a series of major studies for the International Labour Organization have documented how, in the seven South Asian countries comprise seventy percent of the rural population of the nonsocialist underdeveloped world, the rural poor have become worse off than they were ten to twenty years ago. The conclusion is that "the increase in poverty has been associated not with a fall but with a rise in cereal production per head, the main component of the diet of the poor."[14]

Overall, societies have instituted economic apartheid. On the one hand there is a publicly protected, sustained, and controlled sector, including professional and industrial production directly subsidized or indirectly supported by the State, unionized labour, and legally enshrined practices of restrictive corporatism; on the other, there is the formless mass of those in the excluded, low-paid sector, working long hours in precarious situations, in meaningless jobs, and often in deplorable conditions. We are not here speaking of a society with an "elite" and a "base"—such as there has always been and will always be—but of social organization based on a fabulous concentration of resources that excludes and dispossesses a major portion of the population, which makes insecurity, marginalization and poverty systemic.

Waste

There is, however, a critical distortion in GNP that remains unrecognized theoretically. Insofar as high levels of output have to be sustained by central policies, and insofar as these distort spontaneous flows in the allocation of resources away from people's preferences, the situation constitutes artificial production. But this is just another name for waste. It is patently obvious in the string of failed megaprojects and white elephants scattered all over the third world, but it is equally widespread in less visible projects and production systems that only survive thanks to the artificial (yet indirect and thus invisible) support of public policy. Although recorded as wealth (since it is part of GNP), this "output" merely constitutes useless expenditures of human energy and natural resources, with the consequent erosion of welfare through the imposition of useless work.[15] The waste implicit in artificially sustained production (or to be more precise, heteronomously defined consumption) leads to overall dilution of hourly wages,[16] and consequently to a need for harder and longer work to make ends meet.

The long-term result of GNP growth, therefore, may well be increased "family income." But at the same time it increases the *cost* of living through four mechanisms. First, by eroding various cashless sources of well-being it generates needs for commodities to compensate for the loss of nonmaterial sources of welfare, and thus institutes dependency on money (the intensifying monetization of land raises its price, rendering housing increasingly dear; daily commutes are lengthened as megalopolises destroy neighborhoods, or as employment increasingly replaces subsistence livelihoods; babysitters replace family or community care of the young). Second, by secreting various qualitative disvalues, it generates expenses required to redress disruptions caused by industrialization (pollution cleanup costs, psychiatrists to deal with stress, medical costs of environmentally or work-induced ills, social workers to deal with the erosion of the social fabric, etc.). Of course, destruction of positive use-values and the secretion of negative disvalues are never fully replaced by corresponding commodities; and to this extent GNP growth causes deterioration of welfare. Third, in as much as an industrial-intensive society polarizes income levels by concentrating wealth, it is irrelevant for a majority of the population, even actually deleterious, if it replaces the frugality of subsistence routines with the misery and destitution of modernized poverty. Fourth, it sustains production artificially, thus producing useless output and waste.

All of these side effects of economic growth are assuredly a source of scarcity: at a certain level of output, growth starts bringing diminishing returns in terms of human welfare; beyond its optimum point (which will vary according to the geographical and cultural context), it generates increasing *dis*returns, thus secreting more and more of the problems that it was supposed to address in the first place. As scarcity thus spreads, the founding assumption of economic thought becomes reality. It is, however, but a self-fulfilling prophecy.

GNP does not reflect the amount of wealth, and even less of welfare, in a society: it reflects its level of industrialization, together with all of its concomitant problems and distortions.

REALIGNMENTS OF SOCIAL THOUGHT

The State of Intellectual Affairs

Since the collapse of the post-Keynesian consensus, the principles of marginal utility theory (which forms the theoretical basis of the price mechanism through the interplay of supply and demand) still constitute the most cogent diagnosis of the optimal allocation of resources, and, intellectually, the most elegant, given its simplicity, coherence, and comprehensiveness. Whence comes the widespread acceptance of "the market," which now seems solidly established, both politically and theoretically, despite its patent inadequacies and the numerous doubts it raises. Indeed, more than mere intellectual fashion, the principle of economic "self-regulation" implicit in marginal utility theory may well prove to be *the* lasting legacy of modern economics. And as we shall see, this principle has to be taken much more seriously than it has been so far by economists of both the Right and the Left.

But however essential the self-regulated allocation of resources may be as a *component* of a postmodern economic paradigm, the idea of making "the market" the central if not indeed the only organizing principle of social organization, one which subordinates if not excludes other social practices, is highly questionable. It seems at best inadequate, in practice politically difficult, and at worst dangerous. Indeed, its operational prescript—the minimalist State coordinating market relations—has proved ineffective, as the legacy of the Thatcherite experience, which applied it most thoroughly, has by now made clear: one out of two Britons now considers their situation so bad that they declared in a poll that they would emigrate if they could.[17] Not surprisingly, in practice most governments have, on the contrary, maintained active if discreet, or highly indirect State interventionist policies, even many who indulged in the most fiery free-market rhetoric. The best example is, of course, the Republican administration in the United States that quadrupled the fiscal deficit.

The point here is that the theory which informs the decisions ruling modern social organization is still centered on, and limited to, the market's "invisible hand," despite the central role played by the State in the economy as is amply corroborated by historical experience. This is one of Karl Polanyi's key insights: the indispensable intervention of the State in creating and sustaining markets. One example is the social democratic experience which marked Europe's achievements after World War Two. A more recent and clear case are the recipes behind the East Asian economic miracle, which have been outlined in one of the most methodical studies on the subject carried out by the World Bank.[18] It reveals beyond any shadow of a doubt the central role of State intervention in policies that were either irrelevant to market regulation (though not in contradiction with it), such as land reform in Taiwan, or in direct contradiction with the abstract recipes of market-driven allocation of resources. These latter policies included judicious investment in education, systematic "encouraging" of personal savings (for instance by compulsory retirement plans); selective import tariffs designed to promote importation of capital goods on the one hand, and, on the other, to discourage imports in order to protect domestic producers and to give credit subsidies to certain industries in order to promote exports through subsidy programs, and other policies. That they did not adopt the rampant deficit spending of Keynesian demand management, but rather smaller deficits devoted to investment, does not mean that State intervention was any less systematic.

Even the policies of "structural adjustment," thrust by the World Bank and the International Monetary Fund (IMF) onto Latin American and other countries as a response to the international debt crisis, was a *managed* solution, one far from being the operation of market self-regulation. Though State intervention was compressed into areas of social redistribution—including education, health and other policies—the State was obliged to assume responsibility for private failures, socializing the risk costs of industrialization ventures gone sour, and thereby instituting *negative* (albeit indirect) *redistribution*. Even though the State opened its borders to imports, what remained of central policy was reoriented to foster exports. Thus, State intervention was not diminished but simply redesigned in order to generate the hard currency needed to repay foreign debt.

The fact that the role of the State in modern society is often indirect and limited to the "commanding heights" of an operationally decentralized organization does not in any way diminish its massive impact. Indeed, the truly invisible hand in modern social organization is the State. In other words, although State intervention not the market is the central economic fact in contemporary societies, economics offers little or no theory to rationalize this practice based on political or empirical responses that, furthermore, often contradict the prescripts of the market-regulated society. The "market" cannot deal with parks or the environment, for example, any more than collective management can effectively address issues of personal consumption. Not only is marginal utility theory unable to address the residual problem of the public infrastructure and other "externalities" which distort the full operation of the price mechanism, it also has nothing to say about economic redistribution, still less about the articulation of market relations with these other aspects of social organization. Supply and demand theory is coherent and effective for matters involving private exchange (and these cover many more aspects than even liberal[19] thought now recognizes). But its partial perspective becomes decidedly harmful when raised to the level of a totalizing analysis. For it can only prescribe an expansion of market relations, thus minimizing other valid and necessary forms of social and economic relations.

Recent Revisions Within Economics

As we have seen, if there is little in economic theory which represents a clear *principle* for orienting "State intervention" in practice, there is one overriding *goal* that has fulfilled this guiding role: "economic growth." The centrality of this notion is difficult to overstate. Since Keynesian theory constructed the categories which underlie it, the accretion of GNP is taken to represent an improvement in the overall "standard of living," and to foster "job creation"; it is taken as an indicator of society's wealth, one which helps shape policy and arbitrates between a variety of often conflicting goals. Inherited from Keynes' concept of aggregate demand, growth was supposed to ensure economic equilibrium, defined as zero unemployment and inflation.

As we know, these have been the two residual problems of economics. Though fairly secondary and relative to other great achievements of economic science, they have been utterly resistant to resolution (i.e., to *simultaneous* resolution, for one can always be minimized at the expense of another). For this reason they are especially significant, indeed so important that Nobel laureate Paul Samuelson has deemed the mere clarification of appropriate categories for addressing the problem of unemployment sufficient to warrant the Nobel prize.

The persistence and aggravation of unemployment is one of the clearest signs that a change in "paradigm" is required. It has all the traits of that special type of residual problem which cannot be resolved by simply fine-tuning the theoretical system and its consequent policy prescriptions. The history of science is replete with such relatively secondary issues left unresolved by existing theory, whose solutions may have required a complete overhaul of current analysis.[20]

Some mainstream economists have indeed recognized the need for a "paradigm shift."[21] However, few have questioned the basic assumption of GNP growth, which now constitutes the organizing idea in economics. The discipline remains essentially within the same framework progressively constructed over the last two hundred years, first tacitly, and then explicitly since Keynes. But economic growth appears increasingly irrelevant, given the ecological constraints and diminishing "social returns" of industrial expansion. Much contemporary theory which centres around it is thus pointless: just as in basic logic a wrong premise invalidates the conclusions of otherwise impeccable reasoning. Sophisticated econometric models, statistical cost analyses, or studies of tax incidences are irrelevant if the basic goals they aim at do not lead to the overall purposes they are meant to fulfill.

This has become clear to other "alternative" economists, who are explicitly searching for a "new economics," one free from the assumption of "economic growth."[22] Their ideas are so far at the stage of criticism, thereby laying the groundwork for a coherent alternative. But they remain generally inchoate, especially since they have proved incapable of defining alternative goals able to replace GNP as a guide to policy action. Much effort has gone into devising such a revision. The attempts range from Paul Samuelson's calculation of "net economic welfare" (NEW)—computed by factoring into GNP modern "disamenities" associated with it (which are subtracted), and the value of "leisure" (which is added)[23]—to various human development indicators designed to compute welfare by weighing various social considerations,[24] to other attempts to scientifically define and measure people's "basic needs" in order to legitimize, orient and consolidate social spending[25] and, more recently, to "purchasing power parities" (PPP) for international income comparisons that amend GNP figures by means of cost of living differences, rather than uniform dollar-based standards.

These measures, however, remain open to theoretical challenge, and, in any case, lead to divergent and often contradictory prescriptions for action. They are of little practical use. What is significant is the proven challenge they pose to the unifying concept in present thought, for it reveals the radical nature of the revision underway. At the same time, the multiplicity and divergence of the various attempts at correction expose the confusion which exists in the goals of social organization.

The rejection of such alternatives by many mainstream economists stems partly from their well-founded intellectual rigour that refuses to allow value judgements or vague theory to weaken scholarly analysis. On the other hand, the prevailing notion that GNP is itself free from value judgements—which marginal utility theory at least avoids—reveals a similar rigour, one blind to its own consumerist assumptions about social organization. This continued practical reliance on a recognizably ineffective measure reflects the existence of a serious theoretical void, though it is understandable enough given the lack of a coherent alternative. But intellectual attachment to such an inadequate measuring device expresses only too well unthinking resistance on the part of conventional doctrine.

NOTES

1. Indeed, even amid the current enthusiasm about Asia's economic growth, anticipation of vast social and environmental erosion attendant upon its modernization are already raising doubts about its prospects; cf. *State of Urbanization in Asia and the Pacific* (New York: United Nations, October 1993), or J. Decornoy, "Demain, 2,4 milliards d Asiatiques en ville. Un bouleversement humain sans précédent," *Le monde diplomatique* (December 1993).
2. Data from the United Nation's monthly statistical bulletins, reproduced in *La Presse* (Montréal) (September 11, 1993).
3. "La Crise," *Le Monde des débats* (October 1993).
4. Data from the OECD reported in *The Globe and Mail* (Toronto) (June 17, 1994).
5. "Jobs in the Age of Insecurity," *Time* (November 22, 1993); "Les statisticiens mesurent mal les rapports entre le chômage et l emploi," *Le Monde* (February 13, 1992); "Hardships the Job Numbers Miss," *New York Times* (January 8, 1992). For a more extended discussion of the problem in the

case of France see O. Marchand et al., *Économie et statistiques*, 249 (December 1991).

6. "And now the Good News On the Economy," *Wall Street Journal* (April 12, 1993). See introduction and note 2 above.

7. "The Price of Progress. 'Re-engineering' Gives Firms New Efficiency, Workers the Pink Slip," *Wall Street Journal* (Europe) (March 19-20, 1993); for the impact of re-engineering in Germany see H. Henzler and L. Spath, *Sind die Deutschen noch zu retten?* (Munich: Bertelsmann, 1993) as cited in Bernard Cassen, "Impérative transition vers une société du temps libéré," *Le monde diplomatique* (November, 1994), p. 24.

8. "L économie va bien mais les canadiens appauvrissent," *Le Devoir* (Montréal) (April 21, 1988).

9. "Family Life: not enough money, too much stress—Tough times: Even two-income families are being stretched to the breaking point by the mounting economic pressures of the 1990s," *The Globe and Mail* (January 3, 1992); also: "The Incredible, Shrinking Middle Class," *The Globe and Mail* (July 31, 1993).

10. "The Rat Race," *Time* (April 24, 1989).

11. Jean Chesneaux, *Modernité-monde* (Paris: La Découverte, 1989), p.64. See Serge Latouche, *La planète des naufragés, essai sur l après développement* (Paris: La Découverte, 1991).

12. See A. de Romaña, "Post-Crisis Equilibrium: Economic Implications of Human Welfare and Ecological Sustainability," *Interculture* (Montréal) XXII, nos. 3 & 4 (December 1989).

13. Frances Moore Lappé and Joseph Collins, *Food First* (London: Abacus, 1982), p. 113. Cf. Gustavo Esteva:

> Twelve years ago we were impressed by the insights of Paul Streeten [at the World Bank], who had examined experiences of development all around the world and come to the conclusion that it was the success of development strategies, not their failure, that created hunger and misery everywhere. Two years ago we felt our views fully endorsed when we read a statement by Edward Goldsmith, in which he summed up M. Redclift's and J. Porrit's analysis: 'Environmental degradation in the third world is thus the inevitable consequence of present development policies, and third world people are poor not, as one might think, because they are "underdeveloped," but because they have been impoverished by previous development, because they have been robbed by developers of their means of sustenance.'

Cited in "Alternatives to Economics," Don Cole, ed., *Macroeconomics 1989:90* (Guilford: Dushkin Publishing Group, 1989); originally published in *TOES/NA Newsletter* (The Other Economic Summit), 1, no. 3 (1988).

As Esteva recounts it, Streeten's observations later evolved into an alternative development strategy structured around the "basic needs approach" proposed by the World Bank. Peasants reluctantly adopted it, and for three years it was a brilliant economic success. However, because the strategy

> contributed to the dissolution of the peasants traditional routines of subsistence" and "reinforced economic [i.e., market] linkages in the food chain, dependency and scarcity were created...This 'needs oriented' economic policy transmogrified our sustenance activities into [another form of] 'need satisfaction' and the 'production of commodities'...[and eventually] created more hunger, deprivation and scarcity.

After seeing the systematic inadequacy of various "development alternatives," he regrets that "We seem doomed to a theoretical and political limbo."

14. GNP actually measures output and *investment* which is deferred consumption (for it eventually leads to higher output). But this output, and hence the investment that allows it, is useful only insofar as it satisfies spontaneous desires for consumption; if it requires central policy support it constitutes investment for its own sake, divorced from any social utility. It is like building useless factories or infrastructure and sacrificing peoples' consumption, or forcing them to work more: means turn into socially mutilating ends-in-themselves.

15. What is already observable in terms of real (inflation-corrected) income and of disposable (after tax) income, is especially acute when one takes into account not only actually remunerated time, but also the unpaid work associated with employment or access to it. This "shadow work" is linked to the externalities of the economic system (such as increased commuting time, or the time and cost of acquiring the skills and education needed to run increasingly complex technologies, getting a job, etc.).

16. "Britain: Isle of Despair," *Time* (March 15, 1993).

17. *The East Asian Miracle: Economic Growth and Public Policy* (New York: World Bank/Oxford University Press, September 1993).

18. I use the word "liberal" in its European and Latin sense of free-market oriented (as opposed to "socialist"), not in its North American sense of "progressive" (as opposed to "conservative").

19. How certain residual problems can lead to major theoretical overhauls is well illustrated by the changes that physics underwent since first established. Toward the end of the nineteenth century, physical science seemed to have elucidated the basic laws governing the functioning of nature: there were not only impressive theoretical achievements to prove it, but also massive practical successes. Lord Kelvin proclaimed, quite naturally, the consensus of the time: "physics [was] an essentially harmonious whole, a virtually completed science." There were only two minor questions that had not yet been fully resolved, but the definitive architecture of physics was essentially already there. Now we know that the solution of these two "details" required a complete overhaul of the theoretical bases of physics. The first was to be resolved in the theory of relativity; the second eventually was resolved by the development of quantum mechanics during the first quarter of the century. In order

to account for essentially secondary empirical incongruities, physics had to develop theories based on entirely new principles and structures. See Stéphane Deligeorges, "La catastrophe ultraviolette" in S. Deligeorges, ed., *Le Monde quantique* (Paris: Sciences et Avenir, 1984), pp. 21-29.

20. Cf. *The Crisis in Economic Theory*, edited by Daniel Bell and I. Kristol (New York: Basic Books, 1981), in particular Peter Drucker's introductory overview "Toward the Next Economics"; Also K. Wilber and K.P. Jameson, *An Inquiry into the Poverty of Economics* (Notre Dame, London: University of Notre Dame Press, 1983). For a taste of current theoretical disquisitions on the increasingly confused reference axis of economics, see Amartya Sen et al., in *The Standard of Living*, edited by Geoffrey Hawthorn (Cambridge: Cambridge University Press, 1987), and for a good clarification see Serge Latouche's article in Wolfgang Sachs, ed., *The Development Dictionary: A Guide to Knowledge as Power* (London: Zed Books, 1992).

21. The most cogent articulation I have seen of this challenge has been made by economist Herman Daly in *Toward a Steady-State Economy*. He mentions some U.S. antecedents in the profession: Arguments stressing ecologically sound limits to wealth and population have been made by two past presidents of the American Economic Association. See K. Boulding; Resources for the Future, "The Economics of the Coming Spaceship Earth," in *Environmental Quality in a Growing Economy* (Baltimore: Johns Hopkins, 1966) and Spengler. Some time ago, E. J. Mishan [*The Costs of Economic Growth* (New York: Praeger, 1967)], Tibor Scitovsky and Staffan Linder made penetrating antigrowth arguments. There is also much in Galbraith that is antigrowth. In France, Réné Passet also has dealt with fundamental change in economic science, usually from an epistemological perspective, despite his occasional reference to sustainable growth. See *Une Approche multidisciplinaire de l environnement* (Paris: Economica, 1980). I understand M. Passet has dealt with the same problems in *L'économique et le vivant* (Paris: Payot, 1979).

From a more polemical stance, see *The Living Economy: A New Economics in the Making*, Paul Ekins, ed. (London, New York: Routledge and Kegan Paul, 1986). This is a good collection of papers by members of The Other Economic Summit (TOES), an association of theorists and practitioners that has been countering mainstream ideas during citizen summits held parallel with the G7's yearly meetings. Interested readers may also wish to consult C. Buarque, *The End of Economics? Ethics and the disorder of progress* (London: Zed Press, 1993). Buarque is the University of Brasilia rector. See also M. Lutz and K. Lux, *Humanistic Economics: The New Challenge* (New York: Bootstrap Press, 1988).

22. In the 1950s, Kenneth Boulding was one of the first to note the insufficiencies of GNP, as had Simon Kuznets who attempted to measure the economic welfare of leisure. The first systematic challenge to growth ideology appeared in the late 1960s when E. J. Mishan pointed to the *Costs of Economic Growth* (London: Staples, 1967). William Nordhaus and James Tobin's pioneering study *Is Growth Obsolete?* (New York: National Bureau of Economic Research, Columbia University Press, 1972), attempted to systematize an indicator that would correct several GNP inaccuracies by

defining an alternative measure of economic welfare (MEW). This was later polished by Samuelson as net economic welfare (NEW); and somehow manages to compute the value of leisure (which is added on to GNP) and the cost of modern disamenities such as pollution (which are subtracted from GNP). See Samuelson, *Economics* (New York: McGraw-Hill, 1973), pp. 3-6,195-8; see also Robert Eisner, "The Total Incomes System of Accounts," *Survey of Current Business* (January 1985), pp. 24-48.

23. For a summary and further references to the numerous indicators that have been generated (including an "adjusted national product," health-based indicators, and various social indicators) see "Indicators of Economic Progress" in *The Living Economy*, chap. 2.

24. Although the "basic needs" concept had been used in an isolated fashion in the past, it was erected to the level of an "operational" reference axis for planning at a conference convened in 1975 by the International Labour Organization (and summarized in the document *Employment, Growth and Basic Needs*, published the year after). Paul Streeten and Johan Galtung have since contributed major articulations of the concept. See P. Streeten, *Development Perspectives* (London: Macmillan, 1981), and J. Galtung, "The Basic Needs Approach," in *Human Needs: A Contribution to the Current Debate*, Katrin Lederer et al., eds., (Köningstein: Athaeneum, 1980). For a full discussion of the origins and development of the basic needs concept, or, to be more precise, of the conceptualization of life in terms of needs, see Ivan Illich's essay on the question, in Wolfgang Sachs ed., *The Development Dictionary A Guide to Knowledge as Power* (London: Zed Books, 1992).

25. For instance, the PPP now used by the IMF, does not take into account the decline of international purchasing power (of growing importance in an increasingly interrelated world economy), that results from the deterioration of the terms of trade for less industrialized countries. For a long time, those promoting the "comparative advantages" possible from an international specialization of labour have dismissed the traumatic deterioration of the terms of trade observed during the past few decades as a merely conjunctural problem. They noted that a longer reference period of analysis reveals periods in which the terms of trade actually improved. This argument has closed many a discussion with a call for freer trade and greater reliance on "interdependence." It has been a demonstrable mistake. To know whether improvement is the rule with closer-knit trade and deterioration the exception, or the other way around, one simply has to look at the longest reference period available. A recent study has settled the issue confirming that since 1900 there has been an annual decline in the terms of trade of 0.57 percent for the 33 major non-oil commodities. For the basket of commodities important for development countries the rate was faster, 0.67 yearly, a deterioration which is tremendous when cumulated. See Enzo Grilli and Maw Chew Yang, "Primary Commodity Prices, Manufactured Goods Prices, and the Terms of Trade of Developing Countries: What the Long Run Shows," *World Bank Economic Review* (January 1988), pp. 1-48.

9.

COMMUNITY RELATIONS, INDIVIDUAL, SOCIAL AND ECONOMIC CONSTRAINTS IN THE SAVINGS AND LOANS ASSOCIATIONS: African Examples[1]

Jean-Michel Servet[2]

Informal financial institutions emerge, to a large extent, in opposition to the prevailing economic order.[3] Whether or not they succeed, these institutions are often perceived as undermining the State. Institutions give rise to a variety of noninstitutional social relations and forms of repression. Their activities may be discrete, secret, or visible depending upon the constraints imposed by the formal economy which may mask, repress, or tolerate such informal activities. They may even encourage them if they succeed in improving the standard of living of the population, or deal with certain deficiencies within the institutionalized production of goods and services.

A noninstitutionalized economy is defined by its dominant activities. These will differ according to whether the economy is regulated by the State, a collective, or by the private appropriation of the means of production and exchange; whether there are competitive or monopolistic markets, or national planning of the means of production and exchange; whether labour is executed by wage-earners, a small and independent "traditional" community of production, or through forms of slavery or serfdom; whether these jobs are secured or not for the majority of the labour force; and whether or not jobs provide a sufficient revenue to allow for an adequate standard of living as dictated by the norms of consumption of the society considered. In other words, noninstitutionalized economies differ in "developed" countries—socialist or capitalist—and in "developed" and "developing" countries. Moreover, in "developing" countries, the noninstitutionalized economy differs according to whether the prevailing mode of social organization is Statist, cooperative, or capitalist and, according to the manner in which these modes were historically articulated by different States.

The informal savings practices in sub-Saharan Africa provide the main reference for this article. Despite the variety of constraints and the intensity of practices from one continent to another and between different regions within a given continent, there are sufficient similarities for a useful classification. The types of organizations discussed in this paper are not part of a traditional folklore, but are significant social realities. In fact, twenty or thirty years ago, many societies in sub-Saharan Africa ignored the activities of *tontines* (informal savings practices); today, however, these can no longer be ignored since the money involved in such practices often exceeds that which passes through conventional savings banks.

We will explore the relations between individuals, communities, and the State within these savings associations in the societies of sub-Saharan Africa with a brief analysis of the crisis of formal financial institutions which has led to the emergence of autonomous organizations, in other words, to the development of a *counterState*. This will be followed by a review of various forms of informal savings and the functions of village associations and tontines. Finally, we will show how the mode of integration of individuals into groups, either through village associations or tontines, determines the viability of the organization.

THE CRISIS OF FORMAL SAVINGS INSTITUTIONS

The systems of formal savings in sub-Saharan Africa are limited to the following:
  • Development banks which consist of institutions established

after independence as a way to finance, through foreign credits, the necessary infrastructure to develop the economy;

• Commercial banks similar to those found in developed capitalist economies.

Formal saving institutions are currently in a crisis. This is due to both the general crisis in sub-Saharan economies as well as to the operations and the image of these institutions. The crisis runs deeper than what the bankruptcy of this or that establishment would lead one to believe; the population has vehemently rejected the banking system. Too many reports describe banks and financial institutions from a legal or accounting point of view without questioning their nature and the real impact they have upon local economies. Banks are a typical example of transferable activities. Western countries introduced and reproduced their own banking system to finance their local commercial operations. During the period of decolonization, in spite of the emergence of development banks, financial organizations were not fundamentally restructured. These financial systems remain predominantly linked to the production of agricultural products and other primary commodities, and foreign trade.

Thus, the Western imported model has remained dominant. In fact, the imitation of this model is essential for maintaining the confidence of the international financial community. The banks, therefore, introduce a structure which they perceive as necessary for their proper functioning. However, this constraint imposed from outside does not limit itself to the rules of management; it also imposes a cultural model which extends to architecture, buildings, interior design and a dress code (this is so even if the *boubou* is once again worn by the African bank managers). The air conditioner, even when only a simple ventilator, is an attraction for the client who is waiting to be served. Thus, the bank is a model of acculturation for the ruling and middle classes.

Nonetheless, the situation differs from the time when, in Western societies, banks were reserved for privileged elites. Today, in sub-Saharan Africa, the population perceives a link between financial institutions and the State, regardless of their juridical status, even when their interests are not general but rather particular. In fact, their interests are more commonly linked to an individual, or a group of persons. This association with the State is the source of the massive rejection of banks as well as postal savings; although these latter institutions are more firmly implanted in the communities, they do not adequately respond to the expectations of their potential clientele.

The informal sector, including informal finance, emerges often in opposition to formal institutions. Generally, people turn to formal financial institutions failing any alternative, or to settle some operations which appear, rightly or wrongly, to be linked to State or paraState institutions (e.g., payment of electricity or water bills). Cheques serve as a form of guaranteed deposit in businesses which provide credit to clear settlements at the end of the month. Thus, the financial institutions find themselves isolated even within the middle and upper classes. Minor civil servants who receive their salaries in the form of a bank draft, rush to withdraw their earnings at the beginning of the month; when the State, through a system of notes, does not encourage them to do otherwise. Moreover, small savings are rarely deposited in the postal system. In fact, the failure of both the banks and postal agencies is common. The difficulty in withdrawing one's savings from a postal agency only increases a generalized defiance. This has led to the important use of cash, even substantial amounts. The burden of settling accounts in cash is not only linked to informal or illegal activities, but to the frequency of payments, including legal ones, which require cash and, therefore, do not use the banks as intermediaries.

With the exception of bank loans for the purchase of vehicles (something that can be done informally), which are only possible if there is collateral such as a truck, a taxi, or another registered vehicle, recourse to bank credit by households and enterprises is unusual, or even exceptional for a large segment of the population for the following reasons:

• The complex preparation of a loan request document excludes large numbers of individuals who are often illiterate;

• The precariousness of projects greatly limits the profitability of the banks, when they include the fixed costs to study a file and the impossibility of automatically granting loans except if some of its impact is rediscounted by a public financial establishment, which would either put public financial establishments into precarious situations themselves, or require prohibitively high interest rates;

•Due to the absence of the generally required guarantees requested by formal financial institutions, such as an estate or durable goods, the absence or precarious nature of real estate laws is an obstacle to investments; the impossibility of having a mortgage reduces the possibilities of loans, and the constant threat of default creates an endemic instability which prevents the accumulation of capital in productive micro-enterprises.[4] For the most part, the borrowing entrepreneurs are nonsalaried, their revenues are uncertain, and their limited amount of declared revenues restricts the possibility of a personal loan;

• Finally, the failure of formal institutions to recognize or acknowledge collective practices and popular associations which could constitute a socialized model of credit and the development of a novel mutualist (in the sense of French *mutualiste*) or cooperative system.

Africa's financial crisis does not only manifest itself in the relations between economic agents (households and enterprises) and financial institutions, but also in the financial and economic disintegration of the State, and its incapacity to meet its obligations. Tax collection is only partial (this, in part, stems from the refusal to implement a poll tax, and because a large percentage of activities are informal and are therefore not recorded). Conversely, the State is not capable of responding to the basic needs of the population in terms of health and social protection, training and collective assets. At the same time, as we will point out below, the local and informal collective structures are capable of levying contributions and satisfying some of these fundamental needs through their expenses and investments.[5]

This rejection of the formal financial network injects a dynamism into the informal finance sector in which research institutes and international organizations[6] are increasingly interested. Prior to examining the specific practices of savings associations and tontines, it is important to locate these within the larger context of existing informal saving practices.

GENERAL OVERVIEW OF SAVINGS AND THE OPERATIONS OF VILLAGE ASSOCIATIONS AND *TONTINES*

Methods of Saving

Saving is not only monetary.[7] It can, on the one hand, refer to a form of saving-investment that materializes in the construction of a house, the purchase of cattle, loincloth, food supplies, etc.[8] On the other hand, it may also refer to a series of personal or collective gifts (notably dowries, and other gifts at funerals or births, etc.) which are also claims[9] since they assume subsequent countergifts (directly from those who have receive these gifts, or individuals and groups in similar circumstances). These gifts and countergifts may be monetized in which case coins and notes become *special purpose money*.[10]

Monetized informal savings may assume different forms: various types of hoarding,[11] or personal deposits. A deposit may be given either to a person who inspires great confidence, usually a parent or elder, such as a local political or religious authority (imam, chief, priest, etc.); a friend whose economic situation is stable; or to a "mobile banker," who periodically or irregularly collects small sums of money in a district, thereby providing security for the saver;[12] or with a shopkeeper who simultaneously extends loans[13] backed by inventory and relative economic stability.[14]

Finally, at the junction between individual and collective types of saving, there are village associations and multiple types of rotating savings and loans, generally known as *tontines*. These modes of savings are informal since the rules, which the members of a tontine must obey, are formulated by the group itself, and are administered by "customary" jurists who are not recognized jurists. As well, the internal operations of the group take place without the creation of titled claims to legally support its operations.

The financial system is not dualistic. While it is true that a large proportion of the population is excluded from participating in formal financial institutions due to low or irregular revenues, a minority who do have access to these institutions without any difficulty (e.g., bank employees) also take part in informal financial activities. In fact, an individual may make some deposits with a shopkeeper, take part in a tontine, contribute to a village association, and even regularly deposit money in bank, not necessarily to obtain the largest return on savings, but rather as a means of risk diversification.[15]

It is not meaningful to speak of competition between informal practices and the formal system, since in order to have substitutability and the market (the necessary conditions for competition to take place) economic agents would clearly select between alternative organizations, institutions, or practices. Should informal practices be prohibited, they would have recourse to formal institutions. Since these two conditions are not fulfilled, formal and informal practices are largely complementary.

Before we focus more specifically on associational and tontine savings, it should be noted that we have considered only those forms of savings which require a prior deposit. However, savings may also result from previous debt (as is the case in a savings group which receives the first sums of collected money and must then reimburse those who provided the initial advance).

The terms and conditions of loans in sub-Saharan Africa are as multiple, diverse and complex as are the methods of savings. Some, as mentioned earlier, are as simple as an advance without interest given by shopkeepers as a method of insuring the loyalty of their clientele; others are usurious loans which are sometimes referred to as *damned loans* as a result of Islam's prohibition on loans with interest.[16] In fact, very often, the interest is hidden. Linguistic categories do not permit the differentiation between profit (the gain) and the deficit (the loss) through the operations of immediate buying and reselling, the monop- olization of commerce, or traditional relations of dependence, etc. Thus, the practices of savings-deposits have been the subject of multi- ple investigations in the last few years (which have allowed, after a defining phase, for the accumulation of quantifiable data to measure these phenomena); however, the loan mechanisms still remain rela- tively unknown. Knowledge of the methods of indebtedness remains difficult to obtain; this is more hidden or secretive than savings. Local dialects generally have one term which refers simultaneously to both debt and the rope which ties the cattle; indebtedness is considered a source of servitude. Among the diverse forms of informal saving, many are not part of a convivial social life as the large number of studies on tontines and associations would imply.

Village Associations

Village associations bring together people who are identified with the same village, regardless of their place of birth and where they presently live. Each association unites immigrants throughout the diaspora: in the chief district of the region, in local poles of emigra- tion, in the capital, and in many foreign metropoles. Each village has a number of associations which distinguishes between women, men, youth and seniors. These village associations are born out of local initiatives which are not to be confused with the local organizations imposed by the authorities as part of a framework of the politics of cooperative development.[17]

These village associations[18] represent the original modes of collective savings; they periodically collect contributions from their members. This is rarely more than 10,000 CFA[19] from each member per year, and is accumulated through graduated payments which take into account the economic status of the contributing member (for example, émigré members who benefit from regular and higher revenues are expected to contribute larger sums). The amount held by the associations may also be increased by the earnings from the agricultural activity of particular members.

One can speak of collective savings only when collective payments and individual contributions are held in common accounts. The funds are generally collected during meetings; the contribution for each member is generally relatively low. However, the number of members results in the collection of rather large sums relative to the average revenue of these populations (these may be greater than one million francs).[20]

By belonging and contributing to one of these organizations, the individual receives a certain number of benefits, such as the periodic celebrations to commemorate the group, or individual entitlements, such as personal benefits in the case of death, disease, accident, etc. (at which point the savings become a type of mutual insurance). These associations may also finance assets for the community (clinics, maternity wards, place of worship, schools, wells, small irrigation damns, etc.)[21] with the support of Nongovernmental Organizations (NGOs).[22]

Tontines

There exists countless local terms to define the many diverse savings groups to which individuals periodically contribute a predetermined fixed sum, and receive in return the proceeds from contributions of all participating members. Terms such as "tontines" are widely used, or one may hear more local expressions known to a limited number of individuals belonging to a confined social milieu to refer to these practices. In fact, it is impossible to compile an exhaustive inventory of the known types of tontines. Some tontines emerge and develop with the monetization and materialization of the societies (which does not preclude tontines paid in kind). Their forms may also reflect the sociological characteristics of its members. Thus the great flexibility of this type of organization.

A certain number of common features can, however, be identified.[23] Tontines are generally established in urban centres, rarely in rural areas. Tontines may consist of only men, only women, or be mixed. The number of members is extremely variable: five, seven, twenty, thirty, five hundred, or more. The amounts collected begin at a few hundred CFA in tontines found in schools, to several million CFA in the tontines of well-off entrepreneurs, especially among the Bamiléké in the Cameroons. The stakes for each member are either the same, or may differ according to one's ability to contribute if the number of an individual's shares varies. The commitment of members in a tontine may be made verbally or in writing, and the sanctions in terms of delays, nonrepayment, etc., are extremely variable. Members may draw their turn periodically or make requests which are evaluated and settled later by agreement.

It is, therefore, possible to classify tontines by several criteria which do not overlap. The distinction most often made between mutual, commercial and financial tontines is the classification developed by Michel Lelart:

- In a mutual tontine, each participant receives as much as he contributes;
- In a commercial tontine, the organizer (the *tontinier*, the *garde-monnaie*) is remunerated[24] either by witholding the first payment made at each cycle of the tontine or as a percentage of the sum given periodically to each member;
- In the financial tontines, the lot is auctioned.[25]

Another distinction may be made between associative tontines (in which the principles of mutual help and social organization play a key role, or in cases in which there is a purchase of common property) and those tontines in which financial objectives dominate. The terms of membership and the operations of the group will determine whether a tontine is communitarian or, in contrast, simply a variant of financial individualism. Still, the difference between mutual, commercial and financial tontines does not necessarily correspond to this distinction, since the meetings of some financial tontines are the occasions for communal meals and festivities for its members, while many mutual-type tontines actually ignore these practices.[26]

A third distinction may be made between closed tontines in which all the members know each other, and impersonal or open tontines in which the number of members and/or the organizers allow for the anonymity of the participants. In the latter, the authority of the leader provides the guarantee played by the personal relations in a closed tontine.[27]

A fourth distinction may be made between permanent and lasting tontines, seasonal tontines, and single-cycle tontines. A fifth distinction may be established between neighbourhood or village tontine*s*. The latter are neighbourly relations between individuals[28] and professional tontine*s* formed by a group of workers from the same enterprise or the same service-type job, street vendors, or marketplace tontines.[29]

Tontines are, for a large percentage of the population, a source of lending for consumption or a sensible way to finance operating capital for small businesses. The vendor, who generally combines capital and revenue[30] and gives up a fraction of his returns to a *tontinier*, may in this way, periodically dispose of the necessary funds to replenish his stock. However, the hope that tontines would be able to finance capital accumulation in productive enterprises or to accumulate sufficient start-up capital for business is without foundation. Except for those tontines in which the members already have the necessary means to invest significant sums of money in several tontines, the viability of a tontine opposes such risks. Still, the real cost of credit, if the difficulties to obtain a loan from a formal institution are considered, is diminished by the existence of tontines.

THE INDIVIDUAL, COMMUNITY, AND SAVINGS

Several negative reasons for the emergence of informal savings mechanisms have been outlined so far: they develop in response to deficiencies within formal institutions caused not only by the inability of these institutions to adapt to the population's material constraints, but also due to their culture. To fully understand the success of the terms and conditions of savings in associations and tontines, one needs but examine the positive reasons for their development and the mechanisms they employ to avoid the State, and to become an effective collective mechanism without the State. There are several reasons for this which are grounded as much in the particular interests of the individuals who are satisfied to become a member, as in their capacity to integrate individuals in a group on a voluntary and reciprocal basis. In these cases, not only are the social and economic spheres inseparable, but the economic logic relies heavily upon the social. Their dynamic rests very strictly upon the dialectic between the individual and society.

The Economy Embedded in the Social

For village associations, a financial function is one among the many they fulfill. These associations represent, including for those who participate in them, a space for ethnic and cultural solidarity. The activity of accumulating savings for future collective consumption during festivities, or as insurance in cases of disease or death, or as an investment in the village's assets, are all part of a distinct sociocultural identity. The economic aspect is, therefore, embedded in social functions.[31]

In the constitution of a tontine, the economic-financial ends are first and foremost; however, even if the economic aspects are of primary importance, they are not independent of other social functions. To participate in a tontine, may also involve sharing a moment of intimacy between partners which requires a certain degree of trust; in other words, it means to exist socially. In some tontines, altering the sequence of borrowing so as to respond to the immediate needs of individuals in sudden cases of mourning or disease, represents principles of mutual insurance which are embedded in these practices. Members of such a tontine will recall for years the participants, their terms of participation, significant events etc. This is even more pronounced when a meal is part of the reunions.[32] For the tontines between emigrants, it is as much a way to remain in contact with their country of origin as it is a means to integrate into a new society. Even if there exists an important difference between a tontine and an association (since the former is defined by free association whereas the latter requires that all individuals who share a common heritage join), the two types of organizations are, nonetheless, based on alliances and reciprocity, and are distinct from family relations.

Associations and Tontines Reproduce Mechanisms of Mutual Help and Social Traditions

Village associations are able to reproduce the old community through the rights and obligations of their members,[33] even in new spatial settings following migration. This reproduction is simultaneously made easier by revenues earned outside the villagers' activities, and made more difficult through the intergenerational loss of their members who no longer identify with the community. Some scorn the moral sanctions associated with funerals since they are far from their ancestral land, and, therefore, refuse to acknowledge the threats of witchcraft, for example, which weigh upon those who distance themselves from the group. They refuse all or part of their obligations towards their community of origin, which include the personal transfer of revenues to the town or village, aid, and shelter to temporary migrants, participation in rituals and ceremonies, etc., and simultaneously renounce their access to community lands including their own burial sites.

The accumulated wealth of the associations allows the community to maintain a presence both externally and internally: periodic festivities encourage a feeling of belonging to a group; the protection of members contributes to a communal solidarity in cases of individual or familial misfortune, and to accumulating collective investments in a new system of production and exchange. This solidarity requires the renewal of shared memories of hunting, fishing, or communal land clearing.

The tontines may also recall former old social relations. Some societies developed rotating systems of savings and loans before others. Emigration has played a significant role in spreading these practices.[34] However, this presupposes that the ideological and social conditions of acculturation exist.

Certain traces of the origin of tontines may be found in "cultural societies"; these are groups of neighbours or individuals of the same age who help each other plough, weed, and harvest. As in the case of the tontines, these groups consist of various members; an individual may belong to several "societies." In this way, women from certain neighbourhoods or villages form groups to prepare meals. In certain African societies, one finds the establishment of some tontines as a way to anticipate future funerals, weddings or baptisms. The market places found in Nigeria, Cameroon, and Benin, etc., were first developed for monetary purposes. However, even in these contexts, communal obligation and responsibility explain the various networks of small vendors.

In contrast with modern Western conceptions, to accumulate goods or money in banking accounts or savings is not only perceived as behavior which makes no sense, but it is criticized, since true accumulation in these societies is achieved through gifts, that is, through mediation with others. The accumulation of claims, however diversified (including the potlatch) within a large group, is considered a more efficient manner to accumulate savings. Associative and tontine-type savings must, however, be analyzed within the context of a collectivity. In the same way that it is wrong to assume that modern monetization of societies automatically gives rise to formally institutionalized savings, it is also erroneous to assume that individuals spontaneously subscribe to these methods of saving. The tontines and associations, by combining reciprocal debts and claims, may serve to mediate between the forces of individualism in societies which are organized both by markets and exchange, and by tradition.

The Individual/Community Relations Differ in Associations and Tontines

Although these associations pool savings, the tontines also respond to a desire to accumulate personal savings. Participants in a tontine often state their preference to have their turn last. Using purely financial logic, this constitutes a missed opportunity. In the African context of large family solidarity (in which some see the emergence of numerous parasites due to persistent unemployment), the tontines are an efficient way to accumulate savings. A worker, a store-owner, or an artisan cannot refuse to help a family member who asks for help if he has the means to do so. The many commitments undertaken in one or more tontines, reduces the available revenue. In some ways, therefore, the practice of tontines violates a communal spirit of mutual aid.

Still, the tontines, can only function through a collective logic. In fact, the tontine transforms the individual constraints of saving into one which is collective. This explains, for example, the low level of importance given to the issue of nonrepayments. The individual who receives a loan from the tontine pledges his word. If the debtor does not repay his debt, he will be ostracized by his society. This obligation of returning the money to avoid social disgrace is usually more powerful than any other juridical sanction. As well, the individual is aware that he must regularly conform to the obligations he incurred when becoming a member of a tontine in order to be admitted in other tontines.

The guarantee which the tontine provides is based precisely on the underlying coherence of overall debts and claims. Saving is not an individual act that weighs calculations of risk and remuneration over time.[35] Nor does it represent calculation of present and future benefit. Rather, the tontine is bound by trust and community or, in other words, in social relations that define the reciprocal obligations of the tontine. The organizer of a tontine may often assume the place of a defaulter, even if it means that he will have to be reimbursed by the actual defaulting member in the end, and rely, in some cases, on the police and on tribunals. In such a case, direct group pressure, where all members are supposedly equal, is substituted by the leader of a hierarchical organization. Hence, the articulation between the efficiency of game-play and the logic of economic individualism is found: it is up to the organizer of the tontine to oversee its good performance. He must, therefore, demonstrate his power and strength by his capacity to be reimbursed. Thus, regardless of the constraints, group mediation[36] is a necessary condition to materialize savings.

It may be tempting to historically rank village associations and tontines by considering that the former are residues of community, and the latter, a stage in the development of society (F. Tönnies, Max Weber), or to present these as the evolution from status to contract (Henry Summer Maine).[37] However, such analysis is inadequate. The historical illusion emerges in part from the fact that the associations operate on the basis of nonmarket principles that were largely inherited from previous links to communities (the rights and obligations of birth), while the tontines were founded upon market principles (each receives in proportion to what he has contributed). In the historical ordering of community/market, the mistake is as much the result of overlooking the relations between individuals in the old communities as it is the neglect of community relations which exist in societies dominated by the market. These relations may be inherited. They may also indeed be indispensable to the functioning of the market economy by serving as the source for the reemergence of former social relations:

  • First of all, the associations, far from being simple residual elements, constitute dynamic and modern relations of the reproduction of groups. The pressure imposed by the younger generation (due to emigration and a high participation rate) contests the traditional gerontocracy and introduces new democratic models to the villages;
  • Moreover, as noted above, precolonial African societies were aware of the interindividual relations outside their community structures (cultural societies) on which the phenomena of tontines were able to emerge;
  • Finally, we have shown that the success of the tontines is the result of community relations.

Thus, the member of a tontine is not an individual *out of this world*, an individual marginalized from the social network. The modern individualism developed by the tontines is not in direct opposition to the community, but rather is supported by it; it is a continuation of community. However, as a result of the individual consumption and accumulation which results from tontines, the conditions for the destruction of community relations are also present.

Associations and tontines appear, both in the public and private spheres, as forms of social collective innovation within the interstices of the postcolonial State: almost as a counterState. In the context of the crisis of the State, certain third world societies have created new social relations capable of anticipating unknown modes of development and supporting alternative social lifestyles, which may not only help the South to develop semi-formal systems, but may also assist the North in developing new links of financial solidarity between excluded populations.

NOTES

1. This contribution is based upon reflections on the mobilization of savings in developing countries at the Lumière-Lyon 2 University since the early 1980s. (Please see *Cahier monnaie et financement* 19); fieldwork carried out by the CNRS (Paris), "Écologie des communautés villageoises" (Gisèle Ducos director); and the collective work of the *Financement de l'entrepreunariat et mobilisation de l'épargne* network at the Université des Réseaux d' Expression Française/AUPELF, coordinated by Michel Lelart and B. Ponson. Please see M. Lelart, ed., *La Tontine* (London/Paris: Libbey Eurotext, 1990). This paper, presented at the Third International Karl Polanyi Conference, further develops arguments which were first debated at a session entitled "Le développement en question," Thomas More Centre, March 24-25, 1990, co-hosted by Daniel Dufourt, Pierre Dockès, Philippe Hugon, Jean-Jacques Pérennes, and Denis Requier-Desjardins). It was also presented at a conference held within the context of an applied economics seminar at the HEC-Montréal on April 11, 1990. We thank the participants at this session and at the conference for their questions and suggestions.
2. Translated from the original French version by Ann-Marie Field and Marguerite Mendell.
3. Despite the limitations of this term, the word "informal" is used throughout this text for purposes of linguistic convenience.
4. The surplus is used for ostentatious consumption, or for the maintenance of personal relations of dependency, rather than for the acquisition of more productive means of production.
5. Claude Dupuy, "Les associations villageoises au Sénégal: fonctions économiques et modalités de financement," *Tiers Monde* XXXI, no. 122

(April-June 1990), pp.371-372.

6. Please see *Rapport sur le développement dans le monde 1989, Systèmes financiers et développement* (Washington: World Bank, 1989); also, an article which relates a study of a central economic savings cooperative, Jacques Alibert, "Le cas original des tontines camerounaises, phénomène de société," *Marchés Tropicaux* 2236-2237 (1990), pp. 2375-2378.

7. For an explanation of this expanded definition of savings and its relevance in the African context see J.-Michel Servet, "Représentations de la monnaie et des supports d'épargne et limite de la mobilisation de l'épargne informelle en Afrique noire," in M. Lelart, ed., *La Tontine* (London/Paris: Libbey Eurotext, 1990).

8. The purchase of food supplies for future consumption is (for the individual or the group) a protection against the risk of increases in prices or the possible unavailability of supplies; nonmonetary savings may also be a type of speculation in a society which uses widely modern means of payments. See Dipak Ghosh, "Savings behaviour in the nonmonetized sector and its application," *Savings and development* 2 (1986), pp. 173-180.

9. This interpretation was previously proposed by Raymond Firth in *Capital, Saving and Credit in Peasant Society* (London: George Allen, 1964), pp. 26, 27, and 29.

10. J. Michel Servet, "Occidentalisation du monde et rencontre des imaginaires monétaires: une double illusion," in *Comment Penser l'argent?* R.P. Droit, ed. (Paris: Le Monde Editions, 1992), pp. 44-57.

11. In West Africa, the expression *boite condamnée* describes a type of money box which refers to small wooden boxes with a slot on top, and a bottle, or a canary buried in the ground. The practice of returning notes to the central banks in various states of decomposition identifies some methods of hoarding money. It should also be noted that various hoarding techniques are directly related to the body of the saver.

12. It should also be mentioned that there is the activity of the village money-keeper which has been studied by Kiari Liman Tinguiri, "Épargne et crédit informels dans les pays en développement: expériences anciennes et nouvelles et la situation en milieu rural nigérien" (Paper presented at Pratiques informelles comparées: les fondements de la non légalité, Nouakchott symposium, December 8-10, 1988).

13. The store purchases which are made through differed payments (every week, bi-weekly, monthly, or even trimesterly) insures the owner of a stable clientele. See C. Dupuy and J.-M. Servet, "Pratiques informelles d épargne et de prêt: examples sénégalais," *Économie et humanisme* 294 (March-April 1987), pp. 40-54. On the deposits made to shopkeepers, see the results of research done in Ziguinchor (Sénégal) in November 1989 and January 1990 by Maxime Apkaca and "Écologie des communautés villageoises" done within the framework of the EPR, CNRS (Paris) 166, directed by Gisèle Ducos. Please see the interpretations of these loans by Chicot M. Éboué, "Épargne informelle et développement économique en Afrique," *Mondes en Développement* 16, nos. 62-63 (1988).

14. The first three cases generally refer to a tangible deposit, whereby it is the same notes and coins which are deposited and later returned. The trustee

does not use the funds for his personal needs. However, the shopkeeper and "mobile banker" receive larger sums (which are noted in a registry when deposited and for each successive withdrawal). The "mobile banker" levies a small percentage on deposits which are returned on demand and which he has lent for interest or used himself (the case of commercial tontines which is examined below is based on an identical principle); the shopkeeper may use the deposits of his clients as circulation capital for his commerce and returns the amounts deposited without levying interest.

15. J.-M. Servet, "Représentations de la monnaie et des formes d épargne dans le quartier de Colobane," *Rapport CNRS* (CNRS, unité 166, Paris, 1990); "Écologie des communautés villageoises," (Paris: CNRS, February 1990).

16. On the prohibition of the usage of loans by Islam see J.-B. Heinrich, "Les principaux contrat de financement utilisés par les banques islamiques," *Banques* 478 (1987), pp. 1134-1136. This prohibition is more or less respected by Muslim societies, while in many non-Islamic populations there is a similar repugnance toward the remuneration of loans. See the example of the failure of the politics of granting bank credit in Niger's interior delta studied by Bréhima Kassibo and Eveline Baumann, ORSTOM-Bamako researchers.

17. On the failure of this type of group activity in western Africa see Jacques Berthomé, "Les associations villageoises de développement en Afrique de l'Ouest," *Économie et Humanisme* 314 (July-September 1990), pp. 15-19.

18. See the analysis on associations by Claude Dupuy in "Les associations villageoises au Sénégal: fonctions économique et modalités de financement."

19. This sum is equivalent to approximately $40 at the beginning of the 1990s.

20. Approximately worth US$4,000 at the beginning of the 1990s.

21. These savings associations are in a certain way the reflection of the Althusius principle according to which each collective (family, neighbourhood, corporation, State, etc.) must only solve the problems that the inferior level is unable to solve on its own. Please see Michael Kratke, "Het Subsidiariteitsbeginsel anno 1987," *Andersom* (Amsterdam) 9-10 (1987), pp. 3-49, as cited by Philippe van Paris, "Quelle réponse cohérente aux néolibéralisme," *Économie et Humanisme* 306 (March-April 1989), pp. 41-52, 47.

22. "Les associations villageoises de développement en Afrique de l'Ouest," pp. 22-27.

23. A sociological analysis of tontines has been developed in "Un système alternatif d'épargne et de prêt: les tontines africaines," in the catalogue of the exposition, *Banque et Société Humaine* (Paris: Association Française des Banques, 1986), pp. 163-170.

24. See the Benin example studied by Michel Lelart, "L'Épargne informelle en Afrique: les tontines béninoises," *Revue Tiers Monde* 118 (April-June 1989), p. 280.

25. This type of tontine has been studied by Bruno Bekolo-Ebe, "Le système des tontines: liquidité, intermédiation et comportement d épargne," Revue d'économie politique 4 (1989), pp. 619-638; and C. Riesch, "Une tontine à double niveau d enchères," Financement de l entrepreunariat et mobilisation de l épargne, Research note 5, Réseau thématique, no. 11 (Paris: UREF/AUPELF, 1990, p.55.

182 | Savings & Loans Associations: African Examples

26. Christian Rietsch has analyzed the operations of a tontine called "Tontine de l'élite camerounaise en République Centrafricaine" in which the principal lot raised was of 1,400,000 CFA (more than $5,000) with auctions, and where the meetings ended with a reception. See: Christian Rietsch, "Une tontine à double niveau d'enchères," *Financement de l'entrepreunariat et mobilisation de l épargne*, Research note 5, Réseau thématique, p.55 (Paris: UREF/AUPELF, 1990).

27. This distinction was developed by Ibrahim Bah in *Marché financier informel, Étude en milieu urbain (Bamako) et en milieu rural* (Bamako: Bureau d'Études de conseils et d interventions au Sahel, 1988). The distinction between closed and open tontines was made by C. Éboué in *Épargne sans frontière* 10 (February 1988), p. 6.

28. In some instances, the notion of neighbourly relations may be replaced by family relations.

29. This distinction seemed very important in the tontine studies in Casamance, *Représentations de la monnaie et des formes d'épargne*, a study done within the framework of EPR, CNRS 166 in Colobane, Sénégal, January 1990). On the subject of tontines in Sénégal, see the investigations done by Michel Dromain and quoted in his thesis at the University of Nice in 1989.

30. For an original account of the type of behavior in which liquidity dominates over any other consideration, see E. Bloy and C. Dupuy, "Adaptation des règles de gestion aux contraintes du financement informel," in M. Lelart, ed., *La Tontine* (London/Paris: Libbey Eurotext, 1990), p. 16. Originally a paper presented at Journée Scientifiques Financement, développement et culture de l'entrepreunariat, Casablanca, February 16-18, 1989;

31. J.L. Lespes, "Les informalités tontinières: traditions et innovation," in *La Tontine*. Lespes uses the Polanyian concept of reciprocity for the analysis of relations between the members of tontines or associations.

32. As mentioned earlier, this social aspect of the tontine is not limited to the mutual type.

33. J.-M. Servet, "Le système communautaire des Diola de Basse-Casamance (Sénégal)," Cahier AEH (Université Lyon 2) 14-15 (1978), pp. 189-250.

34. Examples of the influence of migration can be observed as much in southern Sénégal (Ziguinchor Servet Mission, February 1990) as in Rwanda (Jean Nzisabira, "Les associations tontinières au Rwanda," Research notes in *Financement de l entrepreunariat et mobilisation de l épargne*; this model is taken from Uganda and Tanzania.

35. M. Lelart, "Les circuits parralèles de financement: état de la question," in *La Tontine*. (Originally presented as a paper at Journée Scientifiques Financement, développement et culture de l entrepreunariat. Paper presented at Casablanca, February 16-18, 1989.)

36. Ph. Hugon, "La finance non-institutionnelle: expression de la crise du développement ou de nouvelles formes de développement," in M. Lelart, ed., *La Tontine*, p.313. It should be noted here that this recourse to group mediation surpasses the methods used in tontines and associations since the latter is found is also used for deposits and personal loans (see above the list of types of savings); the lender may choose to grant a loan without any real guarantee apart from personal relations to the group.

37. K. Polanyi, *Primitive, Archaic and Modern Economies.* George Dalton, ed.
    (Boston: Beacon Press, 1968), p. 82-85; *The Livelihood of Man.* H. W.
    Pearson, ed. (New York: Academic Press, 1977), pp. 48-49.

10.

FORMS OF ECONOMIC ALLOCATION: TRANSITION AND CHOICE[1]

Gian Primo Cella

A MODEL FOR THE THREE FORMS OF ALLOCATION

Karl Polanyi's model of the three forms of allocation, namely principles of integration, between the economy and society (reciprocity, redistribution, market exchange) is well-known and widely employed, though its source is not always acknowledged. The model can be enriched and perhaps improved, but it remains unequalled in its descriptive (and interpretative) power in both historical studies, and in social science interested in forms and criteria of allocation different from the classical market model. Perhaps the limits of this model are due to its explicit descriptive features which may lead to a sort of "restrictive institutionalism,"[2] where the description of a single principle of integration seems to inevitably define a corresponding type of social organization. However, these features allow for appropriate theoretical integrations, taken from the whole of Polanyi's thought as well as from socioeconomic literature critical of the traditional model of economics.

    The brief considerations that follow review the above model[3] and suggest a few solutions to a problem which still remains unsolved: the reasons and mechanisms for a transition from one form to another. This calls for a passing mention of another point which Polanyi leaves in the background: the decision models corresponding to the various forms of integration. These considerations are still in a preliminary stage and should be viewed above all as potential directions for further research. They are here presented as such.

THE POLANYIAN ITINERARY

Polanyi's interest in the different forms of allocation, or rather in the various forms of integration between the economy and society, springs from his opposition to the "ideal" of the market on the one hand, and to the cognitive means of economic science which feed on it on the other. The reasons are "ideal" in many respects, and marked by the author's biographical traits: his personal comments to a *community-oriented* type of socialism, equally far removed from liberalism as from Marxism.[4] But there is also a reaction against the logical error of confusing categories and species, which equates the entire human economy and its market form.[5] This reaction is related to the refusal to accept as necessary to the economy a particular type of rationality, imposed by scarcity. Polanyi's opposition to economic determinism is associated with his disapproval of economic rationalism and "solipsism"; that is, a "self-explanatory" tendency whereby the market's existence is not explained, but viewed as "natural."[6]

In line with these assumptions is Polanyi's aversion toward global, exhaustive definitions of society based on prevailing economic institutions. A classification of society according to the prevailing form is acceptable only if the simultaneous presence of different forms is accepted as a possibility. This possibility is excluded only from the market societies of the late nineteenth century, which had forced relationships between the economy and society into one direction through a clear separation of the former from the latter.

Since *The Great Transformation* (1944), classical anthropology (Malinowski in particular) suggested to Polanyi how ordered production and distribution were ensured in societies lacking the motivation of profit and maximizing "economic principles." As with all the social sciences of the classical period, however, the answer produced no alternative paradigm to the theory put forward by economists, and furthermore it wavered between functionalism and culturalism.[7]

This order was ensured by two behaviourist principles, not immediately economic in nature: *reciprocity* and *redistribution*.[8] To be effective, the behaviourist principles required two coherent institutional models: *symmetry* and *centricity*. Yet, there was another principle, and a third form, namely the domestic economy based on self-sufficiency, which Polanyi later abandoned because of its uncertain, spurious nature.

In his later work, Polanyi deepened his research. The opportunity was offered by his paper "The Economy as an Institutional Process" published in *Trade and Markets*.[9] On this occasion, he claims that the relations between economy and society can be studied through an analysis of the different ways by which the economic process is instituted at different times and places. Hence Polanyi's understandable revival of the various components of neoinstitutionalist thought (North, for instance), albeit within the traditional economic model.

Institutional analysis is certainly more sociological than psychological, as was effectively pointed out by one of the few economists committed to the reconstruction of Polanyi's thought:

> If men appear generous in one place, selfish in another, it is not their basic natures that differ, but their social organization. It is not the presence of this or that motive that is significant in institutional analysis, but instead the institutional structure in which the motives operate. Via definite institutional sanctions, this structure promotes some human proclivities and represses others.[10]

The problems of transfer between different institutional forms and of the choices of subjects involved in them, are mentioned but remain unresolved and in the background.

The Polanyian process of institutional analysis relies on the combination of a limited number of concepts, namely the forms of integration. Their definition in the posthumous work is very precise: they denote the institutional movements connecting the elements of the economic process, ranging from tangible resources and labour to the transport, conservation, and distribution of commodities.[11] According to this definition, *form* proves a more appropriate term than *principle* which Polanyi and his collaborators use interchangeably. As for allocation, the model chiefly indicates its forms, mentioning the corresponding criteria and principles only indirectly. The form reveals a considerable *reconstructive* capacity, especially in economic history. Polanyi recalls this in his foreword to the essay on Dahomey, when he claims that a realistic view of vast socioeconomic changes, regardless of time and place, promotes the search for interpretive solutions.[12]

The basic forms of integration between economy and society, therefore, are reciprocity, redistribution, and market exchange. Reciprocity[13] refers to the movements of related points in symmetric groups, redistribution to the appropriating movements directed toward a center and then away from it, while exchange comprises the bilateral movements between two parties in a market system.[14]

The different forms have clear institutional requirements: reciprocity calls for groups organized in symmetric forms, redistribution needs a central authority, and exchange requires a market self-regulated by prices. These forms do not consist of mere associations of individual patterns of behaviour. In the absence of suitable social conditions, patterns of behaviour alone do not create social effects. As can be seen, this is entirely in line with the criteria of institutional analysis. In other words, the passage from micro to macro occurs via suitable institutions. In addition, Polanyi seems to choose a macro institutional conditioning of behaviour at the micro level. In Alexander and Giesen's typology of the five main approaches to micro/macro relations, Polanyi could be placed in the fourth type, the most *Durkheimian*: "socialized individuals reproduced society by translating the existing social environment into the microrealm."[15]

At the root of Polanyi's position is an anthropological theory[16] of interaction. This enabled a connection to be made between social arrangements and cultural traits on the one hand, and institutions on the other. A significant clarification of the matter was made by H. W. Pearson (1983), among Polanyi's closest collaborators. In his view, the forms of integration also indirectly identify the types of institutional sanctions (social, political, economic) governing relations between participants in the economic process. In reciprocity, sanctions derive from the behavioural expectations imposed by the parental system, the community, the solidarity network, and the obligations of associates. As expectations may or may not be met by diffused behaviour, sanctions pervade the whole range of social life.

In redistribution, sanctions derive from formal rules (subsequently legal and bureaucratic rules) issued by political authorities. Within the market, behaviour is motivated by individual interest; conflict is solved by price movements and sanctions remain specific to, and almost exclusively in the economic sphere.

The historical and anthropological foundations of Polanyi's model are well known and require no further attention in this paper. A brief mention is also sufficient of the important conceptual distinction between different forms of exchange, based on the distinction between the substantial and the "catallactic" viewpoint. This leads, for example, to the division into the exchange of gifts, guided exchange, and market exchange.

Polanyi follows at least two paths to approach his model. The first path is historical and anthropological, characterized by a constant concern with economic institutions. The second path is strictly theoretical (i.e., social theory) and tends to define an economic reference paradigm not confined exclusively to a market society. Each route selects, so to speak, its own enemy. For the former it is the "naturalness" of the market; for the latter, it is classical and neoclassical economic theory, especially in the socioanthropological postulates associated with it.

Considered jointly, the three main forms of integration within the first path imply different relations with society. Reciprocity and redistribution imply processes of incorporation of the economy into society; the opposite occurs in the case of exchange. The historical succession of the three forms is not, however, definitely sealed. Recurrences and cycles are both possible and frequent. In Polanyi's view: even the Welfare State is a movement tending to reabsorb the economy into society.[17]

The second path considers the fundamental distinction between the substantial and the formal concept of "economy."[18] Polanyi's aim is to argue against the profound significance which the formal meaning has been given, broad enough to include every economic event. In his refutation, he even appeals to Carl Menger, one of the founding fathers of neoclassical economics.

In this paper, however, I intend to focus on the first path and its findings. As I noted above, Polanyi lacks an evolutionary view of the forms of economic integration: no form overthrows the others completely and a return to previous forms is always possible, especially to those (i.e., reciprocity) structured most deeply within social relations.

The evolutionary view is considered unacceptable—more or less explicitly—by studies on welfare; on informal and diffused economies; on the role of weak (social) ties in economic relations; on the importance of altruism as a consolidating factor in social relations; and on cooperation strategies based on trust.[19] Significantly, Polanyi's model is a historically and anthropologically adequate scheme for many of these economic and social phenomena. No objection, I believe, has yet proved that Polanyi's scheme is not useful, or is only superficial.

In many respects, the real victims in this field of studies seem to be the theories and studies on modernization. On the historical plane, the events of recent years[20] show that the market may be a winner but it has not triumphed, and that vital "countermovements" are at work, both in the Western world and in societies appearing for the first time, after many decades, on the scene of generalized exchange relations.[21]

Compared to models à la Easton (1960)—essentially dichotomous—the tripartite model has proved more capable of grasping the connections between economic behaviour and social relations. It may be successfully integrated with them in those aspects which concern the form of redistribution, that is the form of politics. No one has surpassed Easton's claim that the distinguishing feature of a social act, which gives it a political slant, is its relationship with the imperative allocation of values in a society.

An interesting development of the "trinitary" formula came from the contributions which, in the wake of research on neocorporatism, singled out a fourth feasible principle of regulation, a fourth form of allocation: an "associative" criterion with its own autonomy and relevance.[22] This can be recognized through the guiding principle of interaction and allocation of resources, and may be defined as an organized arrangement, as opposed to spontaneous solidarity, widespread competitiveness, and hierarchic control.

The authors have no doubts on the theoretical status of this fourth form, even if they misleadingly judge the idea of a corporative and associative social or political global system. My own personal opinion is that a satisfactory definition (and solution) is still lacking as to the specificity and autonomy of this fourth form as related to the adjoining form, namely politics or redistribution. For this reason perhaps Polanyi, always in search of "pure" forms, would probably have dismissed it. Indeed, Streeck and Schmitter (1995) also admit that the delegation of State prerogatives (typical of this form) should be followed at the same time by the acquisition on the part of the State of the ability to form, lead, and control the new self-regulating systems. However, the use of sectorial interests to form a social order extending well beyond the original categories, as well as the belief that associations may become a source of public, social, and economic order, make the assumption of its conceptual autonomy far more plausible. With some caution we can accept this contribution to Polanyi's model, chiefly for its ability to explain changes in the principles of regulation whenever, and wherever organized pluralism is present.

TRANSITION FROM ONE FORM TO ANOTHER

When the Polanyian model of the three forms of integration between economy and society is defined, with appropriate additions, it soon leads to a crucial question: how does the transition from one form to another take place? What kind of social mechanisms are involved in this transition? This calls for a further question, namely whether changes in individual interactions are responsible for changes in institutional macrostructures, or if the latter trigger off changes in "economic" relations (in the substantial sense) between subjects.

This question should be approached in both synchronic and diachronic terms. The optimal theoretical answer should provide a solution to both types of transition. The evident reason is that the diachronic sense alone would inevitably entail the temptation to focus on the major causes of historical change (the "revolutions" of modern times, for instance), those leading to the swift and violent overturn of entire sociopolitical systems. Although these causes do not rule out others, their overall importance would be decisive. But the contribution to the theoretical question would not be as effective in explaining the simultaneous presence of different forms, the unexpected reappearance of a single form in "exclusive" economic-political contexts, and the opportunity to choose among them that is often available to individual subjects.

During the initial stages of investigation, even incomplete answers are acceptable. In fact, Polanyi's research offers no exhaustive explanations in this field. His model remains altogether static. Block and Somers remark that the three forms ought to be seen as comparable answers to the issue of integration is not a satisfactory explanation.[23]

Any contribution aimed at raising its "dynamic" capacity will increase its heuristic status, without necessarily reducing its internal consistency. It is advisable to start from the question concerning the overall transition between forms, leaving aside the relations of microinteractions with macrostructures.

This question was openly discussed in an important paper by D. C. North (1977) that, among other things, proposes a revaluation of Polanyi's contribution to economic history. North's view, according to the principles of recent neoinstitutionalist economic thought,[24] is that "transaction costs analysis is a promising analytical framework to explore nonmarket forms of economic organization."[25] North later added to this a theory of the State, but the picture remained unchanged:

> A theory of transaction costs is necessary because under the ubiquitous conditions and therefore competition, more efficient forms of economic organization will replace less efficient forms under *ceteris paribus* conditions. The State however...will encourage and specify efficient property rights only to the extent that they are consistent with the wealth maximizing objectives of those who run the State.[26]

The role of institutions is decisive, as they "provide the framework within which human beings interact."[27] Their interaction, however, is still directed by economic reckoning.

Clearly defined and respected property rights over goods and services are the precondition for prices to operate in a self-regulating market. The costs of defining and enforcing such rights are known as transaction costs. Under the same heading we can also include information costs. When these exceed benefits, goods and services can be allocated through nonmarket forms.

Pure public goods, for example, may be allocated in the sphere of redistribution because it is impossible to exclude those not sharing in the cost or due to the difficulty of splitting the cost according to the amount of use of a good or service. Allocation may also take place in the form of gifts (even without reciprocity) of private goods whose surveillance and collection costs exceed the benefits available to their owner. To overcome the lack of dynamism in Polanyi's model and to explain changes in the combination of allocation forms, North concludes that it would be useful to develop an ordered classification of transition costs and of the consequent changes in the system. Variations of such costs should produce the pressure needed for institutional readjustment.[28]

In many respects, however, this road may lead to a *non-Polanyian* solution of a typical *Polanyian* problem. This observation is prompted by Granovetter's (1985) critical contribution to recent neoinstitutionalist thought (from North to Williamson). The author takes the typical Polanyian problem of the embeddedness of economic action within the framework of social relations. This problem is decisive for confronting the issue of competition and succession of different institutional forms of integration between economy and society.

Of course, orthodoxy does not worry me nor does it suit this context. Instead, the line of investigation envisaged by neoinstitutionalists may offer a partial answer to the question of diachronic and synchronic relations between different forms of allocation. This solution is probably most suitable for investigating the forms of allocation of different classes of goods (for instance the different types of public property). At the same time it is certainly an "economical" and "maximizing" solution to a problem which remains, or should remain, a typically social and sociological in nature. As Simon recently remarked in his autobiography, "new institutional economics" proceeds by continuing "to pour the new wine into the old bottle of neoclassical reasoning."[29]

Nevertheless, sociological criticism against the use of transaction costs has not been lacking. Beginning with Swedberg,[30] who attacks the approach of promoting social Darwinism (an institution exists, basically, until it allows for good economic performance), up to Frydman (1990) who questions the existence of a higher market where it is possible to work out the costs and benefits of each institutional form. Granovetter's position is divergent from the "substantialists" and the "formalists." His starting point is that the degree of embeddedness of economic behaviour in nonmarket societies is lower than claimed by researchers (Polanyi foremost). But in market societies it is higher than claimed by the investigators of rational economic behaviour. According to Granovetter, "neoinstitutionalists" are merely strengthening the "formalist" side with their economic analysis of social institutions viewed "as resulting from the pursuit of self-interest by rational, more or less atomized individuals."[31] After assembling and disassembling the various lines of interpretation in an unfamiliar fashion, he points out that despite any apparent conflict the undersocialized and the over-socialized views both "have in common a conception of action and decision carried out by atomized actors."[32]

Granovetter argues that social relations—as opposed to institutions (as viewed by neoinstitutionalists)—or anything resembling common morality (and collective conscience?) can explain the different types of integration of economic action within society, and, for example, the production of special "commodities" such as trust.

This type of morality is reminiscent of the "right to give" in the Titmuss study,[33] and of the ethical reference to individual liberties (both positive and negative) supported in Amartya Sen's (1990) observations on worldwide poverty and hunger. It is also connected to the moral constraints invoked by Etzioni in his presentation of a new social science (a brand of socioeconomics), which would not simply influence transactions but sometimes even have the capacity to ban "certain types of exchange behaviour and certain market tendencies."[34] The theoretical and sociological weight of such rights and constraints, however, is still rather unclear.

And yet this opinion can offer an important contribution to a solution of the problem in "Polanyian" terms, especially by a definition of institutions closer to social theory, the insight taken up further on. Despite the reservations expressed by Granovetter himself, a few aspects remain unconvincing: the interpretation of the neoinstitutionalist tradition, for example, is too constrained within the bounds of economic rationalism (North's later writings mitigate his former positions), and inadequate consideration is given to the effect of social relations on the motivation of economic action and on the associated type of rationality.

North's contribution is also taken up by Paci (1989) in his well-known analysis of the long-term cycles of social welfare systems.[35] His arguments are considered useful for rejecting an "uncritical evolutionist view," but according to Paci they seem to merely signal the importance of transaction costs. More promising contributions were made by Hirschman (1982) on the variations between public and private preference cycles, and by Weisbrod (1977) on customer satisfaction, and on the social efficiency of choices in the different institutional and organizational settings of public services. Paci again stresses the difficulty of considering the transition from one form of allocation (and integration) to another in the area of social welfare systems, and the need to reduce our theoretical assumptions: he claims that the idea of a long-term cycle in such systems should be accepted without excessive heuristic ambitions, simply as a working theory.

Even the contributions of the above authors do not appear sufficient to substantiate the assumption of a long-term cycle and of the simultaneous presence of three (or four) forms of allocation (derived from the no-evolution hypothesis). The model suggested by Hirschman does not say much about the simultaneous presence of different forms. Weisbrod's contribution is probably more promising as it allows a tentative answer to both types of questions (and assumptions). While on the one hand it introduces the problem of different classes of efficiently allocable goods within the various forms of allocation, on the other hand it suggests a potential rational cause for the development of different organizational solutions concerning the market and politics: thus the relative dimensions of a third sector will be a function of the heterogeneous nature of demand.[36] All this occurs in situations where the political ability to correct market failure is limited and foreshadows an authentic failure of politics.[37] However the possibility to extend Weisbrod's contribution to other commodities besides welfare still remains doubtful. This can be seen in the features taken on in such cases by the private nonprofit sector: a special specification of the broader category based on solidarity and reciprocity, which makes its competition with the market and political forms simpler and less heterogeneous.

After a closer look, all the above-mentioned interpretative contributions are relevant in a way to the solution of our "Polanyian" problem. This is not due to the indefinite nature of the problem as much as the number of aspects it involves. Overall, however, the contributions remain disappointing on this point; even the authors nearest to an "answer," like North and the neoinstitutionalist writers. While moving in the right direction (considering social institutions in the context of economic analysis), they advocate the use of an explanatory medium (transaction costs) that is elegant in the realm of economic theory, but unsuitable (and "unexplainable") in the field of social theory. As Trigilia rightly noticed, the approach to transaction costs ends up using a timeless, highly generalized analytical model that reduces the opportunities to fully employ the social variables. In this way it becomes a prescriptive rather than an interpretative model: a model unable to account properly for the variation in time and space of the forms of allocation and of integration between economy and society.[38]

RELATIONS BETWEEN MICRO AND MACRO

The nature of a solution to the problem (diachronic and synchronic relations between the different forms of integration of economy and society or between the different forms of allocation) may be more easily determined taking the line—too often taken for granted— of traditional sociological studies on the relations between micro and macro, that is between individual action and the macro social sphere. While in the historical perspective the greatest change occurs in the macrostructures of allocation (or regulation, or integration), in the synchronic perspective the chief agent of change and transition seems to be the individual actor.[39]

Precious information on the mechanism of allocation and on the reasons behind the choice between forms (where available) can be obtained by considering, as well as the above criteria, the decision models applied to the different forms of allocation. These coincide in part with questions like the following: how does the transition from individual economic actions to social economic institutions take place? What tensions and contrasts can be envisaged between the micro level and the macrosphere? What degree (or type) of influence do macrosocial institutions exert on individual economic actions? Does the decision model (or, in other words, the rationality model) remain the same within the different forms or does it vary with transition from one form to another? Expressed alternatively, does the self-same decision model lead to each of the three (or four) different forms in different institutional contexts, or are several models at work under the influence of such institutions?

Again, how does individual rationality connect to social macrostructures? Finally, what type what degree of deviation between macro and micro, do these structures need? Such questions pinpoint a vast and complex line of thought and research, only outlined in these pages. What matters at this stage is the definition of the solutions to the "Polanyian" problem in terms consistent with the problem itself.[40]

It is a well known fact that the Polanyian model ascribes the differences in patterns of behaviour (the word choice is not casual) to the presence of institutional macrostructures associated with the different forms of integration or allocation: social structures (or institutions) of reciprocity, the State apparatus, and the market. The totality of individual behaviours is somehow greater than their sum. This additional element is represented by economic institutions. The process seems to be as follows: social institutions—individual economic behaviour—economic institutions, at least in those societies where the economy is solidly embedded in society. In this light, the market does appear through spontaneous association, but is established with the often crucial contribution of State structures (which proves, in a way, the exceptional historical nature of the economic rational paradigm; see the chapter by De Romaña in this book).

This model contrasts openly with the (formal) economic model, especially with the neoclassical type. In the economic model, the actors are individuals and the macrosphere is reached through the association of a myriad of microbehaviours. The outcome of the macrosphere, moreover, remains totally within the model itself.[41]

The Polanyian model follows a school of social theory dating from Durkheim, if not earlier, in explaining social relations through other social relations. In Blau's words—after his recent unexpected conversion to macrosociology—the *explicans* and the *explicanda* are both social.[42] The deterministic nature of this model is quite evident, and its specifications reveal not only the flaws but also the unquestionable advantages of a purely sociological model (a fact to often overlooked by an ardent antideterminist like Boudon, [1985]). Within these bounds, the social actors are allowed too little space for choice, as Granovetter[43] and Swedberg[44] remind us, quoting Duesenberry's famous remark that economics is a field where actors make their choices, while sociology is a field where subjects have no choices to make!

If we remain close to the "problem" of transition from one form to another, we may be able to explain their sequences (or cycles). We are not likely to find an explanation for the choices subjects make between the different forms of allocation (whenever a choice is available). The answer is likely to fail at the synchronic level. At this point, the Polanyian model must be abandoned "partly," if not radically as suggested by North, through the vehicle of transaction costs.

Partial rejection is possible if the actor is given a choice in the scenario provided by *institutions*, or by the institutional context.

Authors like Burns (1991), for theoretical reasons, and Dore (1991) in his attempt to explain the peculiarity and performance of the Japanese economy, move in this direction. In either case the decision-making model related to rational economic behaviour is considerably weakened. Burns claims that the economic model of exchange and its sociological derivative ignore man's inability, and sometimes his unwillingness, to calculate the rewards and costs of social transactions.[45] Dore remarks that the good performance of the Japanese economy is a consequence of the loss of allocating efficiency,[46] due to a relational negotiation that does not match the market's economic behaviour and derives from a formal associative institutionalization of ethics[47] similar to the "fourth" form suggested by Streeck and Schmitter. Indeed, behind the apparent image, the Japanese have never taken to Adam Smith, nor have they truly attempted to believe in the invisible hand.[48]

This opportunity of choice may be illustrated—in Coleman's terms[49]—with an "algorithm" introducing an institution that imposes a particular structure on the system, for example on the market system. Coleman's representation again risks basing institutions exclusively on individual behaviour, and yet it provides a crucial finding to our issue, considering its source: not every micro/macro transition model based on rational actors necessarily appears in the form of market exchange. Coleman usually mentions instances of *collective behaviour*, but the breach is open.

Transition from the micro level—in our case individual "economic" behaviour—to the macro level (solidarity, politics, the market, associative-cooperative arrangements) can occur, for example, through a model of *individual rational* behaviour independent of the model of formal economy (neoclassical approaches). For once the fateful pair of adjectives "individual/rational" must be taken with no necessary reference to the traditional model of economic rationality.

But what type of model, or rationality, is needed to avoid distorting the "Polanyian" issue? Certainly not the rationality in the economists' neoclassical model, but surely something approaching Simon's *bounded* (nonglobal) rationality in the realm of " behaviourist" models and yet distant from the theory of subjective utility of the "Olympic" model.[50] Even in relatively simple laboratory simulations, man possesses neither the factual opportunity, the adequate structure of values, nor the rational ability necessary to apply the principles of anticipated subjective utility.[51] The role of institutions is to provide alternatives in a context of uncertainty about optimal solutions. In a more realistic world, Simon would say,[52] the decision-maker settles for "satisfying" solutions, far removed from the "optimal" solutions available in a simplified world. Institutional analysis simply confirms the impossibility of optimizing choices in the real world. Moreover, as Elster points out,[53] the preferences involved in a decision may be shaped by compulsion. This constraint is imposed by institutions.

What we require is probably in the sphere of *cognitive* models: "the actor will choose not between *means* properly speaking, but between *interpretations* of the problem," Boudon remarks,[54] showing the difference that can exist between the individualist model of economics and sociology[55] Simon stresses the relevance of the *problem representation*, when he asks in what manner—given a certain amount of stimuli and acquired knowledge—a person will organize this complex mass of information into a definition of the problem instrumental to his efforts to reach a solution.[56]

This orientation (the representation of allocation problems and of the ensuing social relations) has many points in common with that of political philosophers who, in the realm of distributive justice, prefer a contractualist approach to the criteria of utilitarian allocation. As Veca (1986) points out, this approach is founded on our ability to reason about the preferences we happen to have, on the possibility to be responsible for our aims and on our recognition in the process of other fellow beings deserving equal respect.[57]

Cognitive literature[58] reminds us that this is especially true for complex, strategic decisions. In this sense, going back to our first model, it might be a case of choosing between forms of allocation (and of regulation), like those confronting a political decision-maker when asked to privatize a kind of production, or service previously provided by the public sector. But the same complexity could confront the individual actor choosing to assist the elderly through family support, public institutions, or the profit-making private sector. In this light, we may define as complex and "strategic" any decision involving not only a choice between different types of behaviour but also a choice between forms of allocation and between principles of integration, with the consequent institutional requirements.

We have only outlined a course of research and study.[59] The road suggested can only be trusted if it does not distort the "Polanyian" problem. This condition does not stem from a concern for theoretical or doctrinal orthodoxy but from the constant relevance of the problem. Too many alternative models await to tempt those convinced of the usefulness of a social explanation of economic—or better, socio-economic—events.

A FEW FINAL OBSERVATIONS

The starting point of this paper was, again, Polanyi's model of the three forms of allocation, or principles of integration. This start was justified by the relevance of the model to account for a wide range of economic and social facts, especially in contemporary societies urged on by new dramatic needs—first of all those related to the environment. Our brief review of Polanyi's itinerary tried to focus chiefly on the nature of its institutional analysis, combining a limited number of concepts ("forms" and "principles") and assessing the ensuing institutional requirements. An itinerary running along two parallel lines: the anthropological historical line, with its rejection of an evolutionary vision of the forms of economic organization in society, and the strictly theoretical line, critical of the socioanthropological preconditions of classical, and neoclassical economic theory. We then considered an interesting contribution to the model, allowing the addition to the three original forms (reciprocity, redistribution and market exchange) of a fourth possible form involved in the success of "associative" criteria of integration and allocation.

After this review we confronted the fundamental issue, concerning the dynamic part of the model: how does the transition from one model to another take place? This question involves another one, on the decision models of actors, implying three possible relations between micro and macro (that is, different ways for the macro level to influence the microsphere). In answering these questions the Polanyian model is clearly inadequate. Other contributions should therefore be taken up, from neoinstitutionalist thought to writers stressing the unexpected degree of social "embeddedness" in the economic behaviour of market societies.

All these contributions have addressed, to some extent, our fundamental question as they confront a typically "Polanyian" problem though not necessarily posed by Polanyi himself. However, the solution (as the word is used in historical and social sciences) is still far from evident, even in the neoinstitutionalist approach, which comes closest.

A more effective way of finding a solution to this "problem" may be found in the relations (which are too often considered implicit) between the micro and macro levels; that is, between individual action and the macrosocial sphere. At this point, a partial rejection of the Polanyian model is necessary if a single answer must be given as to the different types of diachronic and synchronic transition from one form to another. This *partial* rejection proceeds from recognition of the actor's freedom of choice inside the background provided by the institutional context.

Transition from the micro to the macro levels could occur through a "behavioural" model of individual rationality, with ample *cognitive* traits; that is, through a rationality directed by the different representations and interpretations of allocation problems, rather than by the choice of appropriate means in agreement with the individual's subjective utility.

We have only outlined a course of research that should provide an answer to important questions, which concern more than the historical aspect of social theory. This road ahead will not only concern or involve the number (probably greater by the end of this century) of those who continue to believe that a single *optimal* answer can be given to allocation and regulation problems.

NOTES

1. Translated by Davide Giannoni.
2. G. Berthoud, "Toward a Comparative Approach: The Contribution of Karl Polanyi," in K. Polanyi-Levitt, ed., *The Life and Work of Karl Polanyi* (Montréal: Black Rose Books, 1990), p. 181.
3. For a wider version see G. P. Cella, "Reciprocità, redistribuzione, scambio. Note su Karl Polanyi," *Stato e Mercato*, no. 13 (1985).
4. Cf. the papers collected in K. Polanyi, *La libertà in una società complessa* (Torino: Bollati Boringhieri, 1987a).
5. H. W. Pearson, Introduction to K. Polanyi, *The Livelihood of Man* (New York: Academic Press Inc., 1977), p. 28.
6. "Toward a Comparative Approach: The Contribution of Karl Polanyi," pp. 175-176.
7. Cf. A. Caillé, *Critica della ragione utilitaria* (Torino: Bollati Boringhieri, 1991), pp. 28-32. Originally published as *Critique de la raison utilitaire* (Paris: La Découverte, 1988).
8. K. Polanyi, *La grande trasformazione* (Torino: Einaudi, 1974). In English: *The Great Transformation* (New York: Holt, Rinehart & Wimston Inc., 1944), pp. 62-63.

9. K. Polanyi, ed. *Traffici e mercati negli antichi imperi* (Torino: Einaudi, 1978). In English: *Trade and Market in the Early Empires* (Glencoe, Ill: The Free Press, 1957), pp. 296-331.

10. J. R. Stanfield, "Karl Polanyi and Contemporary Economic Thought," in K. Polanyi-Levitt, ed., *The Life and Work of Karl Polanyi* (Montréal: Black Rose Books, 1990), p. 204; and more extensively J.R. Stanfield, *The Economic Thought of Karl Polanyi* (London: Macmillan, 1986).

11. K. Polanyi, *La sussistenza dell uomo* (Torino: Einaudi, 1983). In English *The Livelihood of Man* (New York: Academic Press Inc., 1977), p. 61.

12. K. Polanyi, *Il Dahomey e la tratta degli schiavi* (Torino: Einaudi, 1987b), p. xxxvii. Originally published as *Dahomey and the Slave Trade: An Analysis of an Archaic Economy*, in collaboration with A. Rotstein (Seattle, Washington, 1966),

13. An open issue remains the allocation of gift forms not requiring implicit or explicit reciprocity, which may be called forms of "creative altruism" using Sorokin's definition quoted by Titmuss in his famous research on blood donation. See R. M.. Titmuss, *The Gift Relationship* (New York: Vintage Books, 1972), p. 212. However, I believe that the permissive institutional conditions may justify their inclusion among the forms of reciprocity.

14. *Traffici e mercati negli antichi imperi*, p. 306; In English: *Trade and Market in the Early Empires*, p. 306.

15. J. C. Alexander, and B. Giesen, "From Reduction to Linkage: The Long View of the Micro-Macro Debate," in J. C. Alexander, et al. *The Micro-Macro Link* (Berkeley, California: University of California Press, 1987), p. 14.

16. Of special interest is Berthoud and Rotstein's contribution in this book, concerning the connection between forms of integration and certain ontological aspects of man, notably the Hegelian-Marxian concept of exteriorization (*äs.serung*).

17. G. Dalton, Introduction to K. Polanyi, *Primitive, Archaic and Modern Economies* (Doubleday & Co. Inc., 1968), xxiii.

18. On the theoretical debate opposing substantialists and formalists cf. recently G. Dalton, "Writings that Clarify Theoretical Disputes over Karl Polanyi's Work," in K. Polanyi-Levitt, ed., *The Life and Work of Karl Polanyi*, pp. 161-170.

19. Cf. M. Paci, *Pubblico e privato nei moderni sistemi di Welfare* (Napoli: Liguori, 1989); A. Bagnasco, *La costruzione sociale del mercato* (Bologna: Il Mulino, 1988); M. Granovetter, "Economic Action and Social Structure: The Problem of Embeddedness," *American Journal of Sociology* 91, no.3 (1985); *The Gift Relationship*; and D. Gambetta, ed., *Le strategie della fiducia* (Torino: Einaudi, 1989).

20. In the third memorable 1889, after the French Revolution and the Second International, Fondazione G. Feltrinelli, *Libertà e cittadinanza sociale. I due '89: Dalla Rivoluzione francese alla Seconda Internazionale* (Milano: Quaderni 41, Angeli, 1991).

21. Cf. Berthoud and Rotstein, in this book.

22. See W. Streeck, and P. Schmitter, "Comunità, mercato, stato e associazioni? Il possibile contributo dei governi privati all ordine sociale," *Stato e Mercato*, no. 13 (1985). An interesting application of this model to the forms

of regulation in various sectors of the economy is made in J. R. Hollings-worth, and L. N. Lindberg, "La regolazione dell economia americana: il ruolo di mercato, clan, gerarchia ed associazione," in M. Magatti, ed. *Azione economica come azione sociale* (Milano: F. Angeli, 1991), pp. 177-211.

23. Fred Block and Margaret Somers, eds., (1984, p.71), citation information unavailable.

24. Cf. C. Trigilia, "Economia dei costi di transazione e sociologia: cooperazione o conflitto," *Stato e Mercato*, no. 25 (1989).

25. D.C. North, "Markets and Other Allocations Systems in History: The Challenge of Karl Polanyi," *The Journal of European Economic History*, no. 3 (1977), p. 709.

26. D.C. North, *Structure and Change in Economic History* (New York: Norton, 1981), pp. 33-34.

27. *Ibid.*, p. 201.

28. "Markets and Other Allocations Systems in History: The Challenge of Karl Polanyi," p. 715.

29. H. A. Simon, *Models of my Life* (New York: Basic Books, 1991), p. 167.

30. R. Swedberg, "Vers une nouvelle sociologie économique," *La Revue du MAUSS*, no. 9 (1990), pp. 52-53.

31. "Economic Action and Social Structure: The Problem of Embeddedness," p. 482.

32. *Ibid.*, p. 485. As Caillé (1991) observes, most simply and effectively, theory constantly repeats that man likes what he likes and cares for what he cares; See *Critique de la raison utilitaire*, p. 84.

33. *The Gift Relationship*, p. 237.

34. A. Sen, "Individual Freedom as a Social Commitment," *The New York Review of Books* (June 14, 1990), p. 20.

35. On the problems of welfare mixture, cf. F. Lesemann, "Les politiques sociales entre la sphère domestique, le marché et l'état: la notion de welfare mix." (paper presented at the Third International Karl Polanyi Conference, Milano, November 1990). For a discussion of the long-term relations between forms of integration in a perspective close to Paci's, cf. B. Hettne, "The Contemporary Crisis: The Rise of Reciprocity," in *The Life and Work of Karl Polanyi*, pp. 208-220, and his diagram, p. 217.

36. B. Weisbrod, *The Voluntary Non Profit Sector* (Lexington, Mass.: Lexington Books, 1977), p. 59.

37. Cf. C. Busana Banterle and G.P. Cella, "Il welfare e l allocazione politica: alcune alternative," in U. Ascoli, ed., *Welfare State all italiana* (Bari: Laterza, 1984).

38. *Economia dei costi di transazione e sociologia*, p. 153.

39. An excellent review of the line of theoretical thought relating micro to macro may be found in R. Münch, and N. Smelser, "Relating the Micro and Macro," in *The Micro-Macro Link*, pp. 356-387. Two extremely convincing solutions (the internalization and establishment of limits) are offered to this relation. For the debate in Italy, see the recent contribution of A. Mutti, "La teoria della scelta razionale: dalla microriduzione alla soluzione combinatoria" (paper presented to A.I.S. Conference, Il rapporto micro-macro nelle scienze sociali, Pavia, december 1990.)

40. This type of solution is attempted by R. Münch, "The Interpenetration of Microinteraction and Macrostructures in a Complex and Contingent Institutional Order," in *The Micro-Macro Link*, pp. 319-336, through an analytical approach clearly derived from Parsons (the well-known AGIL). Münch illustrates the prescriptive conditions in which the various interactions occur and shows that individual microinteractions alone cannot lead to forms of order. Insofar as the results and preconditions of each form (adaptivity, goal directedness, etc.) stretch beyond the interactive situation, they should be viewed as data and, in this sense, as macrostructures (p. 324). In this perspective, there seems to be a transition from one form of integration to another according to the influence each form is able to exert, *outside its sphere*.

41. Cf. *Relating the Micro and Macro*.

42. P. M. Blau, "Contrasting Theoretical Perspectives," referred to in J. C. Alexander, and B. Giesen, "From Reduction to Linkage: The Long View of the Micro-Macro Debate," in J. C. Alexander, et al., eds., *The Micro-Macro Link*, p. 75.

43. "Economic Action and Social Structure," p. 485.

44. "Vers une nouvelle sociologie économique," p. 54.

45. T. R. Burns, "Una teoria strutturale dello scambio sociale," in M. Magatti, ed., *Azione economica come azione sociale* (Milano: F. Angeli, 1991), p. 145.

46. R. Dore, "Buona disposizione e spirito del capitalismo," in M. Magatti, ed., *Azione economica come azione sociale*, p. 167.

47. *Ibid.*, p. 157.

48. *Ibid.*, p. 163. Against the background of these arguments, it is easier to understand the importance (not only in controversy) of Bateson's lethal remark about the "obtuseness" of economic man among all other "imaginary organisms." See G. Bateson, and M. C. Bateson, *Dove gli angeli esitano* (Milano: Adelphi, 1989), p. 263. Originally published as *Angels Fear: Towards an Epistemology of the Sacred* (1987).

49. J. S. Coleman, "Microfoundations and Macrosocial behaviour," in J. C. Alexander, et al., eds., *The Micro-Macro Link*, p. 160.

50. H. A. Simon, *La ragione nelle vicende umane* (Bologna: Il Mulino, 1984). Originally published as *Reason in Human Affairs* (Oxford: Basil Blackwell, 1983), p. 69.

51. *Ibid.*, p. 49.

52. H. A. Simon, "Rational Decision Making in Business Organizations," *American Economic Review* LXIX (1979), p. 498.

53. J. Elster, *Uva acerba* (Milano: Feltrinelli, 1989), p. 7. Originally published as *Sour Grapes* (Cambridge: Cambridge University Press, 1983).

54. R. Boudon, "The Individualistic Tradition in Sociology" quoted in "From Reduction to Linkage: The Long View of the Micro-Macro Debate," in J. C. Alexander, et al. eds., *The Micro-Macro Link*, p. 65.

55. Through cognitive devices, for example, the rational decision-maker on the market may tend to defend himself from the market and its consequences (namely the constant redefinition of choices, positions and prices), See also R. Frydman, "Le marché: un systäme économique incomplet," *La Revue du MAUSS*, no. 9, (1990), p. 161.

56. "Rational Decision Making in Business Organizations," p. 500.
57. S. Veca, *Una filosofia pubblica* (Milano: Feltrinelli, 1986), p. 31.
58. Cf. L. Codara, "Oltre il modello della scelta razionale. I processi decisionali nella organizzazione sindacale" (Ph.D. diss., Università di Trento, 1989).
59. A path that may appear alternative to the decision-maker's use of cognitive rationality at this point, arises from the recognition that certain principles of action are intrinsically incompatible; see *Critique de la raison utilitaire*, p. 91. This recognition is also present in Cheal's observations on moral economy; see D. Cheal, "Economia morale," in M. Magatti, ed., *Azione economica come azione sociale*, p. 349, whereby in pluralistic societies any description of the social order must take into consideration individual choices between alternative courses of action. But these courses are in fact far less alternative than they appear at first sight.

REFERENCES

Alexander, J. C., et al. *The Micro-Macro Link* (Berkeley, California: University of California Press, 1987).

Alexander, J. C., and B. Giesen, "From Reduction to Linkage: The Long View of the Micro-Macro Debate," in J. C. Alexander, et al. *The Micro-Macro Link* (Berkeley, California: University of California Press, 1987), pp. 1-42.

Bagnasco, A. *La costruzione sociale del mercato* (Bologna: Il Mulino, 1988).

Bateson, G., and M. C. Bateson, *Dove gli angeli esitano* (Milano: Adelphi, 1989). Originally published as *Angels Fear: Towards an Epistemology of the Sacred* (1987).

Berthoud, G., "Toward a Comparative Approach: The Contribution of Karl Polanyi," in K. Polanyi-Levitt, ed. *The Life and Work of Karl Polanyi* (Montréal: Black Rose Books, 1990). pp. 171-182.

Berthoud, G. and A. Rotstein, "The Seductive Market," in the present volume.

Blau, P. M. "Contrasting Theoretical Perspectives," in J. C. Alexander, and B. Giesen, "From Reduction to Linkage: The Long View of the Micro-Macro Debate," in J. C. Alexander, et al. *The Micro-Macro Link* (Berkeley, California: University of California Press, 1987), pp. 1-42.

Boudon, R. *Il posto del disordine* (Bologna: Il Mulino, 1985).

Burns, T. R. "Una teoria strutturale dello scambio sociale," in M. Magatti, ed. *Azione economica come azione sociale* (Milano: F. Angeli, 1991), pp. 119-146.

Busana Banterle, C., and G.P. Cella, "Il welfare e l'allocazione politica: alcune alternative," in U. Ascoli, ed., *Welfare State all italiana* (Bari: Laterza, 1984).

Caillé, A. *Critica della ragione utilitaria* (Torino: Bollati Boringhieri, 1991). Originally published as *Critique de la raison utilitaire* (Paris: La Découverte, 1988).

Cella, G.P. "Reciprocità, redistribuzione, scambio. Note su Karl Polanyi," *Stato e Mercato*, no. 13 (1985).

Cheal, D. "Economia morale," in M. Magatti, ed. *Azione economica come azione sociale* (Milano: F. Angeli, 1991), pp. 339-360.

Codara, L. *Oltre il modello della scelta razionale. I processi decisionali nella organizzazione sindacale* (Ph.D diss., Università di Trento, 1989).

Coleman, J. S. "Microfoundations and Macrosocial behaviour," in J. C. Alexander, et al., eds., *The Micro-Macro Link* (Berkeley, California: University of California Press, 1987).

Dalton, G. "Introduction" to K. Polanyi, *Primitive, Archaic and Modern Economies* (Doubleday & Co. Inc., 1968).

———. "Writings that Clarify Theoretical Disputes over Karl Polanyi's Work," in K. Polanyi-Levitt, ed., *The Life and Work of Karl Polanyi* (Montréal: Black Rose Books, 1990). pp. 161-170.

De Romaña, A. L. "The Need for a New Economic Paradigm," in the present volume.

Dore, R. "Buona disposizione e spirito del capitalismo," in M. Magatti, ed., *Azione economica comeazione sociale* (Milano: F. Angeli, 1991), pp. 149-176.

Duesenberry, J. "Comments on "An Economic Analysis of Fertility" by Gary Becker, in Universities—National Bureau Committee for Economic Research, *Demographic and economic Change in Developed Countries* (Princeton, N. J.: Princeton University Press, 1960), pp. 231-240.

Easton, D. *The Political System* (New York: H. K. Knopf, 1960).

Elster, J. *Uva acerba* (Milano: Feltrinelli, 1989). Originally published as *Sour Grapes* (Cambridge: Cambridge University Press, 1983).

Etzioni, A. "Pour une science sociale déontologique," *La Revue du MAUSS*, no.9 (1990), pp. 14-32.

Feltrinelli, Fondazione G. *Libertà e cittadinanza sociale. I due '89: Dalla Rivoluzione francese alla Seconda Internazionale* (Milano: Quaderni 41, Angeli, 1991).

Frydman, R. "Le marché: un système économique incomplet," *La*

Revue du MAUSS, no. 9 (1990), pp. 148-163.

Gambetta, D., ed., *Le strategie della fiducia* (Torino: Einaudi, 1989).

Granovetter, M. "Economic Action and Social Structure: The Problem of Embeddedness," *American Journal of Sociology*, 91, no.3 (1985).

Hettne, B. "The Contemporary Crisis: The Rise of Reciprocity," in K. Polanyi-Levitt, ed., *The Life and Work of Karl Polanyi* (Montréal: Black Rose Books, 1990), pp. 208-220.

Hirschman, A. O. *Shifting Involvements. Private Interest and Public Action* (Princeton, N. J.: Princeton University Press, 1982).

Hollingsworth, J. R., and L.N. Lindberg, "La regolazione dell econo-mia americana: il ruolo di mercato, clan, gerarchia ed associ-azione," in M. Magatti, ed., *Azione economica come azione sociale* (Milano: F. Angeli, 1991), pp. 177-211.

Lesemann, F. "Les politiques sociales entre la sphère domestique, le marché et l état: la notion de welfare mix." Paper presented at the Third International Karl Polanyi Conference, Milano, November 1990.

Magatti, M., ed., *Azione economica come azione sociale* (Milano: F. Angeli, 1991).

Münch, R. "The Interpenetration of Microinteraction and Macrostructures in a Complex and Contingent Institutional Order," in J. C. Alexander, et al. *The Micro-Macro Link* (Berkeley, California: University of California Press, 1987), pp. 319-336.

Münch, R. and N. Smelser, "Relating the Micro and Macro," in J. C. Alexander, et al., *The Micro-Macro Link* (Berkeley, California: University of California Press, 1987), pp. 356-387.

Mutti, A. "La teoria della scelta razionale: dalla microriduzione alla soluzione combinatoria." Paper presented to A.I.S. Conference, *Il rapporto micro-macro nelle scienze sociali*, Pavia, December 1990.

North, D.C. "Markets and Other Allocations Systems in History: The Challenge of Karl Polanyi," *The Journal of European Economic History*, no. 3 (1977).

———. *Structure and Change in Economic History* (New York: Norton, 1981).

Paci, M. *Pubblico e privato nei moderni sistemi di Welfare* (Napoli: Liguori, 1989).

Pearson, H. W. "Introduction" to K. Polanyi, *La sussistenza dell uomo* (Torino: Einaudi, 1983). Published in English as *The Livelihood of Man* (New York: Academic Press Inc., 1977).

Polanyi, K. *La grande trasformazione* (Torino: Einaudi, 1974). Published in English as *The Great Transformation* (New York: Holt, Rinehart & Wimston Inc., 1944).

Polanyi, ed. K. *Traffici e mercati negli antichi imperi* (Torino: Einaudi, 1978).Published in English as *Trade and Market in the Early Empires* (Glencoe, Ill: The Free Press, 1957).

———. *La sussistenza dell uomo* (Torino: Einaudi, 1983). Published in English as *The Livelihood of Man* (New York: Academic Press Inc., 1977).

———. *La libertà in una società complessa* (Torino: Bollati Boringhieri, 1987a).

Polanyi, K. in collaberation with A. Rotstein, *Il Dahomey e la tratta degli schiavi* (Torino: Einaudi, 1987b). Published in English as *Dahomey and the Slave Trade: An Analysis of an Archaic Economy*, in collaboration with A. Rotstein (Seattle, Washington: University of Washington Press, 1966).

Polanyi-Levitt, K., ed., *The Life and Work of Karl Polanyi* (Montréal: Black Rose Books, 1990).

Sen, A. "Individual Freedom as a Social Commitment," *The New York Review of Books* (June 14, 1990), pp. 49-54.

Simon, H. A. "Rational Decision Making in Business Organizations," *American Economic Review* LXIX, (1979), pp. 493-512.

———. *La ragione nelle vicende umane* (Bologna: Il Mulino, 1984). Published in English as *Reason in Human Affairs* (Oxford: Basil Blackwell, 1983)).

———. *Models of my Life* (New York: Basic Books, 1991).

Stanfield, J. R. *The Economic Thought of Karl Polanyi* (London: Macmillan, 1986).

———. "Karl Polanyi and Contemporary Economic Thought," in K. Polanyi-Levitt, ed., *The Life and Work of Karl Polanyi* (Montréal: Black Rose Books, 1990), pp. 195-207.

Streeck, W., and P. Schmitter, "Comunità, mercato, stato e associazioni? Il possibile contributo dei governi privati all ordine sociale," *Stato e Mercato*, no.13 (1985).

Swedberg, R. "Vers une nouvelle sociologie économique," *La Revue du MAUSS*, no. 9 (1990), pp. 33-70.

Titmuss, R. M. *The Gift Relationship* (New York: Vintage Books, 1972).

Trigilia, C. "Economia dei costi di transazione e sociologia: cooperazione o conflitto," *Stato e Mercato*, no. 25 (1989).

Veca, S. *Una filosofia pubblica* (Milano: Feltrinelli, 1986).

Weisbrod, B. *The Voluntary Non Profit Sector* (Lexington, Mass.: Lexington Books, 1977).

11.

THE LACK OF GENERAL ECONOMIC EQUIVALENCY IN ECOLOGICAL ECONOMICS

Juan Martinez-Alier

The ecological critique of economics, which began over one hundred years ago, was academically and politically marginalized. Such ecological economics, by regarding the economy as human ecology, emphasizes the inability of mainstream economics to value the ecological side-effects of production and consumption, particularly the intergenerational side-effects. The economy, seen from an ecological point of view, does not have a common standard of measurement. Because of such economic incommensurability, the economy is embedded in politics.

Marxian economics, despite its focus on reproduction rather than allocation, also failed to value long-term ecological costs. A few forgotten authors introduced ecological concerns in the debate on the economics of socialism in the 1920s and 1930s. This paper builds upon such past attempts in order to find a commonality between ecological economics and socialism, where "socialism" is defined in terms of equality, social or communal control of the means of production, democratic planning, and internationalism. Some social movements are agencies that internalize certain externalities which the economy leaves unvalued. Such egalitarian ecologism is in contrast with the current efforts by international ecological managerialism to define an environmental policy agenda which benefits mainly the rich.

THE ECONOMY AS HUMAN ECOLOGY

In the last few years, there has been, paradoxically, a simultaneous increase in the ideology of the free market (also in noncapitalist economies, as part of the political struggle against the bureaucracy), and in ecological awareness.[1] William Kapp (1910-1976) had already written on ecological issues in a socialist economy in his thesis in Geneva in the mid-1930s. In the 1950s and 1960s, Kapp would become one of the best known ecological economists. He spent part of his career in the United States, perhaps in contact with Karl Polanyi (1886-1964), when both were at Columbia University in New York. Polanyi had written on the economics of socialism in the early 1920s.

With few exceptions, neither mainstream economists, nor critics of economics in the Marxian or institutionalist traditions have seen the economy as human ecology. Ecological economists such as Nicholas Georgescu-Roegen, Kenneth Boulding, William Kapp, Frederick Soddy, Patrick Geddes, Josef Popper-Lynkeus, and Sergei Podolinsky have considered the economy not as a circular or spiral flow of exchange value, a merry-go-round between producers and consumers, but rather as a one-way entropic throughput of energy and materials. The most active economist today in defence of the entropic view of the economy is Herman Daly, a former student of Georgescu-Roegen, but ecological economics actually began one hundred years ago. It provoked counterattacks, such as Max Weber's critique of Wilhelm Ostwald in 1909.

In my view, Karl Polanyi himself, although aware of ecological issues, as shown by many passages in *The Great Transformation,* did not explicitly adopt this entropic view of the economy. Karl Polanyi's connection with ecological economics is rather implicit in the fact that, as a major institutionalist economist, he would sympathize with the view that the intergenerational allocation of scarce resources and waste cannot be understood by a study of market transactions between individuals, separated from the historical study of the social distribution of moral values, and from the historical study of the interpretations of technical change.

To see the economy as entropic does not imply ignorance of the anti-entropic properties of life. Thus, Georgescu-Roegen's ecological economics (1971) would not be opposed to the view that systems which receive energy from outside (such as the Earth) may exhibit steadily increasing degrees of structure and organization over time.[2] While the awareness that *physical-chemical* structures in open systems can be anti-entropic, and the modeling of such processes, are new, the idea of "life against entropy" is over one hundred years old, and it has been very much a part of the ecological view of the economy. Thus, Vernadsky (1863-1945) explained, in a section of his book *La Géochimie* entitled "Energie de la matiére vivante et le principe de Carnot," that the energies of living matter were contrary to the *energies de la matière brute*. This had been pointed out by authors such as the Irish geologist John Joly and the German physicist Felix Auerbach (with his notion of *Ektropismus*). Vernadsky added:

> L'histoire des idées qui concernent l'énergétique de la vie...nous presente une suite presque ininter-rompue de penseurs, de savants et de philosophes, arrivant aux mêmes idées plus ou moins indepen-damment...Un savant ukrainien mort jeune, S. Podolinsky, a compris toute la portée de ces idées et a taché de les appliquer à l'étude des phenomènes économiques.[3]

In retrospect, Vernadsky's endorsement of Podolinsky's work might prove beneficial to the growth of ecological socialist economics, given his importance in the science of ecology within some republics of the Soviet Union. Podolinsky (1850-91) was a Darwinist, though not a social-Darwinist. In fact, he was a radical federalist, a Ukrainian narodnik of the 1870s, a medical doctor and a Marxist.[4] Rightly, Podolinsky did not attribute differences in energy use within and between nations to any evolutionary superiority, but to the inequality bred by capitalism. Now as in the past, the ecological point of view may lead either to egalitarian views, or to social Darwinist views (dating back to Boltzmann's dictum of 1886, "the struggle for life is a struggle for available energy"). My view is that since the exosomatic use of energy and materials is "not in our (human) genes," it is explained rather by our economy and politics. This point must be made again today against the growth of social-Prigoginism, i.e., the doctrine that social systems (for instance, Japan, the European Common Market, or the city of New York?) organize themselves in such a way as to render worries about resource depletion and pollution of the environment obsolete. How are the boundaries of such "social systems" established? The natural sciences do not explain the size and direction of the flows of resources, or the territorial distribution of the human population in the world today. Human ecology is also political economy.

ECOLOGICAL MARXISM

Although the ecological view of the economy leads directly to the issue of unequal distribution, Marxism did not see the economy as human ecology, and this is why there was no Marxist ecological historiography, until recently.[5] Engels' negative reaction to Podolinsky's work in 1882 contributed to the divorce between Marxism and human ecology.[6] Nevertheless, unnoticed by Marxists, old and new ecological movements have been struggling over availability of water and energy (including food energy), over workplace health and safety, toxic waste disposal, conservation of forests by native peoples against paper factories, and higher prices for exhaustible resources from the third world.

Of course, ecological perception in history will not be expressed by the actors themselves in the terms familiar to ecologists, of flows of energy and materials, or of exhaustible resources and waste. This language is the language of scientists, and also of some ecological movements (for instance, part of the German Green movement). It is certainly not the language used in history, or at present, by other, perhaps as yet unknown, ecological movements which have tried to keep natural resources out of the generalized market system; and which have established an ecological economy in opposition to the chrematistic economy. To the extent that the generalized market undervalues externalities, such social movements which try to keep resources out of the market are also, at the same time, ecological movements. This view is developing in India, mainly through Ramachandra Guha, who has written the history of the struggle for communal access to forests from the time of the British Raj to the Chipko Movement.[7] It is also developing in Mexico, through authors such as Victor Manuel Toledo and Enrique Leff. The new ecological history is not divorced from the history of socioeconomic conflicts, and it considers some social movements as agencies that bring some ecological costs into the open. The view that some social movements internalize some externalities[8] also carries implications for an ecological definition of "unequal exchange." To give a Mexican example: social movements could develop in favour of restricting exports of oil and natural gas, and increasing their price, because, at present, exhaustible resources, with a long "production time," are exchanged for imported products produced in much shorter periods.

As regards the metropolitan economies, the traditional Marxian view is that there is a contradiction between the overproduction of capital and the deficiency in the purchasing power of their own domestic exploited working class, or from the external, exploited economies. In ecological Marxism, one would focus not on the overproduction of capital but on the impairment or destruction of the conditions for an expanded "reproduction" of capital.[9] At first sight, this could be related to the view in classical economics that the economy would stagnate because of decreasing agricultural yields at the extensive margin (new lands), and intensive margin (more inputs per unit of land). In fact, Marxist economics, to the extent that it dealt with natural resources, took such a Ricardian view. Thus, in the 1970s it was argued that the increase in the price of oil could be analyzed in terms similar to the increase in prices required in order to cover costs of marginal land in the Ricardian theory of differential rent, and that the resulting increase in rents relative to profits would alter the pattern between consumption and savings (and investment) so as to slow down the accumulation of capital. However, despite the fall in the price of oil in the 1980s, there was less available oil in the 1980s than in the 1970s. The point is that the price of agricultural produce on marginal land must cover production costs, while the price of an exhaustible resource must simply cover the cost of extraction at the margin. Oil is not produced; it is destroyed quicker than its geological "production time." Oil cannot be "reproduced."

Marx did not believe in decreasing returns in agriculture. He saw with his own eyes that production in Britain was increasing even with a decrease in the number of agriculturalists. He was aware of the chemical requirements for agricultural production, and quoted favourably Liebig's argument for small scale agriculture as more conducive to the recycling of nutrients. However, Marx did not discuss whether agricultural prices should not only pay for current production costs but that they should also secure the long-term fertility of the land. In any case, the "reproduction" of fossil fuel is clearly not a matter of prices being high enough. If, in Marxian economics, "ecological values" would need to be transformed into increased prices in order to have a negative influence on capital accumulation, then the ecological critique is also valid against such "ecological Marxism," precisely because social costs, and the needs of future generations, are not reflected in prices. The entropic character of the economy implies ecological costs in the form of depletion of resources and pollution, costs which remain external to the market. They are brought into the open only when they become the objective of an ecological movement.

ALLOCATIONS WITHOUT TRANSACTIONS

Since the economy is entropic, there is exhaustion of resources and there is production. The ecological critique of economics questions the ability of the market to accurately value such effects. Here, the fact that exhaustion of resources is more a problem for the future, while pollution is a problem both for future and present generations, helps to explain why downstream environmental effects are more easily acknowledged than upstream scarcities. The ecological critique points out that because of such a temporal dimension, the economy involves allocations (of waste, of diminished resources) to future generations, without such allocations arising from any transactions. Therefore, the economy cannot be explained on the basis of individual choices and preferences. Methodological individualism encounters the insuperable ontological difficulty of coping with future generations. Because of this, ecological economics is closely linked to institutionalist economics, and it is a mortal enemy of mainstream economics.[10] Is it also an enemy of socialist economics?

Since those not-yet-born cannot participate in a market for diachronic externalities, environmental concerns and reliance on the market are mutually antithetical. Therefore, one would have expected ecological issues to figure widely in the debates on economic planning in a Central European context from the late nineteenth century until the 1930s. However, the ecological discussion was weak in socialist circles because of the lack of an ecological Marxism (and also because of the absence of an ecological anarchism). Only a few authors wrote about a collectivized economy with ecological considerations in mind: Popper-Lynkeus (1838-1921), Ballod-Atlanticus (1864-1933), Otto Neurath (1882-1945), William Kapp (1910-76). As much as I would like to add Kropotkin to this list, I do not think Kropotkin had an ecological view of the economy (thus, Popper-Lynkeus pointed out that Kropotkin's programme of universal greenhouse agriculture forgot to reckon with energy input).

An early participant in the debate on the economics of socialism was the analytical philosopher Otto Neurath. Inspired by Popper-Lynkeus and by Ballod-Atlanticus, Neurath was aware that the market could not give values to intergenerational effects. In his writings on a socialist economy, beginning in 1919, he put forward the following example: two capitalist factories competing in the market, one with two hundred workers and one hundred tons of coal, the second one with three hundred workers and only forty tons of coal. The implementation of a more "economic" process would achieve an advantage. In a socialist economy in order to compare two economic plans, which could both achieve the same result, one using less coal and more human labour, the other using more coal and less human labour, a present value must be given to future needs for coal. A decision must therefore be taken not only on a rate of discount and on the time horizon but also on the evolution of technology (use of solar energy, use of water power, use of nuclear power, to which Neurath could have added weights for global warming, acid rain, radioactive pollution). Because of this heterogeneity, a decision on which plan to implement could not be reached on the basis of a common unit of measurement. Elements of the economy were not commensurable, hence the need for a *naturalrechnung*. One can see why Neurath became one of Hayek's *bêtes noires*. In fact, Neurath managed to antagonize liberals, moderate social-democrats (because he was too radical, not pragmatic enough), and official communists, because he did not worship the Soviet experiment. Thus, he was said to think *auf so primitive chiliastische Weise* that he was *im Utopismus stecken geblieben*![11]

As it will be recalled, Oskar Lange's ingenious market and socialist solution to the objections of Max Weber, Ludwig von Mises, and Hayek, did not include a discussion on the intergenerational allocation of exhaustible resources (which is a different matter from discussing whether coal or oil should be priced according to marginal cost of extraction instead of average cost, as if this would ensure an optimal intergenerational allocation). Dobb's contribution to the debate emphasized growth over the allocation of resources. Both under capitalism and socialism, the assumption of growth allows the discounting of future effects to negligible present values without discrimination against future generations. However, ecological economics questions the assumption of growth, and indeed it questions the very definitions of national income accounting.

Otto Neurath's concept of a *naturalrechnung* was developed because he realized that, from an ecological point of view, elements in the economy became incommensurable. Neurath's idea was received by market economists as could have been predicted. Hayek wrote that Neurath's proposal, in which all calculations of the central planning authorities should and could be carried out *in natura*, showed that Neurath was quite oblivious to the insuperable difficulties which the absence of value calculations would put in the way of any rational economic use of resources.[12] Hayek, in concert with almost all participants in the debate on economic rationality under socialism (on both sides of the divide), was quite oblivious to problems of resource depletion and pollution. Hayek's glorification of the market principle and of individualism led him to dismiss authors who developed an ecological critique of economics—such as Fredrick Soddy, Lancelot Hogben, Lewis Mumford, and also Otto Neurath—as totalitarian "social engineers," "neo-St. Simonians."[13] Otto Neurath was not only an economist, a radical, active in the revolution in Munich in 1919, and a writer in praise of "scientific utopias"; he was also a major analytical philosopher of the Vienna Circle, whose manifesto he wrote himself.[14] Neurath proposed the sketching of many "scientific utopias" such as those of Popper-Lynkeus and Ballod-Atlanticus, from which concrete plans for a socialized economy could be chosen.

ECONOMIC INCOMMENSURABILITY

Here, one of the major polemics of our age has been reopened by pointing out that the market economy by itself cannot provide a guide for the allocation of scarce resources (and of waste). Many feel nostalgia for the freedom of the market when confronted with the prospect of a bureaucracy with the technocratic means of ecological and/or economic planning. However, it has long been noticed that the market economy cannot deal with the externalities which arise from the fact that localized human actions lead to irreversible ecological damage. Some externalities are novel only in the sense that they have not been socially acknowledged, but not in a scientific sense. Hence, for instance, today's German usage of *treibhauseffekt*, retranslated from "greenhouse effect," instead of the original and excellent German word, *glashauswirkung*. The gradual exhaustion of some fossil fuels caused by the demand in a few countries, species extinction because of tropical deforestation, acid rain, the CO_2 build-up in the atmosphere and its effects on climate change, accidents in nuclear power plants and the absence of a technical solution for the disposal of radioactive waste, all such ecological impacts were discussed at least fifty years ago, and some, one hundred years ago. The lack of awareness of these discussions is "socially constructed ignorance."[15] Other environmental effects might be genuinely surprising. For instance, the effects of CFC on the ozone layer were unknown until the 1970s. Similarly, the awareness that a small nuclear war would be followed by a terrible "nuclear winter," and the alarm at the possible ecological effects of genetically-engineered organisms, are not old. Whether noticed (and ignored) long ago or only a few years ago, there is much uncertainty about such effects, at least with respect to their speed, and to their countervailing technical solutions. Economists are unable to put a present value on such effects, duly discounted (at which rate?), and weighed by the (unknown) probability of occurrence. Let us consider two examples: the increased "greenhouse effect" and nuclear power.

Svante Arrhenius explained in his textbook on global ecology[16] that the *glashauswirkung* which helped to keep the Earth warm would increase with the increase in carbon dioxide in the atmosphere, and that in northern latitudes this was to be welcomed. In 1937 it was estimated that fuel combustion had added 150,000 million tons of carbon dioxide to the air in the past fifty years, three quarters of which had remained in the atmosphere. The rate of increase in mean temperature was estimated at only 0.005 degrees centigrade per year: "the combustion of fossil fuel...is likely to prove beneficial to mankind in several ways, besides the provision of heat and power. For instance, the above mentioned small increase of mean temperature would be important at the northern margin of cultivation."[17] The intellectual history of climatic change up to the scare in the United States in the summer of 1988 will perhaps show that some scientists soon took a pessimistic view, but Callendar was, by his own description, steam technologist to the British Electrical and Allied Industries Research Association. His paper was received and discussed openly by the Royal Meteorological Society of Great Britain whose members questioned the statistics, but not the view that increased carbon dioxide would be a positive externality.

Conventional environmental economics, as a branch of mainstream economics, is often useless for environmental management, because the concept of "externalities" merely reveals the inability to value uncertain, even socially unknown or unacknowledged effects, whether of depletion or pollution. Thus, the global warming scare is nowadays used in favour of nuclear power, but the economics of nuclear power also provides good examples of invaluable externalities: present values must be given to the costs of dismantling power stations in a few decades, and to the costs of keeping radioactive waste under control (or to the damage from radioactive wastes for thousands of years). Such values will depend on the rate of discount chosen. Also, there are possible by-products of nuclear power, such as plutonium, which we are unable to be classified either as positive or negative externalities, let alone be attributed a monetary present value. Since the plutonium produced as a by-product of the nuclear civil programme may have a military use, it can be given a positive value, thus improving the economics of nuclear power (in the chrematistic sense). This "plutonium credit" was factored into the accounts of the initial British nuclear power stations.[18]

However, plutonium might come to be seen in the future as a negative externality. Frederick Soddy, who was a well-qualified nuclear scientist, warned against the peaceful use of nuclear energy in 1947 because of "the virtual impossibility of preventing the use of nonfission products of the pile, such as plutonium, for war purposes."[19] However, it was not until the 1970s that the link between the civil and military uses of nuclear energy became a public issue.

POSITIONAL GOODS AND "FORDISM" IN THE PERIPHERY

Fred Hirsch's concept of "positional goods" in his influential book *Social Limits to Growth* (1976) was related to that of externalities. It will be discussed here in an ecological context, although Hirsch dismissed an ecological approach to the economy while trying to explain the persistence of strong distributive conflicts in high-income countries. The book title was polemical against the sudden fashion for "ecological limits to growth" after the oil price increase in 1973. Hirsch argued that, as wages rose in proportion to productivity, mass consumption goods produced through mass production methods became available to everybody (in a Fordist pattern, to use the terminology of another school of political economy). In Western countries, despite the growth of consumption, there was dissatisfaction. One of its roots was precisely, according to Hirsch, the positional character of some goods and services. Veblen's conspicuous consumption comprises one class of "positional goods," the "exclusive" goods bought by the snobs, but Hirsch's concept goes beyond this.

The satisfaction drawn from positional goods diminishes when other people have them because positional goods impose social costs. His examples are as follows: if everybody has a car; if everybody strives after a good education which qualifies him or her for a job at a good wage; or if everybody has a country cottage or a yacht, the satisfaction of these wants remains unfulfilled because of traffic congestion and lack of clean air. They also remain unsatisfied because there will be not enough jobs for all qualified people and because the agglomeration of country cottages or yachts makes them unattractive. Hirsch's emphasis was more on the congestion of European cities, roads, and beaches than on exhaustion of resources, or on world pollution effects.

According to Hirsch, the "material economy" was defined as "output amenable to continued increases in productivity per unit of labour input," while the "positional economy" could not grow without limit because of increasing social costs. This distinction was parallel to Harrod's distinction between "democratic wealth" and "oligarchic wealth." However, from the ecological point of view it appears (and it could have already appeared in 1976) that a "material economy" is also a "positional economy" which shifts costs inside the present generation or shifts costs to future generations. This happens because the increase in productivity per unit of labour, which in some parts of the world has allowed the generalization of "democratic wealth" in the form of mass consumption of goods, has been partly achieved at the expense of exhaustion of resources and pollution of the environment. That is, unless the economy were delinked, or decoupled from the use of energy and materials, and the production of waste, certain forms of wealth will never become universal. Also, some forms of wealth are causes of poverty (now or later). However, in Hirsch's view, the limits to growth were "social," not ecological: "an acre of land used for the satisfaction of hunger can, in principle, be expanded two-, ten-, or a thousand-fold by technological advances... By contrast, an acre of land used as a pleasure garden for the enjoyment of a single family can never rise above its initial productivity in that use."[20] While the second part of this statement is true, the first part is metaphysical since Hirsch provided no analysis of the meaning of "technological advances" in terms of the flow of energy and materials in the economy: modern agriculture has a low ratio of production to fossil fuel input.

Therefore, the relevance of Hirsch's concept of "positional goods" is greater than he himself supposed. For instance, a world with a stable population of ten billion people, and with a North Atlantic car density, would have about four billion cars. This is ten times the present number of cars in the world. A pattern of industrial development without cars would be a novelty in the second half of the twentieth century: the economies of the successful newly industrialized countries (Italy, Japan, Spain, South Korea) were or are still led by the car sector. Mexico, Brazil, Eastern Europe and the USSR, India, and indeed China would like to follow suit. Suitable information on the energetic and material side of production and consumption (which was certainly available by 1975!) would have led Hirsch to think not only of traffic jams. Cars will not become mass consumption goods, because of their thirst for fossil fuels and also because of their environmental impact in terms of CO_2 and NO_x. Fordism in the periphery will be in any case Fordism without Fords, even perhaps Fordism without meat (or at least, not with a North Atlantic meat consumption of over 50 kilograms per person/year). Therefore, distributional conflicts cannot be solved in the world by a universal Fordist pattern of economic growth, not only because of the social limits emphasized by Hirsch, but also because of ecological limits.

Here as always, the technological optimists may use the fact that the future is uncertain in order to argue against an ecological orientation of economic policy. It is not known whether, for instance, a technology based on photovoltaics (with sun energy) and hydrogen as fuel (taken from water by electrolysis) will soon become available.[21] In the meantime, Fordism is not a realistic prospect for the "periphery" of the world, where most people live. It is a reality in the metropolitan countries only because there is no competition for oil coming from the poor, peripheral countries where people lack even the oil they would need (like kerosene or butane gas) to substitute for scarce cooking fuelwood. If you run a car, not only are you preventing *eo ipso* another family from having a car (at least in the future, if not already now), but you are also increasing the "other energy crisis," the lack of fuelwood.

INTERNATIONAL ECOMANAGERIALISM

The main point of this paper, until now, has been that neither the market, nor a planned economy by itself can deal with externalities. However, in this section I shall argue against a purely ecological approach. Policy prescriptions based on ecological analysis make sense only if concrete social contexts are taken for granted, and they are not more rational than such social contexts themselves. Humankind's ability to maintain enormous differences in the exosomatic consumption of energy and material resources, between States and inside each State, requires distinctive human institutions. Because of the lack of genetic instructions on human exosomatic consumption of energy and material resources, because also of peculiar political, social, and territorial human arrangements, human ecology is different from the ecology of other animals. It is a type of study which cannot be reduced to the natural sciences. I shall use as an example the notion of carrying capacity.

"Carrying capacity" refers to the maximum population of a given species which can be supported indefinitely in a given territory, without a degradation of the resource base that would diminish the maximum population in the future. Now, however, what does a "given territory" mean? The territorial distribution of the human population is something which political scientists rather than ecologists should explain. The right to choose one's place of habitation on earth remains the most elusive of human rights. Member States of the new "fortress Europe" (or perhaps, "lifeboat Europe") must require visas for all Africans and Latin Americans. Often, in European countries, the barriers to immigration are not seen as consequences of the difference in standard of living, but as consequences of the pressure of population on resources in poor countries: social inequalities are explained away biologically. Nevertheless, when many European countries were countries of emigration, not so long ago, their population densities were lower than today. Migration usually is the result of "pull" factors, and, in any case, carrying capacity can be increased, if not from domestic resources then by energy and materials subsidies from outside. Across States, frontier police stop migrants who come from territories where they are not necessarily starving, but where there is a comparatively low level of consumption of energy and materials. States, frontiers, and policemen, are products of historical social conflicts. Hence, the Maxwell's demons analogy. Maxwell's demons were unnatural beings who were supposed to be able to maintain, or even increase the difference in temperature between communicating gases by sorting out high speed and low speed molecules. Ecologists are unable to explain the territorial-political distribution of the human population. Sometimes they take it for granted, and then they preach social-Darwinism, as in Hardin's "lifeboat ethics."

The notion of "degradation of the resource base," another important element of the definition of "carrying capacity," is also problematic. Economists claim that the use of resources, even if these are not produced but merely extracted, is not necessarily economic degradation. This is because, before being exhausted, they will be substituted by new resources. Economists also point out that although there is no guarantee of such substitution. Such resources should be used because economic "growth" makes future consumption at the margin less valuable than today's consumption. However, national income accounting disregards the entropic character of the economy (for instance, there is no provision for "amortization" of exhaustible resources destroyed in the economy). "Growth" is defined inside the closed language of economics. Nevertheless, without denying the shortcomings of economics, a so-called ecological rationality is not a better base for policy than the rationality of the market, because ecology cannot evade, anymore than economics, the moral issues of giving present values to future effects, and of adjudicating distributional conflicts today.

Ecologists (and, in general, environmental scientists) are asked to determine standards for human life (instead of pinpointing trade offs): for instance, "safe" doses of radiation, "safe" doses of pesticides, tolerable "CO_2 budgets," and even optimum densities of population (at least in poor countries). Scientists are also asked to deliver new materials and new genetically-engineered plants and animals, with no nasty environmental effects. But scientists are uncertain about such things, and even if they knew for sure, they have no methodology for getting a common standard of measurement that would guide the trade-offs which are really in question. That is, even if reliable scientific information were available, a purely science-based policy from the top down would be impossible by itself. Good ecological data is not a guide for decisions on distribution between different social groups and generations.

Who should set the environmental-economic agenda? The governments of particular States, the EC Commission, the World Health Organization, Greenpeace, the International Monetary Fund (IMF) and the World Bank, the Chipko movement, the German Green movement, and WISE all attempt to direct the debate, although with unequal means and unequal opportunities, in order to set the environmental policy agenda of the world to determine the important issues. This fight is not yet so much about decisions as about the inclusion and exclusion of topics. The temptation of international eco-managerialism is strong: Harich's nightmare of "Babeuf and the Club of Rome," or, in the opposite direction, an "IMF of Ecology." Some try to escape this by praising the market, some by imagining small-scale ecoregionalist refuges, little "ecotopian" communes (presumably protected from large scale immigration by an armed border patrol). They fail to address the important questions of global ecology. The existence of an egalitarian ecologism in the South is ignored in the fierce struggle for the world environmental agenda, from which the rich exclude issues such as their disproportionate contribution to radioactive pollution and to fossil fuel exhaustion, and where the right to migrate from poor to rich countries is never mentioned.

SCIENTIFIC PROGRESS AND TECHNOLOGICAL PESSIMISM

Scientific global ecology is an insecure base for policies from above. This, however, does not stop scientists (and North-Atlantic politicians) from telling other people what to do. Mistrustful of unfounded and prepotent scientific advice, aware also of the deplorable ecological and social consequences of some technologies, some grassroots ecologists turn against science and become holy and holistic, lost in the mists of irrationality (since they no longer possess, on the other hand, a peasant or tribal understanding of nature).

Rational discourse (in favour of science or anything else) is rather a waste of time, if directed against enemies of rationality.

But nevertheless, the point should be made that antiscientific ecological activists mistake science for technology. Reasonable doubts on whether some technologies really mean "progress" become silly doubts on whether science is the right way to pursue knowledge. In fact, ecological knowledge cannot be but scientific knowledge. Members of other political persuasions, so keen on the "scientific-technical revolution" a few years ago, also mistook scientific progress (the advance in scientific knowledge, which undoubtedly takes places) for "technical progress." The progress of science has often shown technologies to be impossible or noxious. Let us illustrate with some examples. Ecological worries about scarcity and ill allocation of energy would be stupid if suitable *perpetuum mobile* engines became available. Scientific progress, in the form of the laws of thermodynamics, showed this to be an illusion. In another example, although nuclear technology grew out of a marriage of science and politics, science shows why radioactive waste is dangerous, and why safe storage is not possible.

More recently, science has provided a critique of current agricultural practices in the overdeveloped countries, explaining why "organic farming" is superior in terms of fossil fuel energy efficiency and also in terms of pollution effects. Science not only provides the data in order to denounce some technologies as impossible, or dangerous, or wasteful; it also concludes that, because of incomplete data and complex interactions, science itself cannot dispel uncertainties about some global environmental effects. The ozone layer issue is probably exceptional in that scientific data might be the base for consensual policies-from-above. In contrast, the valuation of the "greenhouse effect" is embedded in uncertainties and distributional conflicts.

The pathetic enthusiasm for the "cold fusion" titillation in the mass media in the spring of 1989, including the cool *Economist*, shows that people who use more than their fair share of available energy are ready to believe in today's equivalent to the *perpetuum mobile*. The priests of such quasi-religious technological optimism are often scientists in search of money. Technological optimism prevents rational discussion on the intergenerational and contemporary allocation of resources. I believe that the best defence against irrational technological optimism is science itself. Thus, Rachel Carson's *Silent Spring* was, in 1962, a starting point for the scientific critique of modern agricultural technologies.

CONCLUSION

The ecological critique against economics is based on the question of unknown future agents' preferences and their inability to intervene in today's market; and therefore on the arbitrariness of the values given at present to exhaustible resources, or to external effects to be felt in the future. The ecological critique is also based on the uncertainty about the workings of environmental systems which prevents the application of externality analysis. Many externalities are perhaps yet unknown, and some externalities about which we *do* know are not even known to be positive or negative. We are unable to give them a monetary present value. "It is important to keep in mind that we are dealing with essentially heterogeneous magnitudes and quantities for which there can be no common denominator...a commensurability which simply does not exist."[22] There was then a lack of a general equivalency, even inside the market system. But such warnings were repressed, such critiques unheeded.

Strong rational arguments have been brought against so called economic rationality (because externalities escape economic calculus), and also, on the other hand, against ecological managerialism. Often, science cannot yet give convincing estimates on many ecological questions. Even when data overwhelmingly proves some ecological fact, science by itself cannot be the basis for policies from above. Science cannot guide the trade-offs implied by intragenerational and intergenerational allocations of resources and waste. Whether policies are to be based on economics, or on the science of ecology is not the relevant question. As we have seen, neither economics nor ecology can provide a policy. Rather, the question is, should issues of ecological-economic policy, which are also issues of distribution, be decided (*a*) by the market, with unequal purchasing power and in absence of future generations; (*b*) by policies from above (based on technocratic economics or on technocratic ecology); or (*c*) are they to be decided by a politics of universal, and much more equal representation? This third option would be helped by drawing up many different scenarios, well-informed by science which include a sober assessment of technological prospects, and explicit acknowledgment of future generations: a collection of concrete, ecological, scientific utopias in line with those of Popper-Lynkeus, Ballod-Atlanticus, and Otto Neurath. Many such concrete utopias should come from the poor.

Which territorial political units should decide how we should live? How we should treat fellow humans? How we should treat future generations? Is the proper location of decision regional, national or global? Experience since 1945 shows that international agreements among representatives of States, or blocs of States, merely reproduce existing inequalities. Could plenary-meeting ecoregionalism and eco-globalism be combined? Plenary-meeting ecoglobalism is difficult to implement. And, even if it were implemented, it would not guarantee proper regard for future generations. On the other hand, ecoregionalism leaves aside world inequalities in the distribution of resources and population. An ecological socialism was already present in some unacknowledged early social movements and continues today. Ecological socialism is defined not by State ownership of the means of production, but by equality, internationalism, and social and communal control over the means of production. It is still growing as an ideology and as a political movement, much reinforced by the new ecological awareness. Its roots will be among the poor. It will not rely, in its economics, on the market or on central planning because it will be conscious that economic incommensurability places economic decisions openly in the political sphere.

In centrally planned economies, the market was absent not only as allocator of resources but also as provider of incentives to promote the more efficient use of resources. Thus, former communist economies had a greater energy intensity per unit of output than the Western European economies. Today it is seldom remarked that, in market economies, some unvalued externalities are not only sporadic cases of market failure, but rather serious threats to the sustainability of the economy, and indeed, perhaps to the survival of humankind. Now, in market economies within democratic capitalism, an antidote to *some* externalities is their internalization through the agency of social movements. In contrast, in centrally planned economies within single-party dictatorships, no possibility was given for social movements to express themselves. Thus, in Cuba today, there is still no antinuclear movement against the nuclear power station near Cienfuegos.

Against the glorification of the market, and also against an ecological managerialism from the top-down, Enrique Leff (1986), Michael Redclift (1987), and James O Connor (1988) have pointed out that ecological movements increase private monetary capitalist costs (or monetary costs of public firms or agencies), and bring them nearer to social costs. This is a persuasive argument for democratic planning. However, when externalities will be felt only in the future, or are very uncertain, social movements cannot be the voice of future generations that the market economy (or a centrally planned economy) denies.

NOTES

1. Cf. Dieter (Hrsg.) Graf, *Ökonomie und Ökologie der Naturnutzung* (Jena: Gustav Fischer, 1984) for an East German contribution.
2. Cf. Jacques Grinevald, "Vernadsky y Lotka como fuentes de la bioeconomía de Georgescu-Roegen," *Ecología Política*, 1 (Barcelona: n.p., 1991).
3. W. Vernadsky, *La Géochimie* (Paris: Felix Alcan, 1924), pp. 334-5.
4. Cf. his biography in J. Martinez-Alier with Klaus Schluepmann, *Ecological Economics* (Oxford/New York: Blackwell, 1987), chap. 3.
5. Ramachandra Guha and Mahdav Gadgil,. "State Forestry and Social Conflict in British India," *Past and Present* (May 1989).
6. *Ecological Economics*.
7. Ramachandra Guha, *The Unquiet Woods* (Delhi: Oxford University Press, 1989).
8. Enrique Leff, *Ecologia y Capital* (Mexico: Universidad Autonoma de Mexico, 1986); John O Connor, "Introduction," *Capitalism. Nature. Socialism. A Journal of Socialist Ecology*, no. 1 (Santa Cruz, California 1988).
9. "Introduction," *Capitalism. Nature. Socialism.*
10. *Ecological Economics*, chap. 11.
11. Felix Wefl, "Review of Otto Neurath (1925)" in *Archiv für Geschichte des Sozialismus*, hrsg. von Carl Gruenberg, XII (1926). (Reprint. Syndicat, Graz, 1979), p. 457.
12. F. A. von Hayek, ed., *Collectivist Economic Planning* (London: Routledge, 1935), pp. 30-31.
13. F. A. von Hayek, *The Counter-Revolution of Science* (Glencoe: Free Press, 1952; Indianapolis: Liberty Press, 1979).
14. Neurath's writings on socialist economics are cited in Erwin Weissel, *Die Ohnmacht des Sieges* (Vienna: Europaverlag, 1976); Friedrich Stadler, *Vom Positivismus zur "Wissenschaftlichen Weltauffassung"* (Vienna/Munich: Loecker, 1982); and Ingrid Belke, *Die sozialreformerischen Ideen von Josef Popper-Lynkeus (1838-1921)* (Tübingen: J. C.B. Mohr; Paul Siebeck, 1978).
15. J. R. Ravetz, "Usable knowledge, usable ignorance: incomplete science with policy implications," in W. C. Clark and R. E. Munn, eds., *Sustainable Development of the Biosphere* (IIASA, New Rochelle, NY: Cambridge University Press, 1986), pp. 415-434.
16. Svante Arrhenius, *Lehrbuch der kosmischen Physik* (Leipzig: Hirzel, 1903), p. 171.

17. G.S. Callendar, "The artificial production of carbon dioxide and its influence on temperature," *Quarterly Journal of the Roval Meteorological Society* 64 (1938), p. 236.
18. J. W. Jeffery, "The Collapse of Nuclear Economics," *The Ecologist* 1 (1988), pp. 9-13.
19. Frederick Soddy, *Atomic Energy for the Future* (London: Constitutional Research Association, 1947), p. 12.
20. Fred Hirsch, *Social Limits to Growth* (Cambridge: Harvard University Press, 1976), p. 20.
21. Michael Renner, *Rethinking the Role of the Automobile,* Worldwatch Paper 84 (Washington D.C.: Government Printing Office, 1988).
22. K. William Kapp, *Social Costs, Economic Development, and Environmental Disruption,* edited and with an introduction by John E. Ullmann (Lanham, Maryland and London: University Press of America, 1983), p. 37.

REFERENCES

Arrhenius, Svante. *Lehrbuch der kosmischen Physik* (Leipzig: Hirzel, 1903).

Ballod-Atlanticus, Karl. *Produktion und Konsum im Sozialstaat* (Stuttgart: Dietz, 1898).

———. *Der Zukunftsstaat - Wirtschaftstechnisches Ideal und Volkswirtschaftliche Wirklichkeit,* 4th ed. (Berlin: Laub, 1927).

———. "Einiges aus der Utopienliteratur der letzten Jahre," *Archiv für die Geschichte des Sozialismus,* hrsg. Carl Gruenberg, Bd. VI, (1915), pp. 114-128.

Belke, Ingrid . *Die sozialreformerischen Ideen von Josef Popper-Lynkeus (1838-1921)* (Tübingen: J.C.B. Mohr; Paul Siebeck, 1978).

Callendar, G. S. "The artificial production of carbon dioxide and its influence on temperature," *Quarterly Journal of the Roval Meteorological Society* 64 (1938), pp. 223-237.

Georgescu-Roegen, N. *The Entropy Law and the Economic Process* (Cambridge, Mass.: Harvard University Press, 1971).

———. "The Entropy Law and the Economic Process in Retrospect," *Eastern Economic Journal* XII, no.1 (1986), pp. 3-25.

Graf, Dieter (Hrsg.). *Ökonomie und Ökologie der Naturnutzung* (Jena: Gustav Fischer, 1984).

Grinevald, Jacques. "Vernadsky y Lotka como fuentes de la bioeconomía de Georgescu-Roegen" *Ecología Política,* 1 (Barcelona,

1991).

Guha, Ramachandra. "Ideological Trends in Indian Environmentalism," *Economic and Political Weekly* XXIII, no. 49 (Dec. 3, 1988)

———. *The Unquiet Woods* (Delhi: Oxford University Press, 1989).

Guha, Ramachandra. and Mahdav Gadgil. "State Forestry and Social Conflict in British India," *Past and Present* (May 1989).

Harich, Wolfgang. *Kommunismus ohne Wachstum* (Reinbek bei Hamburg: Rowohlt, 1975).

von Hayek, F. A., ed. *Collectivist Economic Planning* (London: Routledge, 1935).

———. *The Counter-Revolution of Science* (Glencoe: Free Press, 1952; Indianapolis: Liberty Press, 1979).

Hirsch, Fred. *Social Limits to Growth* (Cambridge: Harvard University Press, 1976).

Jeffery, J. W. "The Collapse of Nuclear Economics," *The Ecologist* 18, no.1 (1988), pp. 9-13.

William Kapp, K. *Social Costs, Economic Development, and Environmental Disruption*, edited and with an introduction by John E. Ullmann (Lanham, Maryland and London: University Press of America, 1983).

———. *Für eine ökosoziale Ökonomie*, hrsg. von Christian Leipert & Rolf Steppacher (Frankfurt: Fischer, 1987).

Leff, Enrique. *Ecologia y Capital* (Mexico: Universidad Autonoma de Mexico, 1986).

Martinez-Alier, J. with Klaus Schluepmann, *Ecological Economics* (Oxford/New York: Blackwell, 1987;1990).

Neurath, Otto. *Wirtschaftsplan und Naturalrechnung* (Berlin: Laub, 1925).

O'Connor, John. "Introduction," *Capitalism. Nature. Socialism. A Journal of Socialist Ecology*, 1, no. 1 (Santa Cruz, California 1988).

Popper-Lynkeus, Josef. *Die allgemeine Närpflicht als Lösung der sozialen Frage* (Dresden: Reissner, 1912).

———. "Einiges über moderne Utopien. Eine Erwiderung," *Archiv für die Geschichte des Sozialismus*, hrsg. Carl Grünberg, Bd. VI (1915), pp. 309-13 (Reprint, Syndicat, Graz, 1979).

———. *Mein Leben und Wirken: eine Selbsdarstellung* (Dresden: Reissner, 1924).

Ravetz, J. R. "Usable knowledge, usable ignorance: incomplete science with policy implications," in W. C. Clark and R. E. Munn, eds., *Sustainable Development of the Biosphere* (IIASA, New Rochelle, NY: Cambridge University Press, 1986), pp. 415-434.

Redclift, Michael. *Sustainable Development. Exploring the Contradictions* (London/New York: Methuen, 1987).

Renner, Michael. *Rethinking the Role of the Automobile*, Worldwatch Paper 84 (Washington D.C.: Government Printing Office, 1988.)

Soddy, Frederick. *Cartesian Economics: the Bearing of Physical Science upon State Stewardship* (London: Hendersons, 1922).

———. *Atomic Energy for the Future* (London: Constitutional Resarch Association, 1947).

Stadler, Friedrich. *Vom Positivismus zur "Wissenschaftlichen Weltauffassung,"* (Vienna-Munich: Loecker, 1982).

Vernadsky, W. *La Géochimie* (Paris: Felix Alcan, 1924).

Wefl, Felix. "Review of Otto Neurath (1925)," *Archiv für Geschichte des Sozialismus*, hrsg. von Carl Gruenberg XII (1926) (Reprint. Syndicat, Graz, 1979).

Weissel, Erwin. *Die Ohnmacht des Sieges* (Vienna: Europaverlag, 1976).

In conjunction with the *Karl Polanyi Institute of Political Economy,*
Concordia University, Montréal, presents the series:

CRITICAL PERSPECTIVES
ON HISTORIC ISSUES

Volume One

THE LIFE AND WORK OF KARL POLANYI

Kari Polanyi-Levitt, ed.

Polanyi's insights into the social and political impact of the market-driven economy were both timely and prescient, and have guaranteed him a place among the great thinkers of the twentieth century ... a good starting place for those wanting to know more about Polanyi, and a useful source for anyone seeking to understand our "interesting" times.
Canadian Book Review Annual

TABLE OF CONTENTS:

THE GREAT TRANSFORMATION

THE POLANYI RECEPTION

COMPARATIVE ECONOMIC ANTHROPOLOGY

CONTEMPORARY POLITICAL AND ECONOMIC THOUGHT

FAREWELL: In Memorium, by *Hans Zeisel*

264 pages, photographs
Paperback ISBN: 0-921689-80-2 $19.99
Hardcover ISBN: 0-921689-81-0 $48.99

Volume Two

CULTURE AND SOCIAL CHANGE
Social Movements in Québec and Ontario

Colin Leys, Marguerite Mendell, eds

In contrast with the current tendency to see "culture" only as an increasingly commodified instrument of social control in the hands of a power elite, the work collected in this volume reveals cultural transformations occurring in old and new social movements.

The diversity of the topics reflects the multiplicity of political struggles. The editors correctly let the chapters speak for themselves.
Canadian Book Review Annual

TABLE OF CONTENTS

230 pages
Paperback ISBN: 1-895431-28-X $19.99
Hardcover ISBN: 1-895431-29-8 $48.99
L.C. No. 92-70625

Volume Three

FROM POLITICAL ECONOMY TO ANTHROPOLOGY
Situating Economic Life in Past Societies
Colin Duncan, David Tandy, eds.

A collection of international authors' work toward a better understanding of ancient people's attempts at situating economic life within particular societies.

The essays in this volume demonstrate the breadth of Polanyi's influence across many disciplines.
From My Bookshelf

TABLE OF CONTENTS

186 pages
Paperback ISBN: 1-895431-88-3 $19.99
Hardcover ISBN: 1-895431-89-1 $48.99
L.C. No. 93-73927

Volume Four

HUMANITY, SOCIETY AND COMMITMENT

On Karl Polanyi

Kenneth McRobbie, ed.

The articles in this book are based on some of Polanyi's lesser known works: his journalism, letters, articles, conversations, books long out of print, and translations of Hungarian poetry.

TABLE OF CONTENTS

178 pages
Paperback ISBN: 1-895431-84-0 $19.99
Hardcover ISBN: 1-895431-85-9 $48.99
L.C. No. 93-73925

Volume Five

ARTFUL PRACTICES
The Political Economy of Everyday Life

Henri Lustiger-Thaler, Daniel Salée, eds.

In the 1990's, the social, economic and political institutions we have lived with since post-WWII settlements are undergoing massive transformations. The terms of the social contract are being renegotiated, broad segments of the population are increasingly marginalized—faced with the tyranny of ever-triumphant market forces. The artful practices of citizens coping with these changes point to a new political economy of everyday life.

...enjoyable and inspiring...a colourful collection with a wide variety of well-researched case studies, fresh theoretical insights and future perspectives. *Antipode*

TABLE OF CONTENTS

188 pages
Paperback ISBN: 1-895431-92-1 $19.99
Hardcover ISBN: 1-895431-93-X $48.99

Volume Six

EUROPE: CENTRAL AND EAST

Marguerite Mendell, Klaus Nielsen, eds.

Analysts wait with growing apprehension for market "self-regulation" to materialize in the former Eastern block countries. Meanwhile, the vacuum of institutional safeguards of exchange (legal frameworks, trust) are filled by rapidly growing mafias. The people of these countries-in-crisis are faced with coping by means of self-production, barter, and black economic activity. This book considers the social, political and economic complexities which surround the seismic changes going on in eastern europe. Contributors include experienced critics and analysts from East and West.

TABLE OF CONTENTS

300 pages
Paperback ISBN: 1-895431-90-5 $19.99
Hardcover ISBN: 1-8955431-91-3 $48.99
L.C. No. 93-73926

PIERRE-JOSEPH PROUDHON

A Biography

2nd revised edition

George Woodcock

The first full-scale English-language biography of the prominent 19th-century social thinker and "father of anarchism."

A solid and workmanlike effort.
Times Literary Supplement
Woodcock makes a very good case for the consistency of [Proudhon's] teaching.
New York Times

295 pages, index
Paperback ISBN: 0-921689-08-X $19.99
Hardcover ISBN: 0-921689-09-8 $48.99

PETER KROPOTKIN

From Prince to Rebel

George Woodcock, Ivan Avakumovic

This biography surveys and analyzes the most significant aspects of Peter Kropotkin's life and thought: his formative years in Russia, 1842-1876, and the origins of his anarchist thinking; his years as an emigré in Western Europe, 1876-1917, and the ripening of his political thought; and his last years in the Soviet Union, 1917-1921.

490 pages, index, illustrated
Paperback ISBN: 0-921689-60-8 $19.99
Hardcover ISBN: 0-921689-61-6 $48.99

EVOLUTION AND ENVIRONMENT

Peter Kropotkin

Kropotkin's insight, now acknowledged by ecologists, insisted on the selective pressure of the environment.

262 pages
Paperback ISBN: 1-895431-44-1 $19.99
Hardcover ISBN: 1-895431-45-X $48.99

WORDS OF A REBEL

Peter Kropotkin

First published during Kropotkin's imprisonment, this collection contains articles written between 1879 and 1882. The first complete English version.

229 pages
Paperback ISBN: 1-895431-04-2 $19.99
Hardcover ISBN: 1-895431-05-0 $48.99

CONQUEST OF BREAD
Peter Kropotkin

The clearest statement of Kropotkin's doctrines. In his own description: "a study of the needs of humanity, and of the economic means to satisfy them."

235 pages
Paperback ISBN: 0-921689-50-0 $19.99
Hardcover ISBN: 0-921689-51-9 $48.99

FIELDS, FACTORIES AND WORKSHOPS
Peter Kropotkin

As a result of the growing realization that the world's resources of energy and raw materials are finite, the lessons of this book are topical and hopeful.

255 pages, index
Paperback ISBN: 1-895431-38-7 $19.99
Hardcover ISBN: 1-895431-39-5 $48.99

MUTUAL AID: A Factor of Evolution
Peter Kropotkin

Kropotkin counters Huxley's argument that evolution is propelled by a ruthless struggle for existence with the argument that in nature cooperation is as important as competition.

362 pages, index
Paperback ISBN: 0-921689-26-8 $19.99
Hardcover ISBN: 0-921689-27-6 $48.99

THE DECLINE OF THE AMERICAN ECONOMY
Bertrand Bellon and Jorge Niosi

translated by Robert Chodos and Ellen Garmaise

Two prominent economists examine the decline of U.S. industry, covering the post-World War period to the Reagan era.

A convenient summary of a vast amount of research... packed with facts and figures.
The Village Voice

242 pages, index, bibliography
Paperback ISBN: 0-921689-00-4 $16.99
Hardcover ISBN: 0-921689-01-2 $45.99

PRIVATE INTEREST, PUBLIC SPENDING
Balanced-Budget Conservatism and the Fiscal Crisis
William Scheuerman and Sidney Plotkin

Extremely informative about the political trends that exist and about the political economic system of business dealing with government.
The Activist

280 pages, index
Paperback ISBN: 1-895431-98-0 $19.99
Hardcover ISBN: 1-985431-99-9 $48.99

BANKERS, BAGMEN, AND BANDITS
Business and Politics in the Age of Greed
R.T. Naylor

A collection of articles from the shadowy underworld of business, the shady side of politics, and the twilight zone they share.

Based on Naylor's widely read column, this book is designed to give the news behind the news, to put back into the stories the 'awkward' details the main stream media find more convenient to omit.

An eminently readable book, with outré insights into the corrupt underside of world affairs in each chapter.
Canadian Book Review Annual
Without exception, the essays make very interesting reading... Naylor's book is an exhilarating if sometimes frightening roller coaster ride through the real world.
The Alternative Voice

250 pages
Paperback ISBN: 0-921689-76-4 $18.99
Hardcover ISBN: 0-921689-77-2 $47.99

COMMUNITY ECONOMIC DEVELOPMENT
In Search of Empowerment and Alternatives
Eric Shragge, ed.

2nd edition, revised and expanded
Challenges the notion that the economy should only be privately owned and argues that it should both act in the social interest of the local community and be partially controlled by it.

A critical discussion of both the theory and practice of community economic development.
Journal of Economic Literature

141 pages
Paperback ISBN: 1-895431-86-7 $19.99
Hardcover ISBN: 1-895431-87-5 $48.99
L.C. No. 93-072747
ISSN: 1195-1850

BLACK ROSE BOOKS

has also published the following books of related interest

Triumph of the Market: Essays on Economics, Politics, and the Media,
   by Edward S. Herman
Politics of Sustainable Development: Citizens, Unions and the
   Corporations, *by Laurie E. Adkin*
History of Canadian Business 1867-1914, *by R. T. Naylor*
Desert Capitalism: What are the Maquiladoras?, *by Kathryn Kopinak*
Politics of Obedience: The Discourse of Voluntary Servitude, *by Etienne
   de la Boétie*
Free Trade: Neither Free Nor About Trade, *by Christopher Merrett*
Dying From Dioxin: A Citizen's Guide to Reclaiming Our Health and
   Rebuilding Democracy, *by Lois Marie Gibbs*
First Person Plural: A Community Development Approach to Social
   Change, *by David Smith*
Services and Circuses: Community and the Welfare State,
   by Frédéric Lesemann, translated by Lorne Huston and Margaret Heap
The Search for Community: From Utopia to a Cooperative Society,
   by George Melnyk
Canada and Radical Social Change, *edited by Dimitrios Roussopoulos*
The Nature of Cooperation, *by John G. Craig*
Who is this "We"? Absence of Community, *by Eleanor Godway and
   Geraldine Finn*
Local Places: In the Age of the Global City, *edited by Roger Keil,
   David V.J. Bell and Gerda R. Wekerle*
Bringing the Economy Home From the Market, *by Ross Dobson*

send for a free catalogue of all our titles
BLACK ROSE BOOKS
C.P. 1258
Succ. Place du Parc
Montréal, Québec
H3W 2R3 Canada

To order books in North America: (phone) 1-800-565-9523
(fax) 1-800-221-9985
In Europe: (phone) 44-081-986-4854 (fax) 44-081-533-5821

Web site address: http://www.web.net/blackrosebooks

Printed by the workers of
Les Éditions Marquis
Montmagny, Québec